Celebrating Debutantes
and Quinceañeras

CELEBRATING DEBUTANTES
AND QUINCEAÑERAS

Coming of Age in American
Ethnic Communities

EVELYN IBATAN RODRIGUEZ

TEMPLE UNIVERSITY PRESS
PHILADELPHIA

TEMPLE UNIVERSITY PRESS
Philadelphia, Pennsylvania 19122
www.temple.edu/tempress

Library of Congress Cataloging-in-Publication Data

Rodriguez, Evelyn Ibatan, 1975–
    Celebrating debutantes and quinceañeras : coming of age in
American ethnic communities / Evelyn Ibatan Rodriguez.
        p. cm.
    Includes bibliographical references and index.
    ISBN 978-1-4399-0627-9 (cloth : alk. paper) —
ISBN 978-1-4399-0628-6 (pbk. : alk. paper) —
ISBN 978-1-4399-0629-3 (e-book)   1. Minorities—United
States—Social life and customs.   2. Coming of age—United
States.   3. Teenage girls—United States—Anniversaries.
4. Filipino Americans—Social life and customs.   5. Filipino
American teenage girls—Social life and customs.   6. Mexican
Americans—Social life and customs.   7. Mexican American teenage
girls—Social life and customs.   I. Title.
    E184.A1R635 2013
    305.08′073—dc23

                                                    2012041439

Printed in the United States of America

2 4 6 8 9 7 5 3 1

For Vicente R. Rodriguez III and Editha I. Rodriguez

Kahit na magkahiwalay, tayo'y magkasama

Contents

Acknowledgments

As I was writing the final draft of this book, I kept the following quotation from Father Alfred Boeddeker, founder of the St. Anthony Dining Room in San Francisco, California, pinned to the bulletin board next to my writing station: "Start doing what is necessary; then do what is possible; and suddenly you are doing the impossible." Here I offer my meager (and, no doubt, incomplete) thanks to everyone who has wittingly and unwittingly helped me do what was necessary, and possible, and impossible to publish this book.

Those who helped me do what was necessary:
First and foremost, I owe a debt of gratitude to all those who allowed me to sit in their homes, listen to their stories, and be among their families and friends to collect the data that constitute the heart of this project.

I received financial support for my research and writing from the University of San Francisco's Faculty Development Fund and Yuchengco Philippine Studies Program; the Irvine Minority Dissertation Fellowship; the National Academy of Sciences (through the Ford Foundation Predoctoral Minority Fellowship); the Social Science Research Council's (SSRC) International Migration Fellowship; the Murray Research Center's Adolescent and Youth Dissertation Award; the University of California at Berkeley's Chancellor's Opportunity Fellowship, Bancroft Library Award, and Dean's Normative Time Award; and the California Department of Veterans Affairs' Dependents Educational Assistance program.

At the University of California at Berkeley, when I was still unsure that this project was "serious" enough, Ann Swidler met my first tentative proposal with enthusiasm and genuine scholarly interest. Barrie Thorne simultaneously cheered and challenged me forward, and Raka Ray and Evelyn Nakano-Glenn rounded off a committee whose members were always as kind as they are brilliant. Also, while I was at Cal, Nancy Chodorow and my classmates in her "Interviewing Methods" course forever changed the way I approach my interviews and interview analysis.

My SSRC Fellowship was also a turning point: before participating in that program, I had never conceptualized myself as a "migration scholar." I am indebted to the comrades and mentors I worked with that summer— especially our director, Abel Valenzuela, Jr.—who really helped me lay the foundation for this project. The SSRC Fellowship also convinced me that strengthening my Spanish and Pilipino would improve (and reduce the cost of) my research. My teachers and communities at the Cuernavaca Language School and the Tagalog-on-Site programs helped make this goal a reality. I am particularly thankful to Berenice Ramirez and the rest of my accommodating host family in Mexico and to the following people in the Philippines: Ate Lea, Lilibeth, Lorna, Tito Erning, Tita Noning, Imelda Ibatan (my skillful, bilingual transcriber), and the rest of the Ibatan family and Tito Julio, my father's favorite brother.

Those who helped me recognize what was possible:
Henrietta Faast, my teacher's aide from the first through sixth grades, and Charles Henson and Katherine Perrill, two of my middle school teachers, earnestly read each draft of my earliest attempts to be the next Laura Ingalls Wilder and then (I am not ashamed to admit it) the next Amy Tan, and still they told me that they sincerely believed I would one day become "an author." Rebecca Klatch at the University of California at San Diego (UCSD) scribbled on a paper I submitted to her as a college sophomore, "Have you ever thought about grad school?"; then, a while later, Yen Le Espiritu asked me the same question. They may not realize that back then I did not even know what graduate school *was*. I am deeply grateful to all my teachers, and I am grateful to Rebecca and Yen Le for their early faith in my sociological imagination and writing abilities and for the close mentorship they both provided when I was still an undergraduate.

The Ronald E. McNair Postbaccalaureate Undergraduate Research Program at UCSD gave me my first map to graduate school; then the McNair Program at UC Berkeley enabled me to give the same opportunity to a new cohort of underrepresented and first-generation undergraduate students. I thank the administrators of this imperative federal program and the staff who mentored and worked with me in both programs.

I would not have survived graduate school had it not been for the support of the solid, grounded crew of other students and teachers of color who helped reassure me that I belonged: Robyn Rodriguez, Nerissa Balce-Cortes, and Rowena Robles assured me that I was not alone; Asian Women United of California, PANGIT (the Pilipino American Network of Graduate InsurgenTs), and Kapwa were the source of my first true friendships at Cal. These people and organizations reminded me that I was not in graduate school for myself, but to serve the communities I belong to and care about. I cannot express how much they inspired and sustained me.

Julia Alvarez, Linda Trinh Võ, and Karen Mary Davalos provided feedback on earlier drafts of my manuscript. And Janet Francendense, Amanda Steele, my patient copyeditors, and the anonymous reviewers at Temple University Press have been godsends. I thank Janet for her confidence, her empathy, and her patience—I really, truly could not have asked for a better editor to help keep me going even through a devastating loss and to help make this book a reality.

And, finally, those who helped me do the impossible:
My colleagues, friends, and students at the University of San Francisco (USF) have made my "impossible" dream of holding a full-time, tenured post at a reputable institution, in a magnificent city, with *normal* people, an everyday reality—I still pinch myself. I am especially grateful to Stephanie Sears for her generous mentorship, to Pamela Balls-Organista for her invaluable writing retreats and close (and quick!) reading of my book proposal, to Edith Borbon for her careful editing, and to the Arts and Sciences Dean's Office for its steadfast provision of research support. I thank Amy Joseph, Shona Doyle before her, and the entire Department of Sociology for making work more than bearable; Evelyn Ho, Dennis Recio, and Ronald Sundstrom for being great buddies and insightful intellectual sounding boards; Radmar Jao for his spiritual direction; USF's Asian Pacific American Studies and Philippine Studies faculty; and Martha Espinoza, Kelly Kremko, and Christine Mayrina for their stints as my research assistants.

Words cannot describe the amazing ways my closest friends and family have helped me in the completion of this book. But I owe them my best effort. Jennifer Cocohoba has been writing with me since we met in seventh grade. Krysteena Atienza, Eva Huertas, and Bernadette Racelis have motivated me more than they know—I wrote the most personally meaningful parts of this book for Nia, Symone, and Lora, so that one day they could read something that would help explain who they are. Jeannie Celestial told me to "just write," and Jeff Noblejas helped me recognize why I could not leave out the *traviesos*. Sevilla Franco has been a steadfast translator (and magnificent chef). Olga Navarro, René Flores, Pedro Reyes, and Pedro Alberto Reyes have supported me as they would their own daughter/sister/*tía*. And somewhere along the way, Vicky Rodriguez transformed from my little "seastar" into a person I profoundly admire. I made it through my first year of graduate school because I could not stand the thought of disappointing her.

When I confided in my unfaltering partner, Ténoch, that I was ready to drop out of graduate school during my first week, he told me that I should tough it out for a little longer. Without his good sense, the music he fills our home with, and the love and patience he shares with Nala and me, I would have made many more wrong turns.

Finally, Mom and Dad: this book is *for* you and *of* you. Thank you for enabling me to pursue dreams in places and ways we never imagined.

CHAPTER 1

Una Cordial Invitación

Perhaps it was because my sister and I grew up in a brotherless household. Perhaps it was because my mother, in marrying my father, grieved in secret for the dreams she surrendered to fulfill her larger ambition of immigrating to America. Or maybe it was simply economically motivated: Mom and Dad presumed that our working-class, Navy family's money would go a lot further if they did not fill our heads with fantasies of satin gowns, opera-length gloves, and sparkling tiaras. All I know for sure is that, for whatever reason, my parents raised us to run for senior class office rather than try out for cheerleading, to become doctors rather than wait around hoping to marry them, and to dream of sitting in boardrooms and at editing tables rather than being twirled around in grand ballrooms. Needless to say, I was clueless about sweetheart balls, proms, debutantes, and quinceañeras until I was fourteen, when Estelita Diaz handed me my first pearly, custom-embossed, fan-shaped quinceañera invitation. I was totally confused. And captivated. But not nearly as much as I was by her fifteenth birthday party itself.

Estelita's quince began with her own special mass, which was followed by the biggest birthday party I had ever been to—blazing with mariachi, buffet tables overflowing with food, and boisterous guests, who oohed and aahed at Estelita's every move and even cried after she performed a group waltz straight out of Cinderella. And Estelita! Between the day before, when I had seen her at school, and that night, she had metamorphosed into a junior-high princess. She was resplendent in a huge white gown, with tiny glass flowers glittering in her meticulously curled hair. And she wore two things none of us bookish girls had ever tried on in public: mascara and high heels.

After the party, when I gave my mom my bemused report of Estelita's quince, she told me, "Filipinos have parties like that too, when girls turn eighteen." At the time, I remember thinking that this was my mom's inventive way of communicating that Filipinos were just as nice to their daughters as Mexicans, but that I had better get into college before even thinking of having a party like Estelita's. But just as the youngest of my sister's friends finished throwing their quinceañeras, the oldest of our Filipina "cousins" started issuing invitations to their debuts.

At these occasions, groups of young women (who had not necessarily known each other before) were presented at association-arranged balls to appreciative audiences of family and friends but mostly strangers—other girls' guests, former debutantes, and local beauty queens, leaders, and entertainers. Like their Mexicana counterparts, the birthday girls wore bridelike gowns and performed carefully rehearsed cotillions. But unlike the festive, mariachi-filled, rec-room quinceañeras I had grown accustomed to, the debuts my family and I attended were serious black-tie events: hushed sit-down dinners, with unswerving programs steered by baritone emcees in large hotel ballrooms.

Being young, I chalked up these similarities and differences to the diverse tastes of my friends and our devotion to following ephemeral teenage fashions and trends. Seven years later, a feature article on a local African American cotillion evoked nearly forgotten memories of the Mexican and Filipino debutantes of my teen years and made me think that there might be more to these events than girls in white dresses and dance floor promenades. Now, after speaking with debutantes and quinceañeras and attending these events in three different countries over several years, I *know* that there is.

Contrary to popular misperceptions of Filipino debuts and Mexican quinceañeras as overpriced birthday parties and/or ostentatious displays of immigrants' new wealth, these events meaningfully reflect how Filipino and Mexican American immigrants and their children are positioned in the United States, as well as how they imagine who they are, where they have come from, and who they want to become. This is because before and during these events, ethnic, national, class, generational, and gender identities and relationships are played out, challenged, and negotiated in more exaggerated and perceptible ways than usual. This book closely examines these rituals to explain what Filipina debutantes and Mexicana quinceañeras reveal about the individuals, families, and communities who organize and participate in them.

"Supersized": Quinceañeras and Debuts in the United States

Debuts and quinceañeras are larger-than-life events for the Filipina and Mexicana girls (and their parents) who dream of, plan, and celebrate these events. They can cost up to a parent's yearly income to produce; require the collaboration of teams of family, friends, and professionals; and often take at least a year of preparation. Afterward, they are immortalized in immense photo albums, portraits proudly hung in the family *sala*, professional videos and/or DVDs, and cherished memories said to "last a lifetime."

Mexican quinceañeras ("quinces") and Filipino debutantes ("debuts") are usually formal, elaborately planned, and expensive coming-of-age celebrations that mark a girl's entry into society as a young lady. Traditional quinceañeras present an individual girl who is turning fifteen (called the *quinceañera*),[1] accompanied by a "court" she has chosen of seven young men (*chambelanes*) and seven young women (*damas*). Quinceañeras usually include a special mass, followed by a cotillion-like party, and are usually organized by the celebrant's family, which often includes immediate and extended relatives, along with fictive kin such as the girl's godparents, or *padrinos*. Traditional Filipino debuts present up to two dozen debutantes,[2] each accompanied by a male peer escort at the same event on the year of their eighteenth birthdays. They are often annual cotillions organized by local community organizations, although recently, debuts for only one girl, organized by the celebrant and/or her family, have become more common.

No figures exist that document how extensively, and for how long, debuts and quinces have been celebrated in the United States or abroad. But quinceañeras are widely celebrated throughout Latin America, and these events have become common enough in the United States to spawn the creation of various manuals, services, and businesses to help girls and their families prepare for them (Erevia 1980, Salcedo 1997).[3] And while debuts are generally considered "the province of the upper crust" in the Philippines, "debuts have become a part of the Filipino American experience for many families," having "gained favor with middle-class Filipino Americans who desire and can afford the lavish events" (R. Kim 2001).

Because of this image as "lavish" and because of their association with the patriarchy and elitism of the colonizers of the Philippines and Mexico, quinceañeras and debuts have been criticized as being economically impractical and sexist and as valorizing demeaning cultural values—by Filipinos, Mexicans, and nonimmigrants. Outsiders are "baffled" by working-class immigrants who invest so much for just one day (Cantú 2002: 16), and segments of the Catholic Church have condemned the quinceañera custom as "an exercise in excess" and a premature signal of Latinas' "sexual coming-of-age" (Gorski 2008). At the same time, Filipino American historian Dawn Mabalon has written that the pressure to produce "frothy, over-the-top debutante balls" has compelled "some Filipino American families [to] beg, borrow, and steal" (2004: 19). And in 2007, a self-identified "veteran of old feminist and minority-empowering wars" reported that "supersized quinceañeras have hijacked a Latino tradition" and that "these fiestas don't contribute an iota to prepare a young girl for female adulthood in the 21st century. They are a shameful waste of money and reinforce consumerist, patriarchal values" (Prida 2007).

Rituals as *Ventanas*

But if the critics are entirely right, how does one explain Monica Reyes, the young woman who commented after the four-week curriculum required for quinceañeras at her church, "I'd rather wait [to go to parties and date]" (Gorski 2008); Krystal Tabora, whose debut kindled in her a desire to learn more about Filipino culture so she can "uphold tradition" (Downes 2005); Joyce L. Fernandez, a former debutante who characterizes debuts as "an exercise in financial planning and responsibility" (Fernandez 1998); and the former honorees I interviewed, who seem to have turned out to be responsible, successful, and proudly bicultural adults? More significantly, how does one explain the persistence and growth of debutantes and quinceañeras in the United States, along with the fact that they have traveled across oceans and borders with Filipino and Mexican immigrants in the first place? All of this suggests that there are more to these customs than frivolity, materialism, and the romanticizing of colonial cultures and old-fashioned ideas of womanhood. Chicana studies scholar Norma E. Cantú (2002) points out that the creation, perseverance, and evolution of ethnic traditions in the United States can be read as emerging out of community needs and as responses to how groups are positioned within "mobile webs of power" (Sandoval, cited in Cantú 2002: 16). And she writes that these are exceptionally observable in coming-of-age traditions because of their ritual natures.

Rituals have been defined and studied by various social scientists. Classic sociologist Émile Durkheim writes that ritual ceremonies are "dramatic performances" (1995) in which social actors depict and commemorate history, in part, "to maintain the vitality of [a group's] beliefs and to prevent their memory from being obliterated—in other words, to revitalize the most essential elements of the collective consciousness and conscience" (1995: 379). Contemporary anthropologist Paul Connerton writes, "Images of the past and recollected knowledge of the past are conveyed and sustained by (more or less) ritual performances" (1989: 4, 38). He also writes that ritual performances allow us to pass on collective memories from one generation to the next and "to recognise and demonstrate to others that we . . . remember" (1989: 23). Connerton argues that this is crucial in maintaining and asserting group identities, since "our past history is an important source of our conception of ourselves; our self-knowledge, our conception of our own character and potentialities" (1989: 22). Finally, providing perhaps social science's most famous definition of ritual, Victor W. Turner writes that "a ritual is a . . . sequence of activities involving gestures, words, and objects, performed in a sequestered place, and designed to influence preternatural entities or forces on behalf of the actors' goals and interests" (1977: 183).

Turner, Connerton, and Durkheim elucidate how a rich amount of information about Filipino and Mexican Americans can be learned by studying debutantes and quinceañeras. Since rituals are "dramatic performances" of history, studying Filipino debuts and Mexican quinces can help us see how their organizers narrate their experiences in the United States and how "the hegemonic force of U.S. and Mexican [or Filipino] popular culture impels . . . communities to adapt and shift in a fluid manner" (Cantú 2002: 24). Since rituals can be significant expressions and transmissions of identity, investigating quinceañeras and debuts can also help us understand how Mexican and Filipino immigrants, individuals, and communities imagine and re-imagine themselves, their "goals and interests," and how they are perceived. Since rituals charge "gestures, words, and objects" with polysemic social meanings, debutantes and quinceañeras do not just give social investigators *actions* to watch; they also provide an array of *tangible* symbols and spaces that can be examined to help unearth how actors see and explain themselves, their histories, and their environment. Finally, since debuts and quinces are not just *any* rituals but "rites of passage," which Arnold van Gennep defines as "ceremonies whose essential purpose is to enable the individual to pass from one defined position [stage in life] to another which is equally well-defined" (1960: 3), these events provide magnificent *ventanas*, or windows (in both Tagalog and Spanish), into how these groups demarcate and assign meaning to different stages of life and immigrant adaptation; how past and present structures inform immigrant life today; and what all this means for the members of these families, for their communities, and for the United States as a whole.

"Brown Brothers": Mexicans and Filipinos

Mexican and Filipino immigrants and their families compose two of the largest growing populations in the United States: immigrants and what Eileen O'Brien calls the "racial middle" (O'Brien 2008). Mexico and the Philippines have been the top two immigrant-sending regions to the United States for almost four decades. In 2010 (the most recent year for which there are available statistics), more than 11.6 million U.S. immigrants (30 percent of all immigrants) reported that they were born in Mexico, and more than 1.7 million (4.5 percent) reported that they were born in the Philippines (U.S. Census Bureau 2010a). Today there are more than 32.9 million Mexicans in the United States, and more than 3.3 million Filipinos (U.S. Census Bureau 2010c, 2010d). The pan-ethnic groups to which Mexicans and Filipinos belong (Latinos and Asians, respectively) are the two fastest-growing racial groups in the United States, and if their current growth continues, some projections forecast that they "will soon constitute about 35 percent of the US population" (Yancey 2003). Since Latinos and Asians are neither black nor white, such a massive population shift could signify a real "challenge . . . to the hegemonic white-over-black racial order" in the United States today (O'Brien 2008). Investigating Filipinos and Mexicans can help us better understand how those in the "racial middle" perpetuate and/or transform the current racial system, and investigating these groups *together* helps researchers better discern how race works with other social systems (e.g., class, immigration policies, and colonialism) to enable such outcomes.

Filipino and Mexican Americans also offer a fascinating and constructive comparison because, while they are the two biggest immigrant groups in the United States and are both situated in the racial middle, they seem to face vastly different opportunities and challenges to their success in America. And while casual observers tend to chalk up these disparities to Mexicans' and Filipinos' different "values and attitudes," they actually share various normative commitments from the centuries of historical intersection between the Philippines and Mexico.

Magkasama

The interconnected histories[4] of the Philippines and Mexico actually go as far back as 1521. In March of that year, Ferdinand Magellan "discovered" a group of unrelated islands in the western Pacific, which would later be named and claimed as Las Filipinas, for King Felipe II of Spain; five months later, the heart of the Mexica[5] empire, Tenochtitlán, was surrendered to a

Spanish armada led by Hernán Cortés, marking the creation of New Spain in the southern region of North America. Spain's overthrow of the Aztecs subsequently led to three hundred years of Spanish occupation in Mexico (1521–1821). After Magellan's expedition (and execution by indigenous Filipinos), Spain launched three journeys to the Philippines, all from the western coast of Mexico, over the course of a half century, in order to finally seal what would ultimately become a 333-year conquest of the archipelago (1565–1899).

While these centuries as stepsiblings under Madre España were experienced distinctly in each country, they also helped produce similar religious beliefs and practices, categories and structures of race, and understandings of their relationships with the West. To win the cooperation (i.e., labor) of the indigenous populations of Mexico and the Philippines, Spain attempted to destroy all precolonial written literature and history[6] and undertook the total spiritual conversion of each colony's natives. As a result, a unique[7] Roman Catholicism still flourishes in both countries. Today, the Philippines is remarkable for being the only predominantly Christian country among its East Asian and Southeast Asian neighbors, with about 80 percent of its population having been baptized Roman Catholic. Mexico, meanwhile, is home to more than 85 million Catholics (95 percent of its population), making it the second largest Catholic country in the world (*Our Sunday Visitor's Catholic Almanac* 1998). And the erasure of all or most of the pre-Spanish histories of Mexico and the Philippines has made it difficult for the "average" Mexican or Filipino today to recall an "evocative era prior to the Spanish period" to which they can "turn with pride" (Steinberg 1982: 34) and with a profound sense of what some of my research subjects described as "having no culture."

The inferiorizing of native people (especially by native people themselves) was and is compounded by the internalization and continuing operation of the race and class structures and ideologies both countries inherited from their colonizers. The racial *casta* system invented in New Spain, and later transplanted in Las Filipinas, created durable associations between lighter skin and entitlement, beauty, intelligence, and even morality (for more on the creation of the casta system, see Katzew and Deans-Smith 2009; E. Rodriguez 2006). Conversely, it linked darker skin with insignificance, repulsiveness, and a lack of intelligence and morality. Since most native Filipinos and Mexicans are darker skinned, these frameworks, combined with the loss of a precolonial sense of self, has had intensely self-denigrating effects.

In 1821, Mexico finally freed itself from the shackles of Spanish rule, and in 1898 the Philippines did the same. However, shortly after winning their independence, both countries found themselves defending their territories from the United States. After decades of defending itself against a (mostly illegal) Anglo population occupying Mexico's unpopulated northern wastelands (an area that included what is now Texas, California, and the U.S. Southwest), Mexico found itself at war again, when the United States launched the Mexican-American War in 1846. That war ended in January 1848 with the signing of the Treaty of Guadalupe-Hidalgo, which forced Mexico to surrender almost half of its remaining territory—modern-day California, Arizona, New Mexico, and parts of Colorado, Nevada, Utah, and Wyoming.[8]

Only months after its inauguration, the Republic of the Philippines also found itself at war with the United States, its former ally against Spain, after American commissioners at the brokering the Treaty of Paris[9] readily accepted Spain's cession of the entire Philippines—in spite of knowledge that the Philippines had been fighting for national sovereignty since 1896. The Philippine-American War, a devastating three-year armed conflict that ended with the forced surrender of Filipino resistance leaders in 1902, ensued. This was followed by fifty years of American occupation that few in the islands had the vigor to oppose after back-to-back wars had crushed countless Filipino homes, families, lands, livelihoods, and dreams.

Absorption into the United States meant that despite having achieved hard-fought independence from Spain in the 1800s, many Mexicans once again became second-class citizens in places where they had been the earliest settlers, and Filipinos became "little brown brothers" to the United States, wards of the state who needed their American "liberators" to "uplift and civilize and Christianize them" (Ignacio 2004: 64). To justify appropriation of their land, livelihoods, and civil rights,[10] Americans constructed Mexicans as an inferior race. For example, Joel Poinsett, a former U.S. ambassador to Mexico, wrote to then–secretary of state Martin Van Buren that "the Mexicans [are] a more ignorant and debauched people than their ancestors had been" (Poinsett 2002: 14). Filipinos arguably fared worse: "US colonialism stunted the Philippine national economy, imposed English as the lingua franca, installed a US-style educational system, and Americanized many Filipino values and aspirations" (Espiritu 2003: 23). Moreover, images of the Filipino as steeped in superstition, ignorance, and barbarism rationalized American claims that it was "the white man's burden" to undertake such a complete political, economic, and cultural takeover of the Philippines.

Ironically, the pervasive cultural degradation and compulsory Americanization experienced by Filipinos and Mexicans during the late nineteenth century and first half of the twentieth century helped deepen Filipino and Mexican idealization of the West and Western culture, which began under Spain. Compared to their war-ravaged country,[11] the United States seemed to represent "hope and renewal" and "economic security and individual freedom" for Mexicans (Guerin-Gonzales 1994: 11–12). In the American-occupied Philippines, Filipinos similarly came "to regard the American culture, political system, and way of life as more prestigious than their own" (Espiritu 2003: 24). Accustomed to more than three centuries of neglect, contempt, and abuse under Spain, many Filipinos developed an appreciation of, and even affection for, America's program of "Benevolent Assimilation," which, among other things, brought the Philippines well-constructed roads and infrastructure, rapid urbanization, the (re)introduction of inter-island shipping, rapid urbanization, and a common language (Steinberg 1982: 59). Given such conditions, mass migrations of Filipinos and Mexicans to the United States during the twentieth century were almost inevitable.

Lado a Lado: *Pre-1965 Mexican Americans and Filipino Americans*

The first wave of Mexican Americans were recruited by farms, U.S. railway companies, and California gold mines that needed them to help finish the work that Asian immigrants from China had started before they were barred from entering the United States by the 1882 Chinese Exclusion Act. Almost immediately after the Philippine-American War, Mexicans were joined by the first wave of Filipino Americans, which included some *pensionados*,[12] Filipino civil servants (usually from the *ilustrado*[13] class) who had been sponsored and sent to the United States to learn American-style governance to implement back home but were mostly young, able-bodied bachelors who ultimately found work as manual laborers in the United States (these men are now called *manongs*). So, by the turn of the twentieth century, Filipino and Mexican laborers had found themselves working *lado a lado*, or side by side, with their former siblings under Mother Spain.[14]

Because of the status of the Philippines as a U.S. protectorate, Filipinos remained the only Asians who could enter Hawaii and the U.S. mainland after the Chinese Exclusion Act, the 1908 Gentlemen's Agreement (with Japan), and the 1917 creation of the Asiatic Barred Zone (which included India, Afghanistan, and Arabia) effectively banned all other immigration from Asia. And "unlike the immigrants from Asia and Europe, Mexicans could enter and leave [the United States] without passports whenever they wished" (Takaki 1993: 312). Furthermore, between 1910 and 1930, Mexican and Filipino "immigrants seemed to offer a solution to growers' dilemma over how to preserve the American Dream for 'Americans' (whites) and still have a large, cheap labor force to harvest their crops" (Guerin-Gonzales 1994: 23).

Between 1930 and 1965, Filipino and Mexican migration continued to ebb and flow. By 1930, both populations had become targets for growing resentment and hostility from white America. As the nation became enmeshed in the Great Depression, Mexicans were singled out by "governmental programs to deport and repatriate foreigners as a panacea for economic depression" (Guerin-Gonzales 1994: 77), and Filipino immigration was legally limited to fifty people a year by the Tydings-McDuffie Independence Act.[15] Nevertheless, between the late 1930s and mid-1960s, a second wave of Filipino Americans composed of U.S. Navy personnel[16] and their families[17] entered the United States.[18] Then the start of World War II marked the end of Mexican repatriation and the beginning of the *bracero* (guest worker) program in the United States. This brought a third wave of about five million Mexican immigrants to the United States to help fill the need for seasonal agricultural labor and temporary railroad work while many Americans were away contributing to the war effort.[19] After the war, the Philippines finally gained its independence, and the Filipino Naturalization Act made it possible for Filipino immigrants to become U.S. citizens.[20]

The different migration patterns produced through U.S. policies toward Mexico and the Philippines helped continue to shape American perceptions of both groups. By the mid-1950s, the Filipino American community was gradually transformed from a working-class bachelor society into a middle-class community of families, which "did a great deal to reduce white prejudice against Filipino Americans" (Espiritu 1995: 17). In contrast, most working-class Mexicanos found an increasingly unpredictable and inhospitable environment in the United States during the postwar years.[21] Then, the 1965 Immigration Act abolished national-origins quotas and prioritized entry based on family reunification and occupational preferences, completely transforming the U.S. racial landscape as well as the lives of Filipinos and Mexicans in the United States.

Sa Kabilang Mundo/*On the Other Side of the World: Post-1965 Mexican Americans and Filipino Americans*

Although the architects of the 1965 Immigration Act never anticipated that it would alter U.S. immigration in any major way, it did so dramatically. Its family reunion preferences and occupational categories opened the doors to a third wave of Filipino migration, which consisted primarily of the relatives of Filipino Americans and highly skilled, educated professionals who were qualified to meet the occupational preferences of the United States. Meanwhile, the sudden elimination of the final *bracero* program, combined with the 1965 Immigration Act's new national quotas, worsened the problem of undocumented immigration from Mexico by forcing "those who would normally come as guest workers into illegal entry channels" (Ueda 1994: 46). Subsequently, undocumented immigrants from Mexico came to be viewed as primarily responsible for many, if not all, of America's social ills—high taxes, wasted welfare dollars, lost jobs, high costs for education, rising crime, and "the transformation of the very essence of the present civilization of the United States" (Lukacs 1986: 13; Vinson 1992). Meanwhile, Filipinos came to be seen as part of the Asian American "model minority," who had overcome challenges and "made it" in the United States through hard work and adherence to cultural values in line with those of the rest of American society.

By the 1970s, Mexico and the Philippines had become the top two sources of immigration into the United States. But by the 1980s, in spite of their deeply shared histories and values, Filipinos and Mexicans had come to occupy widely divergent socioeconomic positions in the United States and to be viewed by most Americans as almost polar opposites. Today, a sizable proportion of Filipinos are "college-educated professionals who ended up in the US middle class" (Espiritu and Wolf 2001: 163). On the other hand, "on average, adult [Mexican American] immigrants have only a few years of schooling, limited urban job skills, . . . [and] little or no knowledge of English . . . [and are] classified as low-wage service workers or blue-collar workers" (López and Stanton-Salazar 2001: 57, 67). As Figure 1.1 demonstrates, in 2010, the U.S. census reported that Americans of Filipino descent were generally faring about the same as, or better than, other Americans.[22] The median income for Filipino Americans was $51,668, 7.3 percent of Filipinos were living below the federal poverty line, and 37.9 percent of Filipinos had at least a bachelor's degree. Meanwhile, the census also reported that the median income of Mexicans ($23,544) was nearly 55 percent lower than that of their Filipino counterparts, more than a quarter of Mexicans were living below the federal poverty line (26.6 percent), and less than 10 percent held bachelor's degrees.

Largely because of these socioeconomic realities, Filipino and Mexican Americans are now perceived of as vastly unalike, despite histories and cultures that have crisscrossed for nearly five hundred years. For example, in May 2008, a study out of the conservative Manhattan Institute claimed that among immigrant minorities, Filipinos were "the most assimilated," while Mexicans were the least so. The report argued that Mexicans were "faring

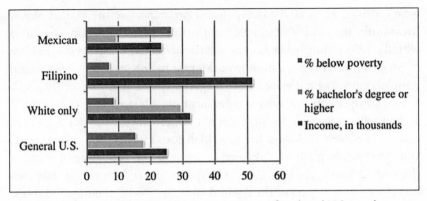

Figure 1.1 Poverty, college degree, and income statistics for selected U.S. populations. *(From U.S. Census Bureau 2010b, 2010c, 2010d.)*

poorly" at "weaving into the American fabric," while their Asian counterparts were "among some of the best and brightest, which puts them on a faster track to assimilation via economic success" (Schulte 2008). Filipinos have come to personify ideal immigrants—successful, assimilable, and inconspicuous. In contrast, Mexicans have come to epitomize the immigrant threat—a drain on public resources, resistant to cultural incorporation, and seeking to "reconquer" the United States (Chavez 2001; Huntington 2004b).

This paradox makes clear that understanding why some immigrant groups seem to be doing better than others requires a search beyond cultural explanations. These attribute the general "success" of Filipinos in the United States to "Asian values," which extol family, hard work, academic achievement, and quiet resolve in the face of hardships, and the general "failure" of many Mexican Americans to achieve the American Dream to their "inherently Hispanic" laziness, sexual promiscuity, obstinacy in the face of new circumstances, and even "contemptuous[ness] of American culture" (Huntington 2004a: 44). Comparing today's Filipino and Mexican Americans can help clarify what *structural* factors enable and constrain immigrant adaptation in the United States, as well as what the unprecedented growth of the Latino and Asian U.S. populations might mean for the country.

Comparatively examining Filipinos and Mexicans is also valuable because this simply allows for more complete and truthful histories of Filipinos, Mexicans, and Americans to be told and made available. Elaine H. Kim writes that "Americans of color share long, complex, and little-discussed relationships," which have been obscured to help preserve Europeans as the central figures in American history (2000: xi). Studying the histories and experiences of ethnic groups together highlights how these groups' stories, fates, and futures are intertwined and dependent on *each other*, as well as white America. It helps decenter Europeans as *the* principal characters in the histories of Americans of color, defies the historical amnesia long imposed on many of them, and shatters "dualistic simplifications [such as] majority/minority, mainstream/margin, native/immigrant, white/non-white" (E. Kim 2000: xi) that often prevent scholars from being able to fully comprehend what and who we are investigating.

Careful Choreography: Methods

This project compares the experiences of Mexicans and Filipinos in the United States by thickly investigating their daughters' female coming-of-age rituals. It represents more than nine hundred debuts and quinceañeras and is based on data collected through three years of fieldwork and in-depth interviews with more than fifty subjects—including current and former female celebrants, family members, and the constellations of people who participate in debuts and quinceañeras, such as "court" members, photographers, and choreographers.

This project was carefully composed—I studied quinceañeras, debuts, and their actors through a combination of methods, in a combination of research sites. I conducted in-depth interviews with individual family members and event participants and group interviews with second-generation Mexican and Filipino American youth. All interviews were located via snowball sampling and were open-ended, tape-recorded, and transcribed. I conducted all of them personally in whatever languages my subjects were most comfortable with—English, Tagalog, Spanish, and/or a combination. I also observed rehearsals, financial transactions, and the "big days" themselves. Most of my work was conducted in Las Querubes, a major metropolitan area in Southern California, and Del Sol, a smaller city outside Las Querubes, between May 2003 and June 2004. However, some preliminary observations and interviews were conducted in the Philippines between August and November 2002[23] and in central Mexico between February and April 2003. I also interviewed and observed participants for three additional events in Bahia, a major city in Northern California, between April 2004 and July 2006.

I conducted thirty-seven "primary interviews" with individuals in California families who had already held or were planning and/or considering having a debut or quinceañera for at least one daughter (see Table 1.1). More specifically, my primary interviews were composed of individual interviews with eight daughters who had already had debuts, six daughters who had already had quinceañeras, six daughters who were planning their debuts, and three daughters who were planning their quinceañeras, and separate interviews with some of the daughters' parents (see Table 1.2).

As well as interviewing members of the nine families in my sample who were planning their coming-out celebrations, I attended and observed selected planning meetings, costume fittings, rehearsals, and/or masses. My subjects also allowed me to examine documents and records of the production, staging, and aftermath of their celebrations, including guest lists, seating charts, transaction receipts, newspaper stories, printed programs, gifts-received lists, cards, photographs, and personal correspondence sent and re-

TABLE 1.1 PRIMARY INTERVIEW SUBJECTS

Name (Pseudonym)	Debut or Quinceañera	Former or Current Celebration
Agao, Barbra	D	C
Agao, Rose	D	C
Aquino, Lauren	D	C
Aquino, Nate	D	C
Arroyo, Berenice	Q	F
Arroyo, Cecelia	Q	F
Azua, Astrud	Q	F
Azua, Dalía	Q	F
Cordova, Erika	D	F
Currabeg, Anabel	D	F
Dizon, Eliane	D	F
Dizon, Nora	D	F
Dobrado, Cassandra	D	C
Dobrado, Sharon	D	C
Favino, Flora	Q	F
Favino, Jasmin	Q	F
Fuentes, Imelda	D	F
Fuentes, Ramona	D	F
Garcia, Adelaina	Q	F
Garcia, Lea	Q	F
Garza, Angela May	D	C
Garza, Juliet	D	C
Gomez, Lila	Q	C
Guzman, Janice	D	C
Hernandez, Olivia	D	F
Hernandez, Ramiro	D	F
Napolo, Klara	D	F
Napolo, Linet	D	F
Saldana, Maria	Q	C
Saldana, Marlena	Q	C
Santiago, Belinda	Q	C
Santiago, Katia	Q	C
Torres, Rosadina	D	C
Torres, Rose	D	C
Valdes, Catalina	Q	F
Valdes, Patrisia	Q	F
Yuson, Marabel	D	F

TABLE 1.2   CHARACTERISTICS OF PRIMARY INTERVIEWEES

| | Filipino | | Mexican | | |
	Daughters	Parents	Daughters	Parents	TOTAL
Former celebrants	8	3	6	4	21
Current planners	6	5	3	2	16
TOTAL	14	8	9	6	37

ceived. This helped me cross-check the costs, networks, and possible systems of (mutual) exchange and support that were involved in planning and participating in these events.

To gain a fuller perspective of Mexican and Filipino youth, especially males and young girls still considering a quince or debut, I also administered five group discussions about coming of age, with a total of eighty-two Filipino and Mexican second-generation individuals, ages fourteen to twenty (see Table 1.3).

Finally, to round out my images of the events, individuals, families, and communities in my study, I conducted fifteen formal "secondary interviews" with selected planning or event participants, including clergy and such service providers as dressmakers, caterers, decorators, and printers (see Table 1.4). And I conducted a number of informal interviews with selected escorts, other "court" members, other immediate and extended family members, and invited guests whom I have not officially counted[24] but whose insights also helped my analysis. Combined with my primary interviews, these and my secondary interviews, which each represent an average of sixty events, enable my work to represent more than nine hundred debuts and quinceañeras.

My multipronged, multilayered (and multilingual) research approach has been informed by Victor Turner (1977) and Stuart Hall and the Birmingham School's theories of rituals (Clarke et al. 1976), Clifford Geertz's ideas on "thick description," and feminist and postcolonial scholars' deliberate foregrounding of subaltern and women's experiences to "decolonize" and

TABLE 1.3   FOCUS GROUPS

Group	Number of Participants
High school class	28
High school class	27
Pan-ethnic Asian student organization	10
Interracial minority student organization	5
Church youth group	12
TOTAL	82

"engender" immigrant and transnational histories and their reconstructions (e.g., Gabaccia 1994; Hondagneu-Sotelo 1994; Hune 2000; Nakano-Glenn 1983; L. Smith 1999; Weinberg 1992). Turner suggests that studies aspiring to uncover the meanings of rituals need to obtain narratives and interpretations of the ritual from *various* participants, since ritual symbols and events can be interpreted in any number of ways, which may sometimes be indistinct from and/or incongruous with each other. Hall and the Birmingham School emphasize a *materialist* ethnography when studying (sub)cultural traditions, since subcultures "adopt and adapt material objects and possessions—and reorganize . . . them into distinctive 'styles' which express the collectivity . . . [and] become embodied in rituals of relationship and occasion and movement" (Clarke et al. 1976, cited in Maira 2002: 38–39). Clifford Geertz contends that cultural ethnographies require gathering "thick descriptions," since "behavior must be attended to, and with some exactness because it is through the flow of behavior—or more precisely, social action—that cultural forms find articulation" (1973: 18). Feminist immigration scholar Pierrette Hondagneu-Sotelo argues that this is especially true when studying immigrant American communities. She writes, "Direct observation yields a more accurate portrayal of people's lives than do methods of self-report" (1994: xxi). She explains that this is because varying degrees of English proficiency, distrust of outsiders, and/or modesty can often render interviews imprecise articulations of immigrant experiences. Finally, postcolonial researchers point out that most work on subaltern peoples "privileges Western ways of knowing, while denying the validity . . . of [indigenous] knowledge,

TABLE 1.4   SECONDARY INTERVIEW SUBJECTS

Name (Pseudonym)	Debut or Quinceañera	Quinceañera or Debut Service	Self-Reported Number of Events Serviced
Agbayani, Edward	D	Filmmaker	3
Arguello, Diana	D	Filmmaker	3
Biagan, Amoldo	D	Deejay/emcee	25
Castillo, Pedro	Q	Priest	30
Dizon, Vikki	D	Choreographer	15
Espalda, Josie	D	Planner	15
Favino, Flora	Q	Parish coordinator	300
Garza, Agnes	D	Planner	4
Gutierrez, Selena	Q	Seamstress	3
Maldivas, Cam	D	Planner	5
Martines, Helen	D	Planner	34
Ortega, Gabriel	Q	Photographer	200
Tiongson, Geraldo	D	Photographer	200
Tomas, Antonio	Q	Photographer	20
Valdes, Lorena	Q	Religious instructor	15
TOTAL Events Represented			872

language and culture" (L. Smith 1999: 183), and feminist researchers point out that (especially because the first waves of immigration from the non-Western countries were predominantly male) women in Asian and Latino American histories have been "rendered invisible, misrepresented, or subsumed . . . as if their experiences were simply coequal to men's lives, which they are not" (Hune 2000: 413).

Bearing these critiques in mind, I foreground and take for granted the validity and legitimacy of women and children's experiences and standpoints in this study of immigrants. And I explicitly aim for the empowerment of my subjects and their communities, and the revision of male- and Western-centered concepts and theories of gender, ethnicity, immigration, settlement, and even feminism, along with utmost methodological and academic rigor. Because I used this approach and a small and self-selected sample, my final analysis is far from definitive. But it is a careful and lucid view of the "partial truths" that my subjects shared with me. Accordingly, I hope it contributes to efforts to "move . . . subjugated voices from the margins to the center," and to "decenter dominant discourses," to highlight and "elevate . . . types of knowledge . . . previously . . . treated as inadequate or lesser" (Mann and Huffman 2005: 65).

Las Querubes and Filipino and Mexican Querubenos: My Research Site and Subjects

The principal people in this study belong to the post-1965 U.S. wave of immigrants and their families and represent the top two immigrant-sending countries to the United States and to California, where the largest share of U.S. immigrants resides and where this study took place. In California, more than 4.4 million immigrants (44.2 percent) report having been born in Mexico, and more than 800,000 (8 percent) in the Philippines (Migration Policy Institute 2009).

The city where I conducted most of my fieldwork, Las Querubes, is a sprawling urban metropolis and home to one of the largest and most multiethnic immigrant populations in the nation. Because of the city's size and diversity, it is impossible to neatly characterize Las Querubes. It includes wealthy districts, dotted with custom-designed mansions, owned by mostly white families; recently gentrified neighborhoods populated by young, middle-class artists and yuppies; working-class ethnic enclaves with constantly changing landscapes, with new skin colors, cuisines, and languages brought in by steady new streams of immigrants; and newer suburbs where many former, upwardly mobile residents of the ethnic enclaves of Las Querubes have been drawn—all set in a vast terrain comprising balmy beaches, swelter-ing valleys, and cool mountains, connected by a tangle of heavily congested streets and highways. Around the time I conducted my fieldwork, nearly 40 percent of the inhabitants of Las Querubes reported having been born outside the United States. Among this substantial immigrant population, about 65 percent had been born in Latin America, more than 26 percent had been born in Asia, and just fewer than 38 percent had been naturalized as U.S. citizens.

The Mexican immigrants who reside in Las Querubes are recognized as having a rich and long history there, and the significance of their presence in Las Querubes is readily apparent. Until the mid-1800s, Las Querubes had been under Mexican rule, but by the middle of the twentieth century, eight out of ten Querubenos (Las Querubes residents) were white. Las Querubes began to undergo major ethnic diversification in the 1970s, shortly after the 1965 Immigration Act widened the doors to immigrants from non-Western regions of the world by nullifying earlier national quotas favoring European countries. As a result, between 1960 and 1990, Latinos grew from one-tenth of the Las Querubes population to one-third. By 2000 (around the time I was conducting my fieldwork), about two-thirds of the city's immigrant residents reported having been born in Latin America, and 40 percent of the city's total population reported Spanish as the language they spoke at home. At the time of my study, I doubt anyone could pass through any four blocks of the city without seeing or hearing Mexican Americans, bilingual English and Spanish-language signs and media, fast-food Mexican restaurants, and/or businesses, places of worship, and organizations that served primarily Spanish-speaking clientele. Consequently, Latino Querubenos, particularly those of Mexican descent, had become well established as a crucial part of the Las Querubes electorate and had helped elect a number of Mexican Americans into prominent leadership positions at every political level.

The Filipino immigrants of Las Querubes have had a far less visible his-tory and presence than their Mexican counterparts. While Mexicans were among the earliest settlers of Las Querubes, it was not until after 1965 that Filipinos grew into one of its major populations. In addition to lifting the national quotas that had impeded U.S. immigration for those "in the East-ern Hemisphere" (Ueda 1994: 170–171), the 1965 Immigration Act revised the occupational and family reunion immigrant preferences of the United States. This enabled a significant wave of Filipino migration into the United States that consisted primarily of the relatives of Filipino Americans and "doctors, engineers, and accountants with professional and special technical skills training, ready to be integrated into the highly skilled US work force"

(Bonus 2000: 44). As a result of the post-1965 wave of Filipino American immigration, Filipinos are now the third-largest population in Las Querubes, after whites and Latinos. However, since many contemporary Filipino Querubenos are not as occupationally or residentially concentrated as their Mexican neighbors—working in various middle-class occupations and often settling in newer, multiethnic enclaves—their political and cultural presence and influence are far less palpable.

Socioeconomically, Filipinos and Mexicans in Las Querubes are representative of the broader Filipino and Mexican populations of the United States (see Figure 1.1). During my year in Las Querubes, I noted that Mexican Americans were often assumed to be recent and/or "illegal" immigrants and were widely perceived of as poor, unable to speak English, and "stupid." Mexicans in my study were highly aware of these stereotypes and shared that they felt that "people see us as an inferior race" and "people think you're poor." Jorge Diaz, the son of Mexican American schoolteachers who immigrated here as teenagers, eloquently told me, "The average American regards the Mexican as uneducated, unclean, and untrustworthy. At best they see them as sometimes-necessary, cheap labor and at worst as a drain on the country's resources. Either way, they're perceived as subservient, intellectually inferior, and 'alien.'"

On the contrary, Filipinos in Las Querubes seemed to be generally viewed as well assimilated and "successful," although culturally and politically inconsequential. Most Filipino Querubenos who spoke with me did not share personal experiences with racism or discrimination but did share the feeling that, in spite of their relatively positive social standing, Filipino Americans were still considered "less than" other Americans. One Filipino immigrant, Linet Napolo, told me: "When we first moved [to Del Sol], I was planting, you know, on a hill. This guy was asking me—you know, he was asking me, 'Are you renting?' You know? I mean, he never think we can *buy* a house!"

Because Las Querubes is such a microcosm of immigrant America, studying Mexican and Filipino Querubenos sheds further light on how immigrants and members of the second generation are experiencing life in the United States, what factors help and/or impede their successful adaptation, and how they are contributing and transforming what it means to be and become "American."

The Program: Book Overview

Chapter 2 further fleshes out the events of this study. It describes popular representations of Filipino American debuts and Mexican American quinceañeras and how the broad range of real-life debuts and quinceañeras in this study both reflect and deviate from these.

In Chapter 3, I begin to explain how quinceañeras and debuts both reflect and contribute to the diverse backgrounds, desires, and social positions of Mexican Americans and Filipino Americans. I examine two of the most apparent ways debuts and quinces differ—in size and expense—to show how families use their daughters' coming-of-age events to maintain, build, and activate key social networks. More specifically, I clarify how large events for individual celebrants enable working- and middle-class Mexican and Filipino families to reinforce and activate already existing relationships with kin and other close relations, how cotillion balls for multiple debutantes help working-class Filipino families fortify existing ties and create connections with new contacts outside their close networks, and how intimate individual quinceañeras and debuts for single girls help lower-working-class Filipino and Mexican families affirm and restrict the quantity and intensity of their strong ties in order to protect their own limited resources. This enhances sociological knowledge on both networks and immigrant outcomes because existing research on networks does not really consider how rituals contribute to building and managing social ties, and while theories of immigrant adaptation explain the significance of social capital for immigrants and their children, they have yet to advance how immigrant families' social networks are built and maintained.

In Chapter 4, I thickly describe how immigrant families use debuts and quinceañeras to mark the passage of Filipino and Mexican American girls into "not just any women" but ethnicized young ladies. The process of training girls to embrace identities as *señoritas* and *dalaga*[25] ("young, unmarried ladies," in Spanish and Tagalog, respectively) through quinceañeras and debuts involves Mexicana and Filipina daughters aligning choices with those of their parents throughout the planning process, prepping through rehearsals and classes, getting physically ready, and, of course, performing on the big day. Each of these practices is ritualized and embodied and therefore powerfully reinforces the understanding that becoming a young woman is tied to better understanding one's "culture" and fashioning oneself into an apt representative of one's family and ethnic community.

Crafting and presenting chaste, dutiful, and self-sacrificing dalaga and señoritas helps immigrant parents challenge Western perceptions of their cultures as "uncivilized" and deficient because they allow organizers to assert their cultures' intrinsic refinement (by representing debuts and quinces as long-standing traditions) and their moral superiority over white Americans (by representing their daughters and, by extension, their families and communities as "proper," while enabling them to construct and repudiate white women, and, by extension, white culture, as morally depraved, out of control, and selfish). And within Mexican and Filipino communities, quinceañeras and debuts allow first-generation immigrants to (re)establish themselves as experts on what is authentically Mexican or Filipino (augmenting parents' control over their offspring), while they enable second-generation daughters and sons to also contribute (in limited ways) to what it means to be Filipino or Mexican in the twenty-first-century United States.

The chapter's close focuses on the formation of second-generation members of immigrant families is vital because understanding the lives of the children of immigrants is key to ascertaining how they and their communities "will be inserted into the economic and social fabric of the nation-state" (Maira 2002: 19). It calls attention to how my subjects concurrently criticize, aspire to fully integrate into, and are helping transform American culture. It also enriches what we know of contemporary American immigrant family life because, while current theories advance that race and gender strongly influence immigrant and second-generation outcomes (Portes and Rumbaut 2001b), they do not adequately explain how immigrant families help *produce* race, ethnicity, and gender. And while these same theories examine how intergenerational relationships can facilitate or disrupt the "normative integration" of second-generation Americans, they do not explain whether and how such relationships can be transformed through various efforts during the adaptation process.

Furthermore, Chapter 4 adds to existing theories on the social construction of race and gender by describing the ways that ritual powerfully contributes to race and gender projects. More specifically, ritual contributes to gender studies by helping affirm the existence of multiple femininities within our society (Connell 1987; Schippers 2007), further illustrating how women's bodies and labor are used and controlled to advance ethnic communities, and specifying how gender is negotiated *through ritual*. While sociological researchers have thoroughly considered how individual gender regimes such as school (e.g., Pascoe 2007; Thorne 1993), work (e.g., Garey 1995; Gerson 1993), and marriage (e.g., Hochschild and Machung 1989) define and shape femininities and masculinities, they have only begun to explore how rituals work within and across gender regimes to produce and/or challenge how we understand and enact gender.

In Chapter 5, I show how assertive females, "playful" and unmarried adults, gay men, and others who do not conform to ethnic ideals for Mexican and Filipino men and women have been suppressed by immigrant communities but are still challenging the boundaries of Filipino and Mexican

America. This clarifies how the ongoing construction of what it means to be Filipino or Mexican American is not straightforward and trouble-free, but rather a project that is contradictory, that is debated, and that compels communities to wrestle with themselves and to constantly reevaluate who does and does not belong, even as they struggle against how they have been constructed by those outside their communities. The chapter underscores the complicated nature of constructing group identities by highlighting how forms of cultural opposition simultaneously can, and sometimes do, reinforce oppressive, essentialist ways of imagining and performing ethnicity, class, and gender.

In Chapter 6, I look closely at my subjects' ardent declarations that the most important result of their participation in debuts and quinceañeras is "the memories you carry with you for the rest of your life." Because of how my postcolonial feminist methodology required me to take such judgments and experiences seriously, I was able to theorize how the memories engendered by debuts and quinceañeras help facilitate immigrant families' social advancement. Positive memories of quinces and debuts are uniquely powerful because they evoke remembrances of identities and reputations that were bodily enacted, ritualized, shared with others, and heavily documented. Such memories can be and are employed to help those who generate them construct and project a desirable sense of who they are for themselves and others. These identities and reputations, in turn, build what I term *emotional operating capital*: affective assets that can help facilitate social advancement by providing actors with the resilience and self-assurance needed to effectively navigate barriers to acquiring, building, and activating the benefits of human, social, and cultural capital. I also put forward that memories are of particular importance to the Mexicans and Filipinos I studied because of the deliberate erasures of their precolonial histories by European imperialists.

Along with the rest of the book, Chapter 6 corroborates and advances existing research on "pleasure, aesthetics, and popular culture" that claims that involvement in such activities is complicated and political, despite being considered "idle" and anti-intellectual (e.g., Kondo 1997). It is consistent with the work of other sociologists (e.g., Bettie 2003; Bourdieu 1984; Gandara 1995) who have found that "a positive perception of oneself and one's family can engender . . . a sense of hopefulness and deservedness" that can play a part in "enabling or restricting mobility" (Bettie 2003: 154). And the concept of emotional operating capital breaks new ground in sociology by offering a new account of how immigrants and their children are able to internally find the motivation and ability to amass and activate cultural and social capital in the United States and to deal with external obstacles to their successful assimilation.

Finally, in Chapter 7, I recap the arguments and questions raised in earlier chapters and reiterate that the processes by which my subjects and their communities are transforming what it means to be American, Filipino, and Mexican females and males are fluid, dynamic, and not necessarily straightforward or always empowering. I also elaborate on what it means for me to declare this project interdisciplinary, feminist, and postcolonial ("a feminist ethnic study") and attempt to cross the divide between what Michael Burawoy (2005) calls "professional sociology" and (traditional) "public sociology." Though I know this book is bound to be read by primarily academic audiences, it could not have been produced without generous immigrant and second-generation "publics." In light of this, I deliberately set aside part of the chapter to present recommendations that may help family and community members, as well as fellow scholars, consider how to design coming-of-age rituals that contribute to producing healthy outcomes for immigrants and their children. I do not mean to uncritically encourage such events, but I do hope to offer individuals and families who feel these events are worth organizing ideas about how to do so in ways that can avoid glamorizing and reproducing patriarchal, elitist, and/or colonial ideals of females and Mexican or Filipino culture.

As stated previously, this book is by no means the definitive work on debuts, quinceañeras, Mexicans, or Filipinos. But it is definitely an open invitation to learn more about the lives and special occasions of the people in my study and about the ways in which they are actively and constantly crafting themselves and their social worlds, as well as helping transform the face and cultures of America.

CHAPTER 2

"No Two Are the Same": Quinceañera and Debut Rituals and Performances

For our interview, Gabriel Ortega, a Mexican American man in his mid-thirties, requested that I meet him on a sunny afternoon, at a multi-story photography shop not too far from where I lived in Las Querubes. The shop was a more considerable distance from his home but was a landmark, and he was purchasing new, hard-to-find photo equipment. This was around the time most professionals were just starting to consider moving to digital; he explained that he was one of the first in the vicinity to take the leap of going completely digital. Gabriel had been working with quinceañeras for nearly two decades—the first two years exclusively as a choreographer and then for the last seventeen as a photographer. So, by the time we met, he had worked about two hundred quinceañeras. For these events, he reported that he was "with the girl every step of the day. The photographer is there when she is getting ready, before she even puts on her dress, all the way to the end." As a result of such close and extensive access to so many quinceañeras over the years, he told me, "I know everything that's going to happen, and everywhere people will be. I can calculate everything. I even know what time they're going to sleep." Accordingly, I felt fortunate to have been able to schedule one of my first interviews with such a seasoned expert and looked forward to him telling me everything about the "typical" quinceañera. So you can imagine my surprise when he declared, "You can't talk about a 'typical' fifteen. No two are the same, just like each girl is unique."

Gabriel was right. And weeks later, I found out that the same held true for Filipino debutantes. I interviewed Geraldo Tiongson, a mild-mannered older gentleman who had been a professional photographer for thirty years. During Gerry's career, he had photographed two thousand weddings, approximately two hundred debuts, and a smaller number of quinceañeras. Gerry reported that he had photographed Filipino debuts with as few as fifty people and cotillions with as many as five hundred. Francisco, his son and business partner, told me he had been to celebrations that "were just like a regular birthday, with friends gathering, and food from the parents," and others that were "like a wedding."

In this chapter, I present Filipino debuts and Mexican quinces, in all their diversity. First, I include a history of each of these traditions by presenting various speculations that others have offered about their origins. Then I examine how quinces and debuts have been represented in two of the most well-known feature films that highlight these events, *Quinceañera* (Glatzer and Westmoreland 2006) and *The Debut* (Cajayon 2001), to help illustrate the basic ingredients of the events and to show how real-life debuts and quinces both mirror and diverge from these film portrayals.

Once upon a Time

Despite the continuing (and some would argue, growing) practice of Filipino debuts and Mexican quinceañeras in the United States, surprisingly little is known about their historical origins. Nicanor Tiongson, one of the Philippines' foremost contemporary cultural historians and critics, surmises that Filipino debuts began their ascension into popularity during the 1970s, when groups in Manila "society" began organizing competing debutante balls, modeling themselves after American ones, with the same Western costumes, music, and form of presenting a group of young women in a lavish and formal setting (2002, pers. comm.). However, stories of debutantes before the 1970s in the Philippines abound, so others speculate that they were introduced during Spanish rule, some time between 1565 and 1898.

A little more has been posited about the origins of the quinceañera. Quinceañeras are thought to be a blend of pre-Colombian traditions and those of the Spanish, who colonized Mexico from 1521 until 1810. Pre-Colombian sculptures, codices, and other artifacts found and studied by archaeologists reveal that natives of Central America initiated and marked young people's passages into adulthood with ritual ceremonies. Mexican historian Mercedes de la Garza writes:

> Al llegar a los 13 años, se celebraba el caputzihil, "nacer de nuevo," ceremonia colectiva para todos los niños y las niñas de esa edad. . . .

"Lo que pensaban [que] recibían en el [bautismo] era una propia dis-
posición para ser buenos en sus costumbres y no ser dañados por los
demonios." (2003: 34)

⎯⎯

At thirteen years old, [pre-Hispanic youth] celebrated a collective *ca-
putzihil*, "rebirth," ceremony, for all the boys and girls of this age. . . .
"It was believed that when they received this [baptism] they each received the character necessary to understand their customs well and
avoid damnation by demons."[1]

During these collective "rebirth" rituals, a priest blessed the ritual space and
the "initiates." Mothers of girls, who, at three years old had been given a *"con-
cha roja sobre el pubis"* ("red shell placed over the pubis"), cut the cord used
to keep the shells on to symbolize their daughters' new fertility and readiness
for marriage (de la Garza 2003: 34). After they returned to their families, the
"new adults" were expected to act as responsible members of their communities; girls, especially, were expected to begin preparing for marriage so that
they could bring new life into the world (de la Garza 2003: 34).

Sister Angela Erevia and Michele Salcedo, authors of the definitive
guidebooks on quinceañera masses (Erevia 1980) and quinceañera receptions (Salcedo 1997), respectively, both posit that today's quinceañeras
are likely a fusion of such pre-Colombian rituals and the European debutante ball. Literary and Latino/a studies scholar Norma Elia Cantú notes
that "the language used in the fiesta as well as the structure to suggest
a more European connection" (Cantú 1995), and Salcedo advances that
debutantes were likely introduced to Latin America by Carlota, the Aus-
trian empress of Mexico, who was installed with her husband, Maximilian,
in 1864, during France's attempt to establish Mexico as a French colony
(Salcedo 1997: ix).

Debutante balls that the French and Spanish transplanted in Mexico and
the Philippines were, in turn, probably adapted from England. In *Girls on the
Verge*, Vendela Vida writes:

Debutante balls originated in sixteenth-century England with Queen
Elizabeth who supposedly started the custom of formally presenting
at court young women who were eligible for marriage. Much of the
ritual's current incarnation, however, dates back to the nineteenth
century, when Queen Victoria began including the daughters of the
Industrial Revolution's increasingly haute bourgeoisie along with
those of nobility and gentry. (1999: 57)

The Spanish aristocracy and bourgeoisie probably borrowed the practice of debutante balls because while it was in their social and material interests to arrange their daughters' marriages to other elites, young girls were expected to stay hidden from the public in order to appear chaste and therefore marriageable. Debutante balls gave members of the upper class an acceptable way to bring their unmarried daughters outside the home, so that their availability for marriage could be announced. Furthermore, they allowed rich families to have their daughters "come out" to an exclusive audience, which helped restrict their marriage markets to other elites.

Although we can only conjecture about when and how Mexicans and Filipinos began celebrating quinceañeras and debuts, we can be certain that they have persisted across time, social class, and borders, while other Mexican and Filipino folk traditions have not. Cantú submits that this is the case because "they serve a particular function in the community on an individual and communal level" (1995). Therefore, I now turn to an examination of modern-day Mexican quinceañeras and Filipino debutantes in the United States.

Representations of Debuts and Quinces in U.S. Culture

It is telling that despite the glaring underrepresentation of Filipinos and Mexicans in everyday U.S. popular culture (for more on this, see Campomanes 2005; C. Rodriguez 1997), only two mainstream films were produced during my study with young adult Filipino and Mexican American characters and actors. And their plots ostensibly centered on the events I am investigating. *Quinceañera*, written and directed by Richard Glatzer and Wash Westmoreland, real residents of the rapidly gentrifying but predominantly working-class Latino L.A. neighborhood of Echo Park where their film is set, tells the tale of Magdalena. Its DVD jacket condenses the movie plot by saying, "As Magdalena's 15th birthday approaches, her working class family prepares for the all-important QUINCEAÑERA—a lavish coming-of-age celebration." A review of its screening at the 2006 Sundance Film Festival, where it won both the Grand Jury Prize and Audience Award, said, "The film provides a honest look at the Mexican-American beauty" and at the "changing . . . face of a Latino community" (Voynar 2006).

The Debut has been called the "first-ever Filipino-American film" (Ebert 2002) and "the first Filipino American film to be released theatrically nationwide" (AMC 2012). At the time of its release, its writer and director, Gene Cajayon, "the Saigon-born, US-raised son of a French-Vietnamese mother and a Filipino father," was eight years out of film school, where *The*

Debut started as a ten-minute short he made for his thesis (Cajayon, Castro, and Mabalon 2001). Centered on the "eighteenth birthday party" of Rose, the main character's sister, it tells the tale of "the struggle between his family's Filipino traditions and his own American dreams" (DVD jacket). Using girls' coming-of-age rituals as windows into the lives of immigrant American families, *The Debut* and *Quinceañera* offer viewers versions of their eponymous rituals that are meant to introduce the uninitiated to these traditions, while offering U.S. Filipino and Mexican audiences recognizable images that seem accurate and authentic. This is why I choose to start with these cinematic portrayals to help me begin to describe these events.

Quinceañera

The film *Quinceañera* opens with the quinceañera of Magdalena's middle-class cousin, Eileen. Eileen's event starts with a religious service at the church where her uncle, Ernesto, is pastor. He initiates the day from a pulpit framed by two columns wrapped with pink streamers. From there, he faces a white rattan throne, decorated with a trellis of pink carnations, flanked by guests on either side of a narrow aisle. The film's first lines are Ernesto saying:

> Buenas tardes. Primero que nada, quiero a darle la bienvenida a la celebración de este día maravilloso en la vida de una hermosa joven, la quinceañera de Eileen Garcia. En este día, ella cumple sus quince años. Y hoy, ella convierte en mujer.
>
> ———
>
> Good afternoon. First of all, I'd like to welcome you to this celebration of a beautiful day in a young girl's life, the quinceañera of Eileen Garcia. On this day, she turns fifteen. Today, she becomes a woman.

As Ernesto issues this welcome, we see that outside, Eileen is jovially trying to line up an entourage of six girls, uniformly dressed in floor-length burgundy dresses with narrow skirts and cap sleeves, and seven boys, all wearing black tuxedoes—six with bow ties. Eileen is in a confection of a dress: a cotton-candy-pink gown with a billowing skirt and a lacy, strapless bodice. Her hair, like that of the other girls, has been tightly twisted in a number of small rows from her hairline, with each twist ending in a coiled, braided bun atop her head—a young twist (no pun intended) on more traditional formal hairstyles.

The mood and movement outside, with Eileen's friends chattering and snapping photos on their cell phones, while her cousin and aunt hand each person a long-stemmed pink rose, is widely divergent from the next scene, which shows the young adults entering the church. As Verdi's "Marcha Triunfal de Aida" trumpets in the background, one couple at a time proceeds solemnly into the church to line up—all females, or damas, on one side, facing their partners, their chambelanes, across the aisle. They step toward each other, and the males spin their partners simultaneously; then all of them step backward to their original places and begin to lift their roses up and toward the center. Following, Eileen makes her grand entrance, holding a bouquet of roses and escorted by the only boy wearing an ordinary tie, her *chambelán de honor*. As they proceed under their floral tunnel, Eileen's expression goes from nervous and apprehensive to eager, though not completely at ease. She finishes her march by taking a seat in her wicker throne and then looks expectantly toward her uncle.

From there, the film cuts to a scene at a park where gardens of multicolored rose bushes branch out like rays of the sun from a large fountain in the center. Cameras are set up on tripods and a professional photographer is taking various formal shots: of Eileen and her parents, Eileen with just the boys, Eileen with just her damas and chambelán de honor, and, finally, of her with all thirteen members of her *corte de honor*, or honor court.

Next, we see all the young people in the back of a limousine that resembles a nightclub. A hip-hop track has replaced Verdi, and a ceiling of LED lights continuously changes colors above. On the mirrored window behind Eileen is a glowing, two-by-two letter H, with the word *Xtreme* shining from within. There is an atmosphere of fun and risk as everyone encourages Eileen to dance with a neon red pole that inexplicably runs from floor to ceiling where the passengers are seated. A male voice eggs on, "Go girl," as a boy places both his hands on the pole and strokes it suggestively. Another boy flashes a five-dollar bill, and Eileen coyly laughs, "Noooo!" The boy with the money then waves it toward her face and pulls it back. Eileen says, "All right then," grabbing at the bill with one hand as she places the other on the pole. The interior dramatically darkens as Eileen begins to swivel her hips while holding the pole. She finishes by quasi-sliding down the shaft and then throwing herself back into her seat, playfully whimpering, "Don't tell my mom!"

Suddenly, we see Eileen and her chambelán de honor stepping tensely in sync to the "Marcha Triunfal" again (this time being played by a live mariachi band), in front of three three-tiered cakes and a buffet covered with pleated white table linens festooned with tulle, carnations, and pink balloons that read *Mis Quince Años*. They are eventually joined by the rest of Eileen's entourage in what appears to be a fluorescent-lit hall. After the camera pans out to show an attentive audience of guests raptly surveying the dance floor, it returns to the corte, deliberate and serious-faced, executing the steps of a highly choreographed *vals*, or waltz. The boys spin the girls around in unison; they switch partners; and they step forward, back, side to side. As they watch the dance, we hear Ernesto tell Eileen's father, "Eileen looks beautiful; you have a lot to be proud of." Eileen's father, Walter, then observes, "Magdalena's quinceañera is coming up soon. . . . Get ready to pay through the nose." Ernesto replies, "Magdalena's won't be like that. She's different—she's a more traditional girl than Eileen."

A few scenes later, the stiff, self-conscious waltz seems like a distant memory. Colored lights are spinning around the now-darkened hall. From behind a set of turntables, a male deejay declares, "Ahora es la hora para bailar y discotear" (Now it's time to dance and groove), and the camera pans the room to show the members of Eileen's corte freaking[2] to a fast-tempoed meringue in small trains. Not an adult eye bats an eyelash at the sexual movements of the young people around them. In fact, if they are not comfortably dancing a traditional meringue beside them, then they are shown sitting at the tables around the dance floor, casually taking shots of tequila, drinking beer, answering the questions of small children, and nibbling at small plates of food. The night concludes later, with the deejay announcing, "Thank you for coming to Eileen's quinceañera. It's a special day for a quinceañera. Thank you, everybody, for showing love."

As Ernesto's earlier comment to his brother-in-law implied and as I observed during my fieldwork, Eileen's cinematic quinceañera is only one way to celebrate a girl's fifteen. Still, Eileen's celebration in *Quinceañera* contained elements that are present in almost all quinces: a church service, a special dress for the celebrant, a special party, and a birthday cake. Unlike Eileen's religious portion, though, most quinceañera church services are special masses, held at a Catholic parish. Also, not all quinceañeras are so elaborately costumed, and there are quinceañeras with no corte, or just a single chambelán; quinceañeras with cortes of up to fifteen other couples; and everything in between. One quinceañera I observed, Katia's, had only chambelanes.

In addition, the venue and size of a quince reception can vary widely. Many, like Eileen's, are held in rented community halls, where the food and drinks are prepared by family and/or personal friends and paid for by parents and/or padrinos,[3] "godparents," who typically consider such sponsorship an honor. Padrinos often sponsor a specific item such as the dress, a religious article used for the church ceremony, or the cake. Cakes are almost always included in a quinceañera, since, as Michele Salcedo's quinceañera guide states, "a quinceañera is not complete without a cake." Salcedo points out this can be anything from a grocery-store-bought "simple sheet cake" to, like Eileen's, a custom-made, "elaborate multitiered extravaganza, with a fountain, bridges, and a fancy topper" (1997: 74–75).

The system of padrino sponsorship, or *compadrazgo*, is why, despite popular misconceptions, quinceañeras are not practices exclusive to middle- and upper-class Latinos. Nevertheless, as Walter noted, many families do end up "paying through the nose" for the occasion, whether it is at a hall like Eileen's or a themed party like Teresita Perez's quinceañera held at Miami's Tropigala Banquet Hall, with a life-sized carousel horse at the entrance and a stage "set with a carousel, two fountains, and two beautiful flower arrangements of pink and white carnations" (Salcedo 1997: 53–54).

Eileen's quinceañera contained several other features common to quinceañeras held outside the home: the rental of a chauffeured vehicle, the performance of a choreographed waltz, an open dance floor, and professional photography. Many real-life parents in my study hired professional drivers to take their daughters, themselves, and/or the cortes from home to church, and from church to the reception. Not all cars were "Hummer limos" like Eileen's, but these were common enough that quince photographer Gabriel told me, "They [the quinceañera and her family] can live in a house . . . that's falling apart, and the big Hummer limo will come. It won't even fit in the driveway; it has to park in the street."

As seen in *Quinceañera*, the formal highlight of many quince receptions is usually the vals. Dancers usually spend weeks to months rehearsing this—usually in backyards and garages, under supervision of an experienced (often, paid) choreographer. Family members typically provide dancers with food, during and after rehearsals. Dalía, a former quinceañera I interviewed, recalled that everyone in her corte was a relative or a friend from school. She said that practices "were easy" because they were held immediately after school, at her home, nearby. Her mother hired the choreographer who worked with them, gave everyone lunch, and drove home any kids whose parents were unable to pick them up. Dalía's mother, Astrud Azua, recalled the result of all those rehearsals, the vals, as "the most beautiful part" of Dalía's quinceañera party. However, Dalía remembered being "uncomfortable in the spotlight" during her vals, and she said that the open dancing was the best part of her reception. Like Eileen's, Dalía's open dancing turned a little amorous later in the evening. She told me she enjoyed it because "I was able to hang out with my friends, finally, and to dance—and make out with!—this guy I liked."

Although Eileen's quince did not show this, oftentimes, before open dancing commenced, the quinceañera program included a few other rituals.

Sometimes parents issued a formal thank-you to guests; a designated person gave a *brindis*, or toast; the quinceañera danced with her father; and/or the birthday cake was cut ceremoniously. At other fiestas, "the young woman changes from flats to high heels in the course of the presentation" to symbolize dressing in "the attire of an adult" and/or "the young woman . . . receives a doll from her *madrina de muñeca* [godmother of the doll]" that looks like the quinceañera and/or is meant to represent her last toy (Cantú 1999).[4]

Finally, like Eileen from the movie, many quinceañeras have professionals record and document their "special day." Midway through *Quinceañera*, Eileen and her damas are shown reviewing the finished DVD of her event at her home. Its opening title reads *Mis Quince Años*, as white petals descend from the top of the screen. The image then changes as a woman's singing begins and the cursive words *Felicidades Eileen May Garcia* move across the screen. Images from Eileen's day finally begin with a shot of what appears to be an ornate heart-shaped "cake or pillow," with *15* in the center. Eileen explains that it is just "cardboard," as her smiling image picks it up and then displays it for the camera. Then the DVD shows a shot of Eileen's tiara. Someone comments, "I didn't even see you wearing it," and Eileen replies, "I know; I broke it in the car on the way to church." In another scene from her DVD, Eileen holds her gown up to her body, and as she spins, a computerized image of a magic wand waves beside her, so that when she turns to face the camera again, she's fully outfitted for her quince. All the girls laugh and then continue to ask questions, comment, and relive the day with Eileen as the video plays on. I discuss the significance of such heavy documentation of quinceañeras and debuts in later chapters (see Chapters 4 and 6).

The Debut

In Gene Cajayon's *The Debut*, the audience does not see the debutante, Rose Mercado, until nearly eight minutes into the film, and we do not see the site of her eighteenth birthday party until about twelve minutes in. This is because "Rose's is a secondary story to that of Ben's, the tortured younger son whose own dreams of art school run afoul of those of his father's for him" (Mabalon 2004: 17). Nonetheless, because Rose's debut is the film's central setting, *The Debut* provides us with a decent illustration of such celebrations and many of their common elements.

Rose's day begins at home, sitting in front of her mother's vanity in a sleeveless brocade top and a satin, wine-colored, floor-length skirt. Her mother, Gina, is in a white *piña* dress,[5] putting the final pins in her daughter's elaborate updo, while Rose admires the results in the mirror. The following shots—of family members loading food into a minivan; of the outside of a Catholic church; and of Rose, Gina, Ben, and a few (mostly female) others decorating a brightly lit room with bleachers and a stage—suggest that Rose's debut is being held in a parish gymnasium. Over what we can presume to be the course of an afternoon, the gym is transformed by everyone's focused efforts. Round dinner tables are draped with teal plastic tablecloths, set with red plastic plates and yellow paper napkins, and decorated with electric tapered candles and tall centerpieces of shimmering gold stars, each topped with an oversized silk butterfly. At least eight massive arches of pink, silver, gold, and blue mylar balloons have been placed throughout the space. At the front of the room, on an elevated stage, the deejay crew have assembled their equipment on a covered table and set up lights that make the curtains behind them radiate red, yellow, and purple. The bleachers are also aglow with white twinkle lights, and along one side of the room, an expansive buffet has been set atop long tables covered with *dahon ng saging* (banana tree leaves) layered on top of white linens. Once the *lechon*, or roast pig, is set down by caterers, the script calls for one of Rose's aunts to declare, "Now it's a party."[6]

The next scene is set in the evening, at the beginning of Rose's debut celebration. The Mercados are greeting guests in a receiving line by the entrance, in front of a gift table, as a photographer snaps away across from them. They kiss and embrace guests quickly until Rose's *tito* (uncle)[7] Lenny calls out, "Kids, your Lolo [Grandpa] Carlos." The line then ceases for several moments as the family welcomes Lolo Carlos, who has traveled from the Philippines to attend Rose's birthday party in Los Angeles. Afterward, several *titas* are shown serving dinner as guests move down a line at the buffet tables. Then we see people of all generations seated together at each table, eating, gossiping, having their photos taken, and catching up with each other.

Several scenes later, Rose has changed into a deep purple *baro't saya*[8] and a black *pañuelo* with silver beading. The close friends and cousins who compose her large court are with her in a locker room, away from the party in the gym, and have changed attire as well. Half of the women are in white baro't saya, and half the men are wearing black *Barong Tagalog* (formal wear for Filipino men)[9] and black pants. The remaining males are dressed in mandarin-collared white silk shirts, tucked into dark pants with *malong*[10] tied over them. The remaining women are in iridescent long-sleeved blouses, tucked into long, brightly colored, fitted skirts, embroidered with gold. In the locker room, the dancers nervously adjust each other's costumes and loudly cheer each other on before sending out Rose's best friend, Annabelle, to introduce them to Rose's guests. Onstage, Annabelle grabs a microphone and tentatively announces:

Coming up next we have a special performance by the birthday girl and some of our friends. We've been working on this for a couple of months now, and I think that we came up with something really nice. So, please take a seat, because you definitely do not want to miss this.

As Annabelle returns the mic, a *rondalla* (a Filipino ensemble of various *banduria*, or mandolin instruments) of five male musicians take their seats in front of the stage, and Rose is escorted to the center of the dance floor by the only male wearing a barong with black-and-white vertical stripes. The room is silent, and we see Gina send Rose's father, Roland, a look of pride and anticipation. Rose and her partner raise their arms and begin to walk forward, to the beat of bamboo castanets that we hear coming from the back of the room. As they do so, they are joined by four male dancers, who, it turns out, are playing the castanets. Rose and her partner encircle each other gracefully as the men start to stomp a beat on the floor and then are joined by the four women wearing baro't saya. Watching from the bleachers, one of Ben's friends observes, "Hey, looks like those Mexican dances my cousins do," just as the rondalla begins, and Rose and her court start to perform a *Jota Manileña*, a lively dance that became popular in the Philippines during the Spanish colonial period. In the audience, the camera shows Rose's lolo nodding approvingly as she and her dancers finish with a flourish.

Guests are still applauding when a large gong is struck by a musician. Ancient sounds of a *kulintang*[11] begin to fill the room, as Rose, now clad in a fitted, long-sleeved, golden dress, reenters the gym. Annabelle follows closely behind, holding an ornate parasol above Rose. On Rose's right ankle is a hoop of brass bells; on her head is a gauzy, floor-length veil that flows from beneath a crown shaped like a gold rooster. In each hand, Rose holds a delicate gold fan that she waves in rhythm to the kulintang, with small flicks of her wrists, and her arms floating around her. The men in her court who are not wearing Barong Tagalog file in, on either side of Rose and Annabelle, carrying ten-foot-long poles of bamboo, which they carefully place in three crisscrosses of four sticks each on the floor. With each man holding one end of two poles, they start to strike the floor with the sticks and then snap them together in a synchronized fashion. Rose begins stoically, gracefully weaving through them as they do so; then the eight remaining girls in her court enter the room and begin doing the same. A male dancer in all purple comes out with a faux sword and shield, wearing a bronze-colored crown on his head. The youth are performing the *Singkil*,[12] and Rose is the lead dancer, the singkil princess. As they move, the center of the gym becomes a flurry of waving fans, floating veils, and bold colors. The dance ends spectacularly, when the music, poles, and dancers suddenly stop, and Annabelle brings her open fans to an abrupt rest at her hips and then looks regally beyond the audience. Her guests give them a standing ovation; Rose's tito Lenny gives her a thumbs-up.

Later, Annabelle is shown, back in her original top and skirt, smiling from her table, as a trio of her girlfriends sing Rose a "surprise" a cappella happy birthday song from the front stage and finish by saying, "Happy birthday, Rose. May all your wishes come true. We love you." Following, an emcee announces, "Up next, we have a special treat for all of you," as Rose's father steps onto the stage to sing to Rose and Gina. As he finishes the second verse, Gina takes Rose by the hand and brings her to the stage, and her father serenades her with the lyrics "Ikaw ang ligaya sa buhay . . ." (You are my life's joy . . .). When Roland is finished, their guests applaud wildly. The emcee then asks, "So, is there anybody else with a dedication for Rose?" After some hesitation, Ben takes the mic and says shyly, "You're the coolest sis any guy can have, and you deserve better. Yeah, that's all. Happy birthday, Rose."

The movie then cuts to the deejays playing a bass-driven R&B track, as one of them says, "It's about time to set things off. . . . Let's see you all grab a partner, and get up and dance." After a few scenes of Rose and all her guests dancing, the film cuts again to just the deejays. This time, one of them is scratching[13] over a hip-hop beat, and when the camera pans back to the dance floor, we see that the titas and titos are no longer dancing—just the young people are. As the music plays, Annabelle and the trio that sang to Rose earlier spontaneously begin performing a modern dance routine. When they finish, they look defiantly at the guys. One of the men turns intentionally toward the turntables, and the male emcee remarks, "Looks like we got a battle brewing here. . . . Let's show these ladies it's a man's world." Four guys then proceed to perform their own dance routine, to which the girls respond with another. The battle ends only after the boys execute another performance that ends with each of them, face to the floor, and legs perpendicular to the ground, in a b-boy freeze. Afterward, the battling dancers amicably praise and hug each other. The emcee declares, "That looked like a tie to me"; then the deejay starts playing a modern cha-cha that brings the titas and titos back out onto the dance floor. The night ends after Rose's family cleans and packs up all their things so that everyone can return home.

At some point midway through that evening, Roland said to his daughter ruefully, "You know, Rose, I'm not like your tito Lenny, or most of the parents out there. . . . I can't even afford a nice debut for you," to which Rose replied emphatically, "I didn't even want a debutante ball; this party's more than enough!" This exchange suggests that, like quinceañeras, debuts come in all shapes and sizes. During my fieldwork, I found this to be true. In fact, at least in Las Querubes, there was arguably more diversity in Filipino debuts because of the group cotillions.[14]

The group cotillions in my study were all annual events, organized by local community associations. These affairs usually recruited about a dozen girls, coming of age during the same year, to be "presented" at the same birthday celebration. Participation in such debuts usually required families to become members of the organizing association (if they were not members already), to help collectively pay for the costs of the event venue and vendors, and to help publicize and fund-raise for the association through various activities, including selling "tickets" to the cotillion (or purchasing them as gifts for their guests). Because of the number of participants, individual girls did not have to choose a court; they had to invite only one male peer, or escort, to join them for weekly rehearsals that cotillion organizers usually set up at rented community spaces. For this same reason, girls and their families had to negotiate many decisions—themes, color motifs, décor, costumes, and the like. Other significant details such as the event location and date, choreographer, photographer and videographer, musicians, dinner, and menu were usually determined by the association. For example, the South Cove Union of Filipino Americans (SCUFA) always held their cotillion in the ballroom of a historic landmark hotel in Del Sol during the late summer. Their cotillion always followed the same program: a promenade of the debutantes with their families, the introduction of each debutante individually before her grand curtsy, a group cotillion to "The Blue Danube," a group serenade to the parents, dinner, a formal cake cutting, and then a father-daughter dance, before open dancing for everyone. However, each year parents (usually mothers) chose a different color for all their dresses, selected unique floral arrangements for the table centerpieces, and determined whether there were to be additional decorations.

Unlike Rose's debut, the group debutantes in my study were all black-tie affairs. For SCUFA's annual ball, escorts and fathers were required to wear tuxedoes, and all the debutantes were required to wear gowns that (though they could vary from girl to girl) had to be white, with full, floor-length skirts. Debutantes for the Leonor Rivera Pilipina Society (LRPS) and the Pilipina Ladies' Association of Southern California (Pilipina Ladies' Association) had to wear Maria Clara gowns,[15] and their escorts were required to wear Barong Tagalog.

Because these occasions brought together the guest lists of so many families, they were usually attended by hundreds of people, most of whom were not intimately familiar with every debutante or family. The more public nature of these celebrations was also evident in the fact that these events were almost always covered in the local media; ethnic Filipino newspapers typically provided brief biographies and photos of each of the girls being presented after each cotillion.

Many of the debutantes I spoke with directly, however, did not have such large, public cotillions. Their debuts were more like Rose's—at smaller venues, with more modest guest lists, and with expenses shouldered completely by the debutante's family. A few were very small. Barbra, one debutante I interviewed, organized her debutante party in two weeks, after her mother convinced her that they should "just have a little get-together" to commemorate her eighteenth birthday. It was held in her working-class parents' modest home. Her dress had been sent from the Philippines, a long chocolate-colored tube that fit closely to her body. Her cake was store-bought, and her mother had ordered most of the food from a nearby Filipino restaurant. There were no extravagant decorations; there was no dance performance. However, eighteen of her female friends and eighteen of her male friends acted as her "Candles" and "Roses" respectively, a common part of many debuts. Each of Barbra's Candles lit a candle on her cake while announcing a birthday wish for her, and each of her Roses danced with her for a few seconds. Barbra recalled this part of her debut as one of the most memorable; "I was surprised, embarrassed, and happy," she told me.

Most of the debuts I heard about were more of a blend of the events organized for Barbra, Rose, and the group debutantes. More often than not, they were events for only one girl, with a "court" consisting of up to thirty or so friends and family. These were usually moderately sized receptions, at a special venue (often a restaurant banquet room or hotel ballroom). Like quinceañeras, debutantes went to great lengths to look exceptional for their debuts, with new dresses, makeup, formal hairdos, special jewelry, and so on. They often practiced at least one choreographed dance with their courts for weeks or months—to perform as a program highlight during their reception. Most frequently, the dance they performed was a waltz; sometimes, they also performed ethnic and/or contemporary dances, as Rose and her entourage did in *The Debut*. If there were no Candles and Roses, then there was usually some period during the program when guests were invited to share "dedications" for the birthday girl, as we saw Rose's friends, father, and brother do. And no matter how big or small, there was always extraordinary food, lively music, a time for everyone to dance, and at least one person capturing everything on film (and sometimes video).

Now that I have identified some of the common features of Filipino debuts and Mexican quinceañeras and, I hope, conveyed the variety of forms that such celebrations can take, I turn to an exploration of the sociological significance of some of the variations in these events.

❦

CHAPTER 3

Lazos/Ties That Bind: Quinceañera and Debut Social Networks

The Santiago family lives just in the shadow of a place frequented by the wealthy, beautiful, and, often, cosmetically enhanced. As I passed this place on my way to interview Belinda Santiago, the female head of the family, I could not help but wonder what it was like for Belinda's daughters to grow up in such close proximity to what, for most people, seems utterly unattainable. As it turns out, Belinda herself had some idea. Recalling her youth in El Salvador,[1] she told me:

> Miraba las quinceañeras de otras personas, de las ventanas. Eran muy bonitas. Eran diferentes de hoy. Había una misa especial, y entonces la fiesta era más privada, más formal, allá. No tenía una porque era mucho dinero para una quinceañera. El día de me cumpló quince años, estaba con mi mama, trabanjando, cortando café. Parecía como un castigo.

> I watched other people's quinceañeras, from the windows. They were beautiful. They were different from today. There was a special mass, and then the party was more private, more formal there. I didn't have one because a quinceañera was a lot of money. The day I turned fifteen years old, I was with my mother, working, picking coffee. It seemed like a punishment.

Consequently, almost as soon as she became a mother to her first daughter in the United States, Belinda began dreaming of how she would give her what she did not have as a girl. "Era un sueño—me encanta la quinceañera" (It was a dream—I love the quinceañera). And though she described life in the United States as *"muy dura"* (very difficult), she noted, "Aquí, pueden tener quinceañeras porque muchos padrinos. Cuando era joven, no había padrinos. Todos fueron los padres" (Here, my daughters can still have quinceañeras because of many godparents. When I was young, there weren't padrinos. Parents had to take care of everything [for their daughters' quinceañeras]"). To illustrate her point, Belinda later shared that eight couples, all of whom she described as among her and her husband's best friends, had volunteered or agreed to take on the expense of some aspect of her youngest daughter's quince, and that, collectively, these padrinos' gifts probably totaled *"unos cinco mil dolares"* (about five thousand dollars).

As Belinda's observations indicate, second-generation females' coming-of-age rituals in the United States are not the same occasions their immigrant mothers grew up with, and, despite sharing their names with the individual girls they celebrate, these events are as much about and for a girl's family and community as they are about their teenage celebrants. This is because, while these events ostensibly mark and celebrate a girl's "big day," they provide immigrant families with matchless opportunities to maintain, build, and activate key social networks. Such work reflects and enables immigrant families to respond to their social positions in the United States.

This chapter describes the ways various quinceañeras and debuts reflect and contribute to the development of distinctive immigrant networks and elucidates how young female bodies make this possible. More specifically, this section illustrates (1) how large individual quinceañeras and debuts with padrinos and other "sponsors" reinforce *and activate* a family's "strong ties," (2) how debutante cotillions that "present" several celebrants at once help families fortify existing strong ties *and create "weak ties"* with people outside a family's immediate network, and (3) how intimate "family only" debuts and quinces for single girls help affirm *and set firm boundaries* around "strong ties" to close friends and family in already existing networks of support.

This enhances existing sociological knowledge of both immigrant networks and outcomes because current research on immigrant outcomes explains the significance of social capital for immigrants and their children but does not adequately theorize how immigrant social networks are managed. The theory of *segmented assimilation* has effectively replaced the earlier master concept of singular assimilation into the dominant culture for contemporary immigrants and their children (Portes and Rumbaut 2001b). And it has distinguished family and the presence of co-ethnic communities as key to enabling members of the second generation to successfully contend with barriers to their assimilation, since such social networks increase access to economic goods and job opportunities, just as they have been shown to do for nonimmigrants (Granovetter 1973). However, despite having established the importance of immigrant social networks and the fact that "social networks are not a natural given and must be constructed" (Portes 1998: 3), sociology has thus far virtually ignored how immigrants' social connections are maintained. In a review of contemporary social science research on immigrant social networks, sociologist Jacqueline Maria Hagan points out that "research on social networks in immigrant incorporation . . . emphasize only the networks' existence, operation, and persistence but pay little attention to their transformations over time" (1998: 55). I would add that existing research almost exclusively focuses on the formation of immigrants' *individual* social networks and not *familial* ones. Moreover, in spite of sociology's emphasis on the value of having both close and distant relationships within one's personal network, immigration scholars have yet to explore how relationships with non-kin and those outside one's ethnic community may influence immigrant and second-generation outcomes. This chapter addresses these oversights by paying attention to and describing how the immigrant families and communities in my study engaged in a range of network-building and network-fortifying work through young women's coming-of-age celebrations.

Big and Strong

Most of the quinceañeras and debuts in my study were large events that involved a single celebrant, entourages of fourteen to twenty-four of the celebrant's peers, groups of adult "sponsors," and guest lists of at least a hundred. Some of the professionals I interviewed told me they had serviced events with as many as five hundred people in attendance; Belinda, the mother mentioned at the beginning of this chapter told me, "Las [quinceañeras] de mis hijas son sencillas. Invitado dos cientos personas—familia y amigos mas cercanos. Para mi, es sencillo" (My daughters' [quinceañeras] are simple. We invited two hundred people—family and our dearest friends. For me, this is simple). Such big events named, activated, and therefore reinforced "strong ties"[2] to close friends and family in already-existing networks of support, by inviting and relying on various family members and/or close friends to be responsible for parts of their quinceañera or debutante celebrations.

Big quinceañeras often employ a system of *compadrazgo*[3] to finance and present the quinceañera mass and fiesta. This is how many working-class Latino families in my study were able to organize fiestas that cost more than $10,000. Belinda told me that for the quinceañera of her youngest daughter,

Katia, she contacted four pairs of *"personas más amigos de nosotros"* (our best friends) to serve as *padrinos de honor* (godparents of honor). These couples furnished Katia's *medalla* (medallion), *anillo* (ring), *cochín* (pillow, which the ring was carried on), *biblia* (Bible), and *ramo natural* (bouquet offered to the Virgin Mary during the quinceañera mass.[4] Implicit in Belinda's invitation to serve as her daughter's godparents of honor was also the expectation that they would be available to offer Katia spiritual guidance as she approached her coming of age. Four additional sets of padrinos were asked to "sponsor" Katia's reception *pastel* (cake), *decoraciones* (decorations—i.e., floral arrangements), and brindis ([champagne] toast—i.e., the reception beverages). "Los padrinos pagan para cada cosa. Es un regalo a Katia, a nuestra familia" (The padrinos pay for each item. It is a gift to Katia, to our family). Other quinceañeras I heard about devised and designated padrinos for everything from *el vestido* (the dress) to *la limosina* (the limousine). Quinceañera photographer Gabriel Ortega told me it was even common to have a *padrino de la cerveza* (beer godfather). All these designations distinguished important adults in a family's network while supplementing a quinceañera's event budget.

As well as invoking support from parents' close friends and relatives, big quinceañeras relied on a number of the celebrant's closest peers to contribute their time and resources, as members of their corte de honor, or honor court. The courts in my study varied in size and composition; however, the most common court comprised fifteen members: seven damas (ladies), seven chambelánes (chamberlains, who served as the damas' partners), and one chambelán de honor, who served as the quinceañera's partner.[5] Court members were usually the quinceañera's siblings, closest friends from school, local cousins and godsiblings, and other court members' significant others. While quinceañeras generally had no input in the selection of their padrinos, quinceañeras usually chose and invited their own court members.

Damas and chambelánes were primarily responsible for participating in the mass, and for learning and performing the waltz, or vals, performed during (and usually the unequivocal highlight of) the quinceañera reception. Thus, they were typically required to attend at least one *ensayo* (dress rehearsal) at the parish where the quinceañera mass would be held to practice their parts in the mass and to learn what the church wants participants to know about the history and significance of the quinceañera tradition. Flora Favino, quinceañera coordinator for Prince of Peace parish in Las Querubes told me, "It's important that the quinceañera and her parents aren't just blindly following tradition. They have to understand how this thing [the quinceañera] started—how the tradition started, the importance of the tradition, how it is linked to religious life."

Without question, however, court members' foremost obligation to a quinceañera usually consisted of attending "practices" and purchasing their attire and accessories for the vals. Dresses, rentals, and accessories usually cost at least $150 per court member. By the end of their obligation, court members had often each devoted at least fifty hours of their time, talent, and support, over several months, to their friend's or relative's quinceañera (attending weekly dance practices and a "dress rehearsal"; renting and/or purchasing clothing for the mass and performance; commuting between school, home, and the practice locations; and participating in the actual event). Sixteen-year-old Josh reported that he had been in seventeen quinceañeras by the time he spoke to me as part of a focus group. "I've been doing this since I was eight or nine years old," he recalled. When I asked this quince *veterano* to describe the responsibilities of a chambelán, he said:

> To look good—nah, not really! But you need money, like between fifty [and] a hundred dollars, to rent a tux—maybe a hundred dollars, on average. Sometimes, it's pretty expensive. To be organized. Going to practice on time, and learning the steps—you don't wanna mess up [during the vals performance]; that's embarrassing to the whole thing. I feel like it's a lot of responsibility.

In return for their participation and sponsorship, a quinceañera's corte de honor and her padrinos were formally recognized in various ways, which included having their names printed in the quinceañera invitations, having a special part in the mass or reception program, being assigned special seating at the church and/or the reception *salón*, and being distinguished and addressed as honorary kin to the quinceañera celebrant and her parents.[6] This is in large part why, considering the sometimes-significant financial and emotional costs of being a padrino, dama, or chambelán, no one who spoke with me described his or her role as a burden. On the contrary, they all told me they would have never considered declining an invitation to contribute to such a special occasion and that they considered such requests "an honor." As Josh said, "For friends, you wanna do it, to be included, and not excluded, or left out. It's a cool, honorable thing."

Big debuts for a single girl also required the mobilization of numerous close family members and friends. Like their Mexicana counterparts, individual debutantes throwing large celebrations had to assemble courts of their peers to perform a formal waltz, as well as one to five additional modern dances. Debutante courts varied in size[7] but typically consisted of eight ladies, eight male escorts, and the debutante's escort, who had generally been chosen from among the celebrant's siblings, closest friends from school, close cousins, the teen children of her parents' closest friends, and other court members' significant others. Since none of the debuts in my study had a formal, individualized mass, the only responsibility of a debutante court member was to perform during the debut. This was a sizable duty, however, since the court's performances often were the most anticipated, featured, and lengthy parts of a debut.

Fulfilling their obligation to the debutante usually required court members to attend a series of practices and to purchase or rent their attire for the performances.[8] Since there were often multiple dances to be learned and performed for the debut program, most court members ultimately invested at least \$200 in performance apparel and at least sixty hours of their free time after school, extracurricular activities, and work to attend weekly dance practices and at least one dress rehearsal; to get measured and/or to buy their clothing and accessories for the performance; to commute between school, home, and the practice locations; and to participate in the actual event. And although it was not expected, at almost all the debuts I attended, court members also prepared their own songs or dances to perform and dedicate to the debutante, which meant that they ultimately contributed many more hours and personal resources than I am able to estimate.

When I asked Francisco, who had been in a number of debuts, to tell me his primary responsibilities as a court member, he told me:

> Being punctual and just being there. It can get stressful, even though it's supposed to be fun. Two to three weeks before [the debut], it's crunch time—like, practice three times a week. The hardest one [debut] I was in was when I was a freshman during college. I was commuting between Maneha and Macintyre [suburbs of Las Querubes, about an hour apart] during finals week. But it was for a friend. . . . You're just making the event as memorable as possible, letting a friendship grow.

Unique to quinces, large debutantes did not designate padrinos to sponsor any event elements. However, they typically designated eighteen male guests to serve as Roses and eighteen female guests to serve as Candles. While debutante court members were almost always asked to participate months beforehand, Candles and Roses were typically selected only a few weeks in advance and generally consisted of the debutantes' close (but not closest) friends, adult relatives, and parents' close friends—many of whom had already assisted the debutantes and their mothers by helping to make giveaways (gifts to reception guests), making and/or serving food (during practices, and at the debutante reception if it was not professionally catered), helping to decorate the reception site, and volunteering to check in reception guests (welcoming guests to the reception and giving them printed programs and their table assignments).

Candles and Roses played notable and highly visible roles in debut programs, but these did not demand any substantial investments of their money or time. Usually some time after the waltz and dance performances, and immediately before the cake was cut and served, Roses were called to each present a long-stemmed rose to the debutante and then to dance with her for less than a minute. Afterward, Candles were each called on to publicly announce a birthday wish for the debutante and then to light a candle on her birthday cake. At Janice's debut, among the birthday wishes her Candles shared were: "When times get rough, please don't forget about the people who care for you the most" and "Don't hold back into living your dreams." The actual roses and candles were provided by the debutante's family, and I never observed or heard of rehearsals being held for the dancing (which was not choreographed, unlike the waltz and other routines performed by the debutante and her court) or cake lighting.

In return for their participation, Candles, Roses, and debutante court members usually had their names printed in the debut program (although court members' names were usually more prominent than the names of the Candles and Roses), played a visible and special part in the reception, and/or were assigned special seating in the reception venue. This is in large part why, like their quinceañera counterparts, court members, Candles, and Roses all regarded the invitation to contribute to a debutante's eighteenth birthday a privilege. As Francisco reflected, "It's an intimate thing to be in a cotillion because you're part of a central thing that means something to her. Out of hundreds of people, she picked you to be in a cotillion [court] of seventeen or eighteen."

Devising, inviting, and directing a court, padrinos, Candles, and Roses makes it possible for quinceañeras, debutantes, and their immediate families to identify, activate, and therefore fortify their family's strong ties. Finding padrinos, Candles, and Roses requires parents and daughters (often for the first time) to distinguish their closest and most reliable family and friends and to invite their assistance in arranging their celebrations and supervising and guiding the quinceañera celebrants as they come of age. Asking others to invest so much personal energy, time, and/or money in people outside their immediate families can be perceived of as unduly demanding. But organizing a large debut or quince gives immigrant families a socially appropriate means for doing so by making such requests appear unavoidable and as honors rather than impositions. This is because large quinces and debuts are seen as *necessitating* a number of familial and extrafamilial adults to fill customary roles. It is also because, as I have already shown, despite the fact that significant participation in a quinceañera or debut costs considerable time and money, within co-ethnic communities, being called on to be a padrino, court member, Candle, or Rose signifies one as well thought-of and worthy of immense trust and respect. This is especially so in the case of padrinos, since the invitation to become one is also, in effect, an invitation to become a co-parent and part of the quinceañera celebrant's extended family.

Additionally, big debuts and quinces are public rituals and therefore help families further reinforce the bonds between themselves and the people they have invited to participate. Large debuts and quinces are held outside the home—in parishes, recreation centers, and hotel banquet rooms—and in front of scores of guests (at least a hundred). And they ritualize the celebrant's coming of age. Anthropologist Catherine Bell writes that

> ritualization is a matter of various culturally specific strategies for setting some activities apart from others, for creating and privileging a qualitative distinction between sacred and profane, and for ascribing such distinctions to realities thought to transcend the powers of human actors. (1992: 74)

Large debuts and quinceañeras are held in a special place, mandate participants' and guests' use of distinctive attire, and designate certain articles and activities as symbolizing and/or facilitating the celebrant's transition from girlhood to womanhood. Through such ritualization, debuts and quinces create and privilege celebrants and their events as sacred. This lends exceptional power and weight to the naming and presentation of padrinos, courts, Roses, and Candles; it allows the bonds between them, the celebrants, and the celebrants' family members to be experienced and seen by them and others as true and deep because they have been sanctified through the quinceañera or debut ritual.

Strong ties such as those that are identified, tested, and intensified during debuts and quinceañeras are important to sustaining immigrant families. Social networks have been described as the "linchpin" in helping migrants get ahead; current research indicates that immigrant social networks "provide newcomers with emotional and cultural support and various other resources, including initial housing and information about job opportunities" (Hagan 1998: 55; Waldinger 1997). Studies also show that over time, strong ties help immigrants bring other family members into the United States, maintain transnational connections, supervise their children's physical and moral development, establish and sustain ethnic entrepreneurships, and successfully navigate U.S. legalization and/or naturalization bureaucracies (e.g., see Hagan 1998; Massey 1987; Portes 1998). Finally, studies of *nonimmigrant* networks corroborate the value of strong ties, suggesting that such relationships contribute to immigrants' physical and mental well-being as well. Sociologist Bonnie Erickson writes, "Research has long shown that having close friends and family is good for a person's health. People who say they have someone they can count on feel less depressed, get less physically ill and live longer than those who do not" (2003: 28).

All of the subjects in my study reported that they felt that their friendships were emotionally beneficial. Some mentioned the utility of their strong ties. For example, at least one immigrant in my study, Rose Torres, used strong ties with members of her ethnic community to help her find her first job in the United States and then figure out how to petition for other family members in the Philippines to join her in the United States. And strong ties among the Mexican American community of Las Querubes no doubt contributed to the flourishing quinceañera industry I encountered while conducting my research.

Though there were professionals (e.g., choreographers and planners) who catered primarily to debut clientele, nothing in the Filipino American community paralleled the quinceañera goods and services sector I came across. The world-famous Style Quarter of Las Querubes contained at least five city blocks of shops devoted to *quinceañeras y novias* (quinceañeras and brides). Families could spend entire afternoons here shopping for dresses, tiaras and jewelry, items for the church, decorations, and *recuerdos* (souvenir giveaways). None of these businesses heavily advertised themselves—most customers just knew to find them in the Style Quarter, and/or had heard about them from friends. However, about twice a year, the most successful business owners reserved booths at "quince expos," large regional events, designed to bring together

> almost two hundred different vendors: bringing the best variety of photographers, dress shops, travel agencies, videographers, florists, DJs, limousine providers, cadet troupes, choreographers, quinceañera planners and hairstylists within easy reach of every Latina bride and quince girl. (Strategic Events 2011)[9]

After I left the field, I learned that the success of such businesses was not confined to Las Querubes. A 2011 news article reported on the quinceañera industry in Texas and described it as "booming . . . despite the recession" and "opening new doors for people. . . . who . . . decide . . . to get a piece of the pie" by opening new businesses catering to quinceañera celebrants and their families (Garza 2011). All this helps underscore the tangible benefits of strong ties for many first-generation Americans.

Alejandro Portes and Rubén Rumbaut write that strong ties are especially consequential for working-class immigrants with less human capital (education, job experience, and language knowledge). They write that "among immigrants of limited means, this . . . social capital is vital" (Portes and Rumbaut 2001b: 65). In my study, the families who organized large quinceañeras were generally working class,[10] with parents in blue-collar occupations, while the families who organized large debuts were solidly middle class and even upper class. This helps explain why the quinceañeras I observed both drew in more family and community networks to participate and seemed to institutionalize those relationships more significantly and deeply. While large debuts usually invited the involvement of a court of peers (with substantial responsibilities) and Roses and Candles, who had relatively few duties and responsibilities, large quinceañeras required the participation of a court of peers (with substantial responsibilities) and an extensive set of padrinos, who not only performed significant duties but also shared part of the financial burden of the celebration with the quinceañera's parents. And while large debuts were ritualized in recreation centers, dance halls, and hotel ballrooms that were *conditionally* designated as sacred during debut celebrations, quinceañeras were ritualized at church, which is a space that is perceived as *always* holy. The greater number of strong ties pulled into large quinceañeras, the larger commitments requested of them, and the more powerfully their bonds to the celebrants and their families are formalized through the quinceañera celebration reveal how working-class immigrant families make use of their daughters' coming-of-age events to activate and solidify relationships that they rely on more considerably.[11] This reflects the socioeconomic differences between their working-class families and the middle- and upper-class families who typically throw large debuts. This in turn mirrors the larger Mexican and Filipino immigrant populations in the United States.

Since the 1965 Immigration Act radically transformed the face of U.S. immigration by removing national-origins quotas and installing occupational preferences for highly skilled and highly educated workers, Mexico and the Philippines have become the first- and second-largest immigrant-sending countries to the United States. However, their populations are vastly different in terms of human and economic capital. National figures indicate that "a sizable proportion" of Filipinos are "college-educated professionals who ended up in the US middle class" (Espiritu and Wolf 2001: 163), while, "on average," Mexican American immigrant adults "have only a few years of schooling, limited urban job skills, . . . [and] little or no knowledge of English . . . [and are] classified as low-wage service workers or blue-collar workers" (López and Stanton-Salazar 2001: 57, 67). Furthermore, the U.S. Census Bureau reported that in the year 2010, the median income of Filipinos was $75,349, 7.3 percent of Filipinos were living below the federal poverty line, and 37.9 percent of Filipinos had at least a bachelor's degree (U.S. Census Bureau 2010c). Meanwhile, the Census Bureau also reported that the median income of Mexicans was $39,103, 26.6 percent of Mexicans were living below the federal poverty line, and only slightly more than half (56.6 percent) of Mexicans reported being a "high school graduate or higher" (U.S. Census Bureau 2010d).

My data show that families throwing large quinceañeras and debuts for a single celebrant call on numerous individuals in their close personal networks to participate in their events but that large quinces for one girl draw on a greater number of connections and more profoundly recognize and involve these individuals. This suggests that the greater the size and extent to which a debut or quinceañera for a single girl calls on others, the greater the organizers' need for and dependence on their networks of mutual support (which is strongly connected to a family's socioeconomic position), and it reveals the important role that female coming-of-age rituals play in helping to fortify and maintain strong ties among immigrants and their communities.

Large and Wide

While most of the celebrations I studied were concerned with managing a family's strong ties, the large debutante cotillions in my study demonstrate that immigrant daughters' coming-of-age events can also be employed to develop weak ties with acquaintances and other social contacts who are seen infrequently and to whom they feel little or no emotional obligation. Such affairs, which commemorate the eighteenth birthdays of several Filipina girls during the same occasion, peaked in popularity among Filipino American immigrant families during the 1980s and early 1990s, and thus were the most common type of debuts celebrated by the former debutantes (in their mid-twenties and early thirties at the time of their interviews) in my sample.

The year I conducted my research, the Leonor Rivera Pilipina Society (LRPS), a local organization for Filipina women, was gearing up to celebrate more than thirty-five years of successfully introducing debutantes to Del Sol's Filipino American society. Since 1968, LRPS, with founder Helen Martines

("Missus M") at its helm, has presented nearly four hundred debutantes, including Helen's two daughters, three granddaughters, and three other women in my study. Two other organizations that arranged group cotillions were also represented in my sample: the Pilipina Ladies' Association of Southern California (Ladies' Association), which had held an annual cotillion in Las Querubes almost every year between 1978 and 1999, and the South Cove Union of Filipino Americans (SCUFA), which started its annual cotillion in 1978.

About a year before each cotillion, community associations begin recruiting debutantes and their families. All of the organizers who spoke with me said that recruitment relied almost exclusively on word of mouth, though SCUFA did occasionally place announcements in church bulletins and local ethnic newspapers to find families to participate. Regarding recruitment, Eliane Dizon, former SCUFA cotillion organizer, said, "We approach only good candidates with debutante potential. Our debutantes are between sixteen and twenty [years old]—seventeen, ballpark.[12] They're good girls, grade-wise; [they're] willing to participate and respectful to their parents." Josie Espalda, five-term former president of the Ladies' Association, whose eldest daughter was among the debutantes presented at the organization's inaugural ball, said, "We select women from good families. Their parents are leaders of the [Filipino American] community, professionals, and of Filipino descent." Only Missus M provided an application that outlined specific criteria for becoming an LRPS debutante. These conditions were "a special intimacy with the Lord," "Filipino descent and heritage" and a respect for "Filipino family values," "financially affluent and supportive" parents, "a strong mother-daughter relationship," and a "3.0 GPA."

In spite of all the associations stipulating that potential debutantes possess particular family (i.e., "good") and socioeconomic (i.e., "affluent") backgrounds, their cohorts ultimately were more representative of the local Filipino American population, including girls of mixed Filipino heritage, from working- and middle-class backgrounds, with strained intergenerational relations, and from single-female-headed households. Furthermore, no one I spoke with (organizers, debutantes, or parents) could recall a family ever being disallowed from participating in a cotillion. Eliane told me that SCUFA had "never turned down a debutante." This discrepancy between the associations' rigorous criteria and their open admissions practices may have been because only a self-selected group of girls and families usually responded to the organizations' recruitment efforts. I also believe that it was probably because of these groups' desires to convey an image of selectivity while having to depend significantly on enlisting a sufficient number of women every year for the success of their event and organization. Josie said:

It's not profitable to have very few girls because we're fund-raising, and the hotels are so expensive [to rent a ballroom from] these days. In the seventies and eighties we had big ones almost every year. We were the only club in the community that had done debutantes. But now, different clubs sponsor different debutante balls, and it's been divided.

Once the associations had gathered an adequate number of debutantes, each girl's family was required to pay a participation fee: $500 to join the Ladies' Association cotillion and $300 to become an LRPS or SCUFA debutante. Typically, this gave each cotillion committee approximately $3,000 to start putting deposits down for a venue and vendors. Since 1968, the LRPS ball has been held in the same ballroom, at a distinctive hotel with a panoramic view of Del Sol's marina. SCUFA always held their cotillion in the same iconic Del Sol hotel, and the Ladies' Association usually held their ball in one of two renowned Las Querubes hotels. At this point, organizers also typically finalized the dinner menu and booked the cotillion's choreographer, photographer, videographer, and printer (for event tickets and the souvenir program). Eliane explained, "We tend to use the same people [vendors]. We call . . . on people we kn[o]w to help save money, family friends—we ha[ve] a pool of people."

An orientation meeting to explain to parents and girls the kind of commitment required by them from the organization is typically held six months to a year before each ball. Between that time and the cotillion, girls are expected to find an escort, a male peer or family member who will attend weekly rehearsals with them to learn and refine the waltz that will be performed during the debut. As they do this, organizers expect that the youth will also learn about Filipino culture. LRPS requires attendance at a series of formal workshops that one of my subjects, Missus M, described as intended "to preserve and promote Philippine interest and culture in . . . homes, schools, and [the] community, . . . to gain a higher level of education, [and to] effectively project ourselves in the real world."

Meanwhile, families are expected to become involved with one another, as well as with other organization members and community projects. They have to work closely with the other debutantes' parents (usually mothers) to make collective decisions, such as the event's color motif and additional decorations. Independently from one another, they have to buy, make, and/or hire someone to craft their daughters' gowns and their own dresses; they (sometimes with their daughters) have to find local business "sponsors" to buy souvenir program ad space; they have to pay for several debutante-related photography and video sessions; and they have to invite forty to one hundred guests to the cotillion, to whom they sell or for whom they purchase $35–$55 tickets. The year of Ramona's presentation as an LRPS debutante, her mother, Imelda Fuentes, invited and paid for forty guests—"relatives from Los Angeles, . . . my friends, . . . and Mona's close friends from school." Consequently, the total cost of Mona's debutante was around $3,000 (adjusting for inflation,[13] this would be about $5,700 today)—about half of what Imelda estimates she would have had to pay for a comparable debut for Mona alone.

As the event date grows closer, cotillion organizers usually settle the evening's program, purchase decorations and birthday cakes, invite emcees and guests of honor, design and print their souvenir programs, distribute press releases to get local media coverage, and select any award recipients to be announced the night of the ball. The annual cotillions themselves are usually several hours and attended by 350 to 400 guests who consist of the debutantes, members of each debutante's immediate and extended families, each debutante and her family's friends, other organization members, and any organization VIP guests—local celebrities, elected officials, businesspeople, and other role models of Filipino and non-Filipino descent.

The bringing together of multiple families and community members at large cotillion events for several celebrants enables daughters and their families to meet and establish numerous weak ties. Large cotillions require debutantes and their families to be introduced to a large number of new people outside their usual close networks. For instance, over the course of their debutante year, LRPS "debs" and their families must meet and become acquainted with their co-debutantes and their immediate families, their co-debutantes' escorts, the LRPS cotillion organizers and general members, their monthly workshop speakers (who are often leaders in the Del Sol Filipino community), local businesspeople to whom they were trying to sell ad space in their programs, the extended families and close friends of their co-debutantes who attend the annual ball, and their cotillion's VIPs or guests of honor—individuals Missus M describes as "people who serve the Filipino community as role models in the fields of business, community service, education, international [work], medicine, government, the military, sciences, arts, and politics."

These acquaintances generally do not burgeon into deep friendships, but they are still of great value because they bridge debutantes and their families into new, dissimilar networks, giving them access to information and opportunities they might otherwise have been unaware of. Mark Granovetter explains that having numerous bridging weak ties is important because individuals with few weak ties will be deprived of information from distant parts of the social system and will be confined to the provincial news and views of their close friends. This deprivation will not only insulate them for the latest ideas and fashions but may put them in a disadvantaged position in the labor market, where advancement can depend . . . on knowing about appropriate job openings at just the right time. Furthermore . . . weak ties . . . are actually vital for an individual's integration into modern society. (1983: 202–203)

Additionally, he argues that weak ties are vital for positive social integration, since such relationships "have the effect not only of linking culturally different groups but of reducing . . . alienation and increasing social solidarity" (1983: 221).

Strengthening weak ties through cotillions for multiple debutantes therefore offers immigrant Filipino families not just a way to more securely establish themselves in the United States; it also increases the ability of second-generation daughters and their parents to improve their chances of success and mobility. This is especially noteworthy, given that opportunities for developing indirect contacts are infrequent and uncommon, especially among those in lower socioeconomic classes, since they are the least likely to find themselves in contexts where they can meet people far removed from their personal networks.

One former debutante, Olivia, shared how the social contacts she gained through her group debut created opportunities for her and other members of her family to become more socially successful. She said:

I guess my debut did help a little in the end. Me and my sister both got scholarships from the Union [the South Cove Union of Filipino Americans, which organized her cotillion] when we went to college. And I think it helped my dad become more active in the Filipino community. Before that our family wasn't really involved in a lot of Filipino things, but afterwards he became a leader in the Union, and through that, he was able to meet some local political people and do stuff like that.

Remarkably, debuts for several girls also allow participating families to secure their strongest ties as well, although this is done in a manner different from how such work is done through large coming-of-age events for one celebrant. While the latter entails organizing families to assemble a sizable number of people from their closest networks and committing these individuals deeply in the planning and performance of debut and quince celebrations, cotillions for multiple celebrants bring together far fewer family members and close friends and require measurably less commitment from them. None of the cotillion balls represented in my study required that debutantes find peers and request that they serve in an entourage, since cotillion organizers recruited four to twelve debutantes annually and determined that the debutantes, along with their chosen escorts, would serve as each ball's court and perform the cotillion waltz together. Nor did any of the cotillion balls in my study call for anyone outside the debutante's immediate family to help financially sponsor any considerable aspect of the event. While parents paid for their families' photo and video packages, and their own, their daughters', and sometimes escorts' performance attire and accessories, organizing associations collected dues and ticket payments from participating families and cotillion guests to subsidize the costs of everything else: the venue, the waltz choreographer, the event photographer and videographer, production costs for printed tickets and souvenir programs, the emcee, event decorations (including flowers), cakes, and the costs of any special gifts for their workshop facilitators, awardees, and guests of honor. Nonetheless, strong ties to the relatively few close family and friends who were invited to contribute their time and resources to those taking part in group cotillions—namely escorts, who were asked to attend rehearsals and sometimes pay for their performance attire, and guests, who were asked to attend the ball and sometimes pay for their ticket—were still effectively reinforced, since even modest participation and attendance at these events were perceived as honors. This view stemmed from escorts' and guests' understanding of the cotillions as special events for the debutante, her family, *and* the greater co-ethnic community, and from their knowledge that families had to be selective in choosing to invite them, since each family was allotted only a limited number of seats for their guests by the organizing association.

Of course, the degree to which these strong ties between debutantes, their families, escorts, and guests were reinforced through cotillion balls for several girls is considerably less than the degree to which such ties are fortified through large debuts and quinces. And this reflects the fact that while most of the large individual coming-of-age celebrations for one girl were organized by working-class Mexican families and solidly middle- and upper-class Filipino families, most of the families participating in the group cotillions in my study self-identified as between working and middle class at the time of their debutante. Thus, the immigrant families involved in group cotillions were not as reliant on their strong networks as their working-class counterparts. However, they were not so solidly middle class that they could afford to shoulder the costs of a large individual debut on their own or to pass up the extraordinary opportunity to establish new connections to a diversity of people outside their immediate networks who might link them to knowledge and information that could help improve their position in U.S. society.

The fact that cotillions for multiple girls facilitate both the bolstering of a relatively small number of strong ties and the creation of new weak ties implies that the immigrant families who join such events are distinct from those who organize large coming-of-age functions for single celebrants and that group debutante balls benefit participants in unique ways. Not surprisingly, I observed the most upward mobility between generations among families who took part in such cotillions. It was among past group debutantes—many of whom were daughters of military servicemen and homemakers—that I found the most graduates from four-year institutions, the most women who had taken leadership positions in college, and the most women who owned homes.

Small and Cautious

The most uncommon type of debut and quince in my study was comparatively small, with fewer than thirty guests who primarily consisted of the celebrant's family and the family's dearest friends. Such coming-of-age parties were described by their celebrants as "nothing really," as "just a little get-together," and as "not real" debuts and quinceañeras. (This may have contributed to the low number of such events in my sample—i.e., those who had comparably sized fifteenth and eighteenth birthday celebrations may have been more unlikely to participate in my study, since they do not consider such parties "real" quinceañeras or debuts.)

Ostensibly, the small parties in my study were not much different from what one might expect from any other family birthday celebration. They usually were held at the debutante or quinceañera celebrant's family home, served the same type of food that would be prepared for any other family special occasion, and did not require the celebrant or anyone else to wear anything extraordinary. Most important for the focus of this chapter, they did not require the celebrant or her family to solicit an unusual amount of help from others.

Jasmin's quinceañera is representative of such small coming-of-age parties. On the day of Jasmin's fifteenth birthday, the family went to an ordinary mass and then had "a simple party at home" with "a nice birthday cake" and some of Jasmin's favorite home-cooked food for dinner. Although she feels that a girl's fifteenth birthday is special (she advocated for her parish to offer special masses to help families celebrate these events when it was still highly unpopular to do so),[14] Jasmin's mother, Flora Favino, was strongly against organizing an elaborate party that would require the family to depend on financial resources from others. She ardently explained, "I think that we should provide for our daughters according to our own means. The whole asking for a 'padrino of this,' a 'madrina of that' [to help pay for a quinceañera] turns me off; I dislike it."

Despite their outward mundanity, these small celebrations still hold exceptional meaning for the celebrants and their families. For example, while Barbra Agao told me that her debut was "just a normal birthday with some other special stuff," she could not hide how special that day was, and still is, to her. During her interview, Barbra and I looked through her debutante album, and she just beamed as she recalled everyone who was there, the details of her party program, and how it all made her feel. As she pointed out close friends and relatives in photos, Barbra shared, "The best thing about my debut was seeing my friends there, and my family. It means a lot to me, knowing that they cared enough to come there, rather than go anywhere else." By the time we reached the end of her album, she acknowledged, "I guess it was a pretty big day."

While these quinceañeras and debuts were relatively small, they nevertheless played a valuable role in helping the families who organize them identify and recognize their strong ties to close friends and family in already existing networks of support. However, unlike their larger individual counterparts, small and cautious celebrations restrict the number of close friends and family who are invited, as well as limit the extent to which such networks are called on. At the same time, while group cotillions cap the number of guests each deb can invite (most of whom are typically family and good friends), especially to accommodate the inclusion of more distant but potentially valuable new connections, small individual quinces and debuts do not forgo bolstering strong ties to establish weak ones—they simply seem to activate fewer relationships and do so less intensely.

The choice to hold a small debut or quince is a strategic one, made carefully by the lower-working-class families who choose to organize them. This is because, while strong ties can aid with the cultural and economic survival of working-class immigrant families, the emotional and financial obligations to which they bind individuals and families can also be experienced as burdens. In fact, financial considerations and self-sufficiency were consistently cited as the most important reason for having a small debut or quince. Carol Stack's ethnography of a poor African American community, *All Our Kin*, compellingly reveals that while the black families in her study "need[ed] a steady source of cooperative support to survive" and therefore invested considerable time and resources into building and maintaining "kinship-based exchange networks," the demands made on those in extremely strong networks often negated their upward mobility (1974: 32, 124). Cecilia Menjívar also pays attention to and reports on the "underside of networks" in her study of Salvadoran migrants in San Francisco. She argues, in contrast to earlier immigrant studies that emphasized only the benefits of networks based on kinship and friendship for migrants, that involvement in some social networks is impossible for many impoverished immigrants because they do not have the "means to repay favors," and it can actually *harm* them—in some cases, jeopardizing employment, creating tension in family relationships, and undermining access to other benefits (2000: 118, 30). In response to such conditions and risks, Menjívar found that some of the immigrants in her study were forced to "curtail obligations toward friends and relatives and cause temporal limits within which they are expected to reciprocate favors to be exceeded" (2000: 118). More recently, Bindi Shah challenged the idea that strong co-ethnic networks indubitably "lead to successful adaptation among the second generation" (2007: 40). She observes that "social norms" held and enforced by immigrant community networks can be experienced as culturally and socioeconomically confining for second-generation Laotians:

> For example, according to [a] Mien social worker . . . Laotian families in the USA still uphold the intrinsic value of children and large families and encourage early marriage and child-bearing. . . . [Therefore,] traditional courtship and fertility patterns continue in some Laotian communities (see [J.] MacDonald 1997). Thus, in this case the norms related to marriage and child-bearing would not help Laotian adolescents engage with school nor encourage educational performance and achievement. (40)

On the basis of such findings, Shah concludes that although "for some second-generation immigrants family solidarity may provide resources to resist assimilation, for others it may be a source of alienation or pressure to conform to some idea of ethnic authenticity" (2007: 31).

Because of their low socioeconomic positions, those who organized small debuts and quinces in my study had the least resources available for actively participating in support systems of strong ties because of such networks' ensuing obligations and informal ways of enforcing exchanges of assistance.

Nevertheless, these families perceived value in arranging debuts and quince-añeras for their daughters for several reasons. First, intimate coming-of-age celebrations for individual girls do not completely avoid reinforcing existing relationships with good friends and family; rather, they help families *restrict* the number of people in their closest networks. This allows them to avert any unnecessary reliance on others, especially so that few will feel entitled to call on them, which could strain their limited means. Second, families who coordinated small debutantes and quinceañeras, more so than families orga-nizing large celebrations or participating in cotillions with other debutantes, emphasized the religious and spiritual aspects of coming of age. For example, Barbra was the only debutante who mentioned intentionally attending mass the day of her debut "just to thank God for my family, and for my life and to ask for guidance as I become older and more mature." And Flora Favino insisted that one benefit of having a no-frills quince for her daughter was that rather than have her daughter get caught up in trying to produce a huge, flamboyant party, Flora was able to use her daughter's coming of age to help emphasize to her daughter "the principles of our faith" and to teach her that turning fifteen meant becoming more responsible for "living a good Chris-tian life" and "contributing to her faith community by living her adult life in accordance with God's commandments." Flora stressed:

> I don't like it when the focus is on the party. I've seen what happens when all they [daughters and their parents] are concerned about is the *salón*, and sometimes it's a disaster. The real meaning of the quince-añera is what happens in the church, when a girl who is becoming a woman commits her life to growing herself in the presence of God.

Finally, daughters conveyed that despite their families' desire to avoid arranging a large debut or quince, it was still important to them to observe their coming of age, to somehow mark their transition from child to adult. Although most parents seemed satisfied that the smaller size of their daugh-ter's birthday parties did not rob the occasion of its customary significance, most daughters did expressed at least some disappointment. One daughter confided, "It kinda sucked that it was just me. It didn't feel like it was real."

Putting the "Work" in Networks

This chapter has illustrated how the debutantes of Filipino American im-migrant families and the quinceañeras of Mexican American immigrant families offer organizers and participants invaluable opportunities to build, maintain, and fortify critical social networks. I visually summarize my findings in Table 3.1.

I advance that large debuts and quinceañeras for individual celebrants offer working-class Mexican families and solidly middle-class Filipino immigrant families a means to reinforce *and activate* relationships with kin and other close relations. Cotillion balls for multiple debutantes help working-class Filipino families fortify existing strong ties *and meet and establish relationships with new associates* outside their immediate family network. And intimate individual quinceañeras and debuts for single girls help lower-working-class Mexican and Filipino immigrant families affirm *and restrict* the number and intensity of strong ties they have with close friends and family. I also put forward that only reinforcing strong ties, regardless of whether a family is working or upper class, can lead to ethnic and/or socioeconomic insulation, which strengthens, but does not necessarily improve, a family's existing social status. Over time, in fact, sociologists have found that this can disadvantage some working-class immigrant families (Portes and Jensen 1989; Zhou and Logan 1989). "Migrants can become so tightly encapsulated in social networks based on strong ties to coethnics that they lose some of the advantages associated with developing weak ties with residents outside the community" (Hagan 1998: 65). On the other hand, selectively fortifying strong ties while forming new weak ones can create the kind of varied networks immigrant families can use to increase their opportunities for social advancement, which may help explain why the former group debutantes in my study have experienced the most social mobility among those in my sample. Since there was not an ample number of women who organized "small and cautious" celebrations in my sample, I can only posit that by limiting the number of strong ties their families had to manage, their families have

TABLE 3.1   TYPES OF CELEBRATIONS AND OUTCOMES

Subpopulation	Type of Celebration	Network Outcomes	Social Outcome
Working-class and upper-class Filipinos and Mexicans	Large individual	Reinforces strong network → *Network insulation*	*Reinforces status*
Working-class and middle-class Filipinos	Large group	Reinforces strong network + Creates weak network → *Network variation*	*Opportunities for upward mobility*
Lower-working-class and working-class Mexicans and Filipinos	Small individual	Restricts strong network → *Network protection*	*Limits risks of downward mobility*

minimized their chances of experiencing downward mobility by protecting their limited resources from becoming overdrawn.

While there are certainly more motivations for and outcomes to organizing a debut or a quinceañera, recognizing the extent and variety of network-work that is performed through and during these occasions is significant because of how it highlights important characteristics of the immigrant populations they involve. Further, they improve existing sociological knowledge about how immigrant social networks are created and managed. The fact that the overwhelming majority of Mexican American families in my study organized large individual quinces, while Filipino American families in my study celebrated their daughters' eighteenth birthdays in a variety of ways, reflects the greater dependency many immigrant Mexican American families have on family and close friends because of their working-class and lower-working-class statuses. And it mirrors the greater range of socioeconomic statuses represented among Filipinos in the United States, along with their clustering in the middle class.

Such differences between the ethnic groups are, in large part, the result of post-1965 U.S. immigration policies, which have essentially made immigrating as a skilled professional (or the family member of one) the most viable method of legally entering the United States for Filipinos and have simultaneously promoted the undocumented immigration of unskilled Mexican laborers and their families by removing previously available avenues for the legal migration of working-class people into the United States, such as temporary worker visas for farmworkers.

The decreasing popularity of group cotillions among working-class Filipinos in favor of large individual debutantes also mirrors the larger Filipino American immigrant community. It signals the shrinking numbers of working-class Filipino immigrant families who have been able to settle in the United States, especially since the 1990s, when income provisions began to limit the number of family sponsored preference visas granted to Filipinos and when the last U.S. military bases in the Philippines were closed, dramatically reducing the numbers of Filipinos who were recruited and enlisted into the U.S. military. And it indicates the decline of Filipino American participation in ethnic community associations. It is beyond the scope of this study to conclude what has led to Filipino American disinterest in such groups; however, it would not be unreasonable to surmise that this is at least in some small part because of the promotion of greater individualism and personal consumption both in the United States and the Philippines during the 1990s and early 2000s. Regardless, the gradual disappearance of such organizations should be cause for some concern, since (as illustrated by outcomes experienced by some of their past cotillion participants) their ability to connect new immigrants to valuable resources in their ethnic and local communities greatly facilitates the successful integration and social mobility of Filipinos in the United States.

Examining the network-building labor involved in organizing and participating in debuts and quinceañeras not only calls our attention to the experiences of those who are coordinating them but also deepens our understanding of the fact that social networks are not innate to immigrant communities and must be actively established and sustained. First, it supports contemporary scholarship that demonstrates that female bodies and labor are central to the organization of family networks. And it affirms earlier studies that show that the needs of young family members often help mothers activate and expand family social networks. My research also backs up relatively recent work that shows that efforts at maintaining networks also involve policing and even dissolving ties that can potentially strain individuals and groups with limited means. And my findings help verify studies that show that social position (which can change over time) shapes the strategies chosen to build and manage a family's social networks. As already described, social class and the type of coming-of-age ritual coordinated (which reflected a family's network strategy) were definitely linked in my study. And it is no accident that upper-class Mexican and Filipino Americans and families with nonimmigrant parents do not appear in my sample.[15] Such families have other opportunities available to them for connecting to valuable weak ties (such as college), have far less of a need to participate in dense networks of mutual support, and thus rarely express interest in organizing or participating in traditional debuts or quinceañeras. Additionally, my work confirms the important role that community organizations play in connecting participants to valuable weak ties outside their families and close associates. Finally, the findings outlined in this chapter add a new understanding of the significance of rituals and ritualization in creating and invigorating new and existing social networks for immigrant families.

CHAPTER 4

Pagdadalaga/Blossoming:
Becoming the Debutante

The camera lingers on Olivia Hernandez for a second as the emcee, Willis, announces that her parents, Ramiro and Adele, are about to present her to the captive audience sitting inside the expansive ballroom of the Palacio del Rey, the century-old hotel where every South Cove Union of Filipino Americans (SCUFA) debutante has been "introduced to society" since 1978. Olivia's hair is in a chignon that cascades into a bouquet of brown ringlets, adorned with shimmering combs. The skirt of her white gown billows around her; its poufy cap sleeves form small clouds at her shoulders. Her satin-gloved right wrist is cradled in her father's arm, her left in her mother's. Her face looks porcelain-smooth, punctuated only by the bold plum of her lips and by big, dark eyes that betray a hint of nervousness and self-consciousness. With a small tilt of her chin, she, Ramiro, and Adele step into the center of the spotlight to parade slowly around the ballroom floor. Willis announces Ramiro and Adele's birthplaces and occupations, when and where Olivia was born, how long their family has lived in Del Sol, Olivia's college plans, and her aspiration to become an optometrist. After Olivia's parents deposit her onstage, to be seated with her nine fellow debutantes, Willis booms, "We have come together on this special occasion to acknowledge all ten of tonight's beautiful debutantes taking their first gracious step from childhood into their lives as young women." As we watch this scene together, eight years after that "special occasion," Adele visibly beams with pride and wistfulness. When Olivia asks her, amused, "Why are you still emotional?" Adele responds, "It's special to me, to watch when you became really a dalaga."

In spite of the infinite ways Filipino debuts and Mexican quinceañeras have been reworked and configured in the United States, they all share a prominent common thread: the understanding that these events commemorate a girl's passage *de niña a mujer* (from girl to woman). This chapter explores how quinces and debuts try to accomplish and memorialize this transformation. And it underscores how these efforts reveal the construction of distinctly Mexican and Filipino versions of womanhood, especially in response to how these groups feel and live their racial identities in the United States.

Social scientists have long understood gender and race as identities that are continually produced through individuals' and institutions' ordinary and extraordinary activities. Summing up a considerable body of literature, Joshua Gamson and Laura Grindstaff write, "Gender is neither a fixed nor essential property of the self but an outcome of ongoing performances in various interactional and institutional contexts" (2010: 252). Michael Omi and Howard Winant similarly assert that racial categories are neither natural nor predetermined; rather, they are "formed" through "racial projects," which "simultaneously interpret . . . , represent . . . , or expla[in] racial dynamics, and [attempt] to reorganize and redistribute resources along particular racial lines" (1994: 56). Female writers of color have advanced both gender and race studies by criticizing investigations of gender that neglect race, as well as investigations of race that overlook gender (e.g., Anzaldúa 1999; P. Collins 1990; Espiritu 2001; Moraga and Anzaldúa 1981). They call our attention to the fact that in addition to being socially constructed, race, gender, and class are mutually constituted.

Building on the work of all these scholars, this chapter examines quinces and debuts as ethnicized gender projects, especially to show how the immigrant families in my study construct their daughters' gender identities to help them make moral claims to recover some of "the power denied to them by racism" (Espiritu 2003: 158). I point out how immigrant parents distinguish the women they want their daughters to become as specifically Mexicana or Filipina and hold up la Virgen de Guadalupe and Maria Clara de los Santos, respectively, as feminine ideals. Then I describe how choosing, preparing, and executing a quince or debut contributes to the gendering of Mexican and Filipino American young women into señoritas and dalaga. I argue that this enables working-class immigrants to dispute perceptions of ethnic inferiority and makes it possible for middle- and upper-class immigrants to make their ethnicity visible in positive ways. And I show that while such work relies on critiques of (white) "American" culture, it is also aimed at improving immigrants' perceived social positions (i.e., furthering their integration) in the United States.

This chapter is necessarily extensive because it would be absurd to separate discussions of the construction of gender from the construction of race while considering ethnicized femininities. And splitting this chapter into two separate discussions, one on Filipino Americans and another on Mexican Americans, would run completely counter to the comparative project at hand.

"Cuando la Niñez Termina"

Parents, guides, and young women's magazines—considered the ultimate authorities on debuts and quinces by the second generation—universally characterized these events as marking the passage of girls into young womanhood. For example, when I asked her to tell me what a debut was, Filipina mother Rose Torres explained:

> A real debut is when a girl turns eighteen, and she has the eighteen—you know, the nine pairs [of girls and escorts]—and they have the cotillion. It's more common in the Philippines, 'cause it came from there, the debut. . . . Here [in the United States], they observe only the sixteenth birthday. Among Filipinos, the parents do it for their daughters when they turn eighteen, to present them to society, to show they are ready to be an adult.

Similarly, Belinda Santiago, mother of two quinceañera celebrants, told me, "Me encanta la quinceañera. Es algo muy bonito cuando la niñez termina y una hija empieza a ser una señorita" (I love the quinceañera. It's something beautiful when childhood ends and a daughter begins to be a young lady). Belinda's sentiment was echoed in various written materials about quinceañeras. Michele Salcedo's definitive guide to *quince años* planning defines the quinceañera as "a celebration that recognizes the bright promise of [a young girl's] future, acknowledges her transition from a child to a woman, and lets her know that to those who care about her, she is someone very special, that she is loved" (1997: xiv). And one quinceañera videographer's monthly newsletter explained:

> La transición de adolescentes en mujeres se celebra de diferentes maneras y a diferentes edades en el mundo. En Latinoamérica tiene

un arraigo muy especial y se celebra cuando las chicas cumplen XV años. . . . Las chicas pueden presentarse como adults en eventos sociales apropiados.

———

The transition of adolescents to women is celebrated in different ways and at different ages throughout the world. In Latin America, this has very special meaning, and is celebrated when girls turn fifteen years old. . . . Girls can present themselves as adults at appropriate social events.

Filipino vendors likewise maintained that girls' coming of age was the chief rationale for organizing debuts. Cam Maldivas, an event planner and mother of a former debutante, said, "It's the [Filipino] tradition, at eighteen years old, for the female to be introduced to society as a mature person, to show that she is no longer a child."

"Not Just Any Woman": La Virgen and Maria Clara

Significantly, the organizers, participants, and professionals who spoke with me distinguished the women they wanted their daughters to become from "just any women," especially "American" ones. Belinda Santiago said she appreciated the lessons her daughters were learning about becoming "*una mujer real*" (a real woman) while preparing for their quinceañeras because she considers herself "*más como una madre hispana*" (more of a Latina mother) and because "*quisiera que mis hijas reconocieran que sean hispanas, aunque las crecen en los Estados Unidos*" (I would like my daughters to recognize that they are Latina, even though they are being raised in the United States). She approved of the message the church taught her daughters that "*la mujer mexicana . . . es algo especial*" (the Mexicana woman . . . is something special). And she agreed with other immigrant mothers and the church that la Virgen de Guadalupe should be her daughters' "model of a valiant woman."

"La Virgen" is considered "the Mother of all Mexico" and is everything the biblical Mary is—and more. In the Bible, Mary is God's "favorite daughter," who unquestioningly puts herself at God's service when she is told she will bear God's son, despite being a virgin. Nuestra Señora de Guadalupe is said to have been a dark-skinned incarnation of Mary who appeared in 1531 on a Mexico City hillside, Tepeyác, to Juan Diego, a poor, childless *indio* (native Mexican). According to official (Vatican) and popular (folk) accounts, la Virgen asked Juan Diego in Nahuatl, the Aztecs' native language, to tell the bishop to build a temple on Tepeyác. After the bishop's initial refusal to believe Diego, Mary instructed him to fill his *tilma*[1] with roses. Later, when Diego unfolded his cloak before the bishop, a life-size figure of la Virgen appeared on it, and the bishop accepted the miracle as a sign that Diego was speaking the truth.

Regardless of its veracity, this story has captured the imaginations and hearts of countless Mexicans who understand la Virgen's manifestation in Tepeyác as a sign of Mexico's "chosen" status. Her image contains several Aztec symbols, so she is seen as specifically Mexicana. For example, the sash tied around her waist has been interpreted as the same kind of belt Mexica women wore when they were with child. In 1945, Pope Pius XII formally declared la Virgen "Queen of Mexico and Empress of the Americas," and today, practically five centuries after her first appearance, she is still venerated as the most significant religious figure in the country. Even those who doubt her legend celebrate her as a symbol of Mexican national identity and characterize her as having taken "upon herself the psychological and physical devastation of the oppressed *indio*" (Anzaldúa 1999: 52) and as "pure receptivity" who "consoles, quiets, dries tears, calms passions" (Paz 1950: 25). Therefore, as a model of womanhood, the Virgin of Guadalupe is celebrated as a selfless, loving mother and a symbol of chastity, obedience, forgiveness, and peace.

To many of the first-generation Mexican parents who spoke with me, la Virgen and "Mexican culture" offered divergent ideals from those their daughters encountered in America. For instance, Belinda clarified that she wanted her children to maintain their Latina identities because "American" children

> tienen mas libertad. Aquí tienen se va a bailar a medianoche. Entonces, empieza cosas mala. Muchachos bien jovenes tomando alcohol, drogas; piensan ellos solamente sobre el dinero para comprar carros, una casa. Los hispanos, no.

> ———

> have more freedom. Here, they go dance until midnight. Then they start bad things. Very young kids are taking alcohol, drugs; they're thinking only about money to buy cars, houses. Latinos, we're not like this.

First-generation Filipinos who organized debutantes also aimed to offer young adult Filipino Americans an alternative model of femininity. For instance, Imelda Fuentes, the mother of a Filipina debutante, said:

> The debutante is important to show that they [Filipino American young women] are not just the *basta-basta*, you know. They are not—

what do you call this?—women without education, you know. In the debutante, you are being dignified by your peers, and by your people because you are *mahinhin*—you are educated. You [do] not exactly belong to a society, but you have the qualification of a Maria Clara. You are not just like the ordinary American [girl]; you are a Filipina.

Maria Clara de los Santos was the female ideal to which nearly all the Filipino parents in my study referred. In fact, the Leonor Rivera Pilipina Society (LRPS) is named after the real-life woman thought to have inspired the Maria Clara character, and the Pilipina Ladies' Association's annual cotillion was actually called the Maria Clara Debutantes' Ball. Though only human, Maria Clara exemplified ideals similar to la Virgen for Filipinos. She was the beautiful young love interest of the brave and righteous Crisostomo Ibarra in the novel said to have launched the Philippine Revolution, *Noli Me Tangere* (Rizal [1887] 2004). Author and national hero José Rizal rendered Maria Clara as a beautiful, sincere, self-denying woman who stayed faithful to her true love despite distance, scandal, humiliation, and even death. As a child, Maria Clara was described by Rizal as "everybody's darling." After she "turn[ed] woman overnight," she was betrothed to marry Ibarra, a favorite childhood friend. However, during a sudden period of political tumult that pitted Ibarra against powerful enemies and forced him into hiding, Maria Clara was betrothed to another man in order to enhance her father's "good connexions." She submitted, reasoning:

> My father requires this sacrifice from me. He gave me a home and affection when it was not his duty to do so. I repay this debt of gratitude assuring him peace by means of this new relationship. (Rizal [1887] 2004: 535)

When Ibarra resurfaced, he wrongfully accused Maria Clara of betraying him. Instead of growing angry, Maria Clara patiently made clear her innocence and explained to him that despite her second engagement, "I will not forget that I swore to be faithful" (Rizal [1887] 2004: 535). Afterward, Ibarra fled again and then was (falsely) reported dead to Maria Clara. Upon hearing this, she begged to be put in the nunnery or to die. The novel implies that she then lived out her days in a convent, a "timid virgin," grieving in the night, begging for "protection against the assaults of hypocrisy" (Rizal [1887] 2004: 565).

Today, Maria Clara survives as the archetypal Filipina woman. She is naturally beautiful and is always conscious of her dress and comportment. Even on one of her worst days—the day her second engagement was announced—Rizal wrote, "[she] greeted and received [her guests] ceremoniously, without losing her air of sadness" (Rizal [1887] 2004: 527). Like her obvious namesake, Maria Clara is characterized as an unselfish, unquestioning daughter, willing to "sacrifice" to ensure her father's peace. She is strong, enduring physical illness and profound heartache throughout Rizal's story. She is a pure ("virginal"), patient, honest, and loyal sweetheart. And when she realizes that she cannot be with the "one love" who could complete and fulfill her, she does the only other thing she can do: she voluntarily surrenders her life to God.

Like la Virgen, Maria Clara is a model of femininity that debut organizers understand as superior to that which American culture offers young women. Josie Espalda, mother and former cotillion chairwoman for the Pilipina Ladies' Association, explained, "Being a Maria Clara widens their [debutantes'] knowledge about their ethnicity and about being Filipino, a *dalagita*. Filipino girls are different from other ones. They don't just go wild. They have respect, from being members of Filipino families."

"Kids Here Are Wild"

The promotion of ethnic-specific ideas about femininity by the immigrants who spoke with me is one way they attempt to project themselves as morally above white Americans, particularly because they feel they are seen as economically and culturally lesser than them. Sociologist Michelle Lamont has compellingly demonstrated that "morality" is often used as a tool by underprivileged people to assert and maintain "a sense of self-worth and dignity" (2000: 51). For example, in her study of middle- and working-class men in two countries, she found that working-class men who felt positioned beneath the middle and upper classes used "hard work, personal integrity, and traditional morality . . . to put themselves above others and help them compensate for their low socioeconomic class" (2000: 51). These workers disassociated "moral worth" from "socioeconomic worth" and argued that "caring" (e.g., solidarity, egalitarianism, generosity, and close interpersonal connections) and personal responsibility were better indicators of success than money. The development of this "alternative measuring stick" for success hence allowed workers to "locate themselves above, or side by side with" people more socioeconomically successful than them (Lamont 2000: 147).

Sociologist Yen Le Espiritu introduces an explicitly gendered dimension to Lamont's thesis when she argues that one way less advantaged groups contend that they are "above or side by side with" more advantaged groups is by guarding female sexuality, to "reclaim the morality of the community" (2003: 167). She writes that

> female morality—defined as women's dedication to their families and sexual restraint—is one of the few sites where economically and politically dominated groups can construct the dominant group as other and themselves as superior. (2003: 160)

Although they did not appear consumed by it, the immigrants in my study were aware of their marginalization as minorities in the United States. I discuss this in greater depth later in this chapter; for now, I advance that consciousness of their "secondary status" as people of color in America led the families in my study to construct white American women as promiscuous ("wild," "more free"), materialistic ("only thinking about money"), and unaccountable to their parents and families ("they start bad things" and have less "respect"). For example, when I asked Catalina Valdes, a Mexicana mother, how she would describe Americans, she responded:

> America is, like, free. They don't care. The girls [in the United States], they don't respect herself. Right away they will go to be with any kind of man, no big deal. Oh my God—for me? I don't think so. A proper woman needs to respect herself. Oh, yes. This is like [how] I talk a lot to my daughters, oh my goodness. Values. Respect is the most important of all—for any human being.

Here, Catalina equates American freedom with recklessness and a lack of "values" and self-respect (especially for women). She juxtaposes this with what she teaches her daughters, connoting that she, and by extension Mexican culture, is morally superior—more "caring" and concerned with instructing children about "the most important" things they need to know, not just as students or aspiring workers but as human beings.

Sharon Dobrado, a lively Filipina mother, also had strong ideas about white Americans. She observed:

> Kids here [in the United States] are wild. I don't like how they answer [talk back to their parents]. You know, in the Philippines, they have to hide their feelings not to upset the older people. There's more respect. Kids here . . . cannot be disciplined, or they [Americans] call it abuse. They [kids] won't be scared. They don't care. They get whatever they want. . . . When they're eighteen, they move out already. In the Philip-

pines, until you get married and you have kids, you still live with your parents! Americans let their kids do what they want; they're so indepen-dent, you know. Even if they fall down. That's one of the first things I learned in America! When they [kids] fall down and they scratch them-selves, [parents] don't help them! They let them stand by themselves. In the Philippines, once you fall—gosh! Everybody's, "Oh my God! Come on, help!" Like, "Put a Band-Aid [on it]! Clean it!" That's how they are. That's how we take care of kids. Here they don't care.

Here, Sharon characterizes Americans, as Catalina and the other mothers in my study did, as "wild," ill-mannered, undisciplined, and overly indepen-dent. This allows her to contend that Filipinos are more vigilant of children and generally more concerned with making sure their sons and daughters are more respectful and protected. She even suggests that Americans care less about their children's physical well-being, implying that Filipino parents are more inclined to shield their children from harm.

Their daughters' coming-of-age celebrations offered Sharon, Catalina, and the other immigrant parents in my study a substantial opportunity to further advance claims regarding greater morality of their cultures, since these events made it possible for them to literally present young adult Filipi-nas as Maria Claras in the making, and young adult Mexicanas as disciples of la Virgen—obedient, chaste, and willing representatives of their families' and communities' decency and success.

Becoming the Debutante

Having demonstrated that the process of organizing and executing a debut or quinceañera is explicitly conceived of as helping to prepare Filipina and Mexicana girls for lives as young ladies and as a way for Filipino and Mexi-can parents to fashion their daughters into representatives of their cultures' moral superiority, I now turn to detailing how the quinceañeras and debuts I studied helped produce racially gendered bodies. In particular, I examine how the following practices help shape the minds and bodies of girls into dalaga and señoritas: (1) aligning choices, (2) prepping, (3) getting ready, and (4) performing for a debut or quince.

Aligning Choices

The countless ways in which debuts and quinceañeras are celebrated in the United States reflect the myriad choices entailed in organizing one. One look at *Debutante and Bride Philippines* magazine's "Debut Planner" bears this out (see Figure 4.1). To arrange a debut or quince, decisions must be made regarding a date, a budget, a color motif, a theme, venues, vendors, court members, padrinos, Candles and Roses, a dress and accessories, guests, invitations, seating, decorations, favors, and of course whether to have one at all. But these decisions are rarely, if ever, made exclusively by debutantes and quinceañeras. Rather, they have to be arrived at with parents and other significant adults.

Most of the Mexican American women who spoke with me shared that they conceded most of the important choices regarding their quinceañeras to their mothers. For instance, when I asked Dalía, a Mexicana who had celebrated her *quince años* almost a decade and a half before I interviewed her, if she had "any specific responsibilities" for her quinceañera, she said:

> Not really. My mom did all the planning. She coordinated everything. I did some things: I picked the music, the invitations, my chambelánes, my damas. . . . For my quinceañera I couldn't really do anything. What could I do? I couldn't sign any contracts—my mom had the money, so she decided what to rent and buy.

Katia, whose family allowed me to shadow her quince, likewise recalled that other people made most of the major decisions for her birthday party. She said that while she had momentarily considered asking for money or a trip for her quince, she ultimately decided to throw a quinceañera because her "parents insisted. They said it would be nice and that I could get presents." The church was predetermined because she and her family were already parishioners of Prince of Peace, and her mother chose the *salón* where her reception was held a year in advance. Her mother also chose and booked Katia's quinceañera limo, photographer, flowers, food, music, giveaways, and most of the two hundred people on her guest list. Proceedings for Katia's mass were established by the church; the items used in her mass were gifts that people, "family, friends of my parents," offered, so she accepted them without question. Her older sister, Ana, had celebrated her quinceañera two years earlier, so Katia let her have considerable input on the few remaining things she could decide: her chambelánes, her hair and makeup, some of her personal guests. "I didn't really have to do that much, 'cause my parents took care of everything, and people [padrinos] were offering to help."

Almost all event-related decisions for Filipinas in group cotillions were made by their organizing associations. But even the individual debutantes who spoke with me related having a little more decision-making power than

The Debut Planner

6 Months Before:

- Plan a budget with your parents. The most important part in planning your debut is setting a limit on how much your parents want to spend. Your checklist should include:
  - venue rental fees (if any)
  - food cost per person
  - flowers and/or balloons
  - giveaways
  - gown(s) for you and the cotillion
  - the cake
  - the choreographer's fee
  - rehearsal venue rental rates
  - snacks for the rehearsals and entertainers
  - equipment (screen projector)
  - mobile disco and spinners
  - stylist's fee
  - cost of invitations and calligraphy
- Decide on the number of guests you want to have.
- Reserve a venue. Remember, hotel ballrooms are difficult to reserve. Before you do anything else, you have to decide where you want to hold your debut. If you want a garden setting, book a caterer and reserve the date. Have the following information ready: Date and Time and Number of Guests.
- Make a preliminary guest list. Write out the names as you would like them to appear on the invitation envelope (for calligraphy), complete address (for delivery), and contact numbers (for RSVP). This way, you only work with one master list.
- Decide on your color motif.
- Interview prospective designers for your gown and . . . the cotillion's.
- Make a list of possible members of the cotillion. Invite your relatives and friends to join the cotillion. Warn them that rehearsals may fall on weekends. Ask them for their availability, exam schedules, etc. This is important as you have to get a commitment from them early on. They have to know what to expect as well.
- Interview prospective choreographers.
- Have your invitations printed as early as possible. Once you have confirmed your venue and cotillion members, have the invitations printed. Allocate at least three weeks for your invitations to be printed. You may also want to order additional envelopes, just in case mistakes are made when addressing them.
- Interview and get quotations from different florists. Have the following information ready:
  - budget
  - types of flowers you prefer
  - color motif
  - style of centerpiece (low or topiary)

The florist should be able to guide you on flowers available locally and which ones are in season so as to bring down the cost. Should you want ceiling work to be done and entrance decorations to be done as well, mention this to your florist as the price of the package may go up. Remember, most florists provide mock-up services, so take advantage of this. Ask them to supply the eighteen roses as well, if your venue package doesn't include this.

- Interview prospective photographers and videographers. Look at samples of their work, then decide.
- Select a videographer to present your video interviews and pictures.

4 Months Before:

- Finalize your guest list. Arrange the names according to addresses. Group your guests according to the area where they live to facilitate the distribution of invitations.
- Select possible menus based on your budget. Arrange dates for possible food tasting, if you wish.
- Interview possible cake makers, get quotations, and compare prices.
- Decide on a florist, videographer, and photographer.
- Decide on a choreographer and make a preliminary schedule of rehearsals.
- Finalize designs and designer for your gown(s) and . . . the cotillion's.

3 Months Before:

- Schedule fittings for your gowns and . . . the cotillion's.
- Start taping for the video presentation.
- Finalize your menu and make the necessary down payments.
- Look for a makeup artist. Don't forget to have a picture taken after each trial so you can remember how each makeup artist made you look.
- Begin rehearsals for the cotillion and any special number you may want included.

(continued on next page)

Figure 4.1 Debutante's planning checklist.

(Re-created from Debutante and Bride Philippines, *July 1998, p. 27.)*

The Debut Planner (continued)

• Make a down payment on your cake.
• Make a down payment for your videographers and photographers.
• Make a down payment to your chosen spinner.
• Decide whether or not you want to hire professional entertainers and contact them for their availability.
• Decide on your giveaways.

2 Months Before:
• Decide on your makeup artist.
• Give the invitation envelopes to your calligrapher.
• Conceptualize the decor with the florist if you haven't done so and make the down payment.
• Have your giveaways packaged if you feel you cannot do a good job yourself.

1 Month Before:
• Send out your invitations.
• Go for final fittings and rehearsals with the cotillion.

2 Weeks Before:
• Call the guests who did not respond and confirm their attendance. Give the final head count to the banquet officer of the hotel or to your caterer. Remember to remove 20 percent from the total number of people who confirmed for your guaranteed number of guests. Hotels and caterers provide a ten-percent allowance. You will find that there will be people who said they were not coming but show up and there are more who confirm their attendance and show up [with extra guests].
• Get your gowns and . . . the cotillion's from the designer.
• Reconfirm all your reservations: the cake (delivery time), florist, photographers, videographers, equipment rentals, mobile and spinners, etc.
• Pick up your giveaways.
• Buy a token gift for your parents to thank them for giving you a debut.

1 Week Before:
• Last-minute rehearsals.
• Try to get some rest.

Figure 4.1 *(continued)*

their Mexicana counterparts. When I interviewed Angela, she cataloged everything that she had to do for her celebration:

> Let's see, I'll name every step: finding a photographer, videographer, making the floral arrangements, getting the dress design, finding the place, practices, getting my choreographer, printing my invitations and actually inviting people, renting tables, printing the program, deciding of the program, giveaways, cakes, Roses, Candles, acknowledgments . . .

But Angela eventually revealed that her mom had found the photographer online, and, she added, "My mom has someone in the office who's a really good graphics designer," who designed her debut invitations. Her mom also threatened to kick out court members who could not consistently make their weekly practices and rejected Angela's initial idea for giveaways—"My mom didn't want it, so she was like, 'We're giving CDs,' and I'm like, 'Fine.'" Out of her 243 guests, Angela ultimately invited "I think 50, outside of my court because my mom invited 180." And when they were choosing cakes, Angela said, she "was like, 'I want this one,' and my mom was like, 'Okay, but let's try another one,' and then—so, the one that we decided was the English cake, 'cause my mom didn't want to pay extra." Even Angela's acknowledgments were prepared by her mother. Angela admitted, "I didn't know who to thank, so she wrote it down all for me on the program." Angela reflected:

> My mom, she likes it her way, and if it's not her way, she doesn't think that it's good, like perfection-like. I was like giving her my input, but in the long run, it doesn't really matter. So my main thing [responsibilities] was like menial—like Candles and Roses. You know, for the most part I didn't have a say in anything. It's kind of sad. . . . It's still all beautiful. It wasn't what I expected, but in the long run it's still beautiful.

Angela concedes that while she offered input on many of the decisions for her debut, "in the long run" her mother's opinions were the ones that counted. But she doesn't necessarily state that she disagreed with her mother's choices—in fact, she says, "It wasn't what I expected, but . . . it's still beautiful." So Angela ultimately came to understand that she and her mother compromised on most of her debutante decisions and that she did not feel that her mother completely overrode her preferences.

One result of being expected to make so many event-related decisions, while having to ultimately defer to their parents' preferences and rely on their parents' pocketbooks, is that young women come to understand being a dalaga or señorita as involving aligning their personal aspirations with those of their parents and families. That is, decision making for debutantes and quinceañeras trains Filipinas and Mexicanas to take into consideration, and even prioritize, how family and community might benefit from their choices. This enables second-generation daughters to develop greater empathy and respect for their parents' financial and cultural efforts in the United States and to learn to forgo individual preferences and advancement for the sake of others. LRPS founder Helen Martines ("Missus M") shared how she explained this to her debutantes:

> You know, your basic mother and parents are trying to do the best they can for their kids. Sometimes this is not what you [a second-generation daughter] want to do, and you start arguing with your mother and father: "Oh! Because you're from the old country, you don't understand why we do this!" You just listen and observe: all

they are trying to do is protect you. You have to understand where your parents are coming from and the hardships they encounter.

These are critical lessons to be learned in immigrant families, since they counteract the self-absorption and individualism that first-generation parents feel is so dangerous for their American-born daughters. And it helps to restore some parental control within immigrant households.

> When children's acculturation has moved so far ahead of their parents' . . . key family decisions become dependent on the children's knowledge. Because they speak the language [English] and know the culture better, second-generation youths are often able to define the situation for themselves, prematurely freeing themselves from parental control. (Portes and Rumbaut 2001b: 53)

Before her *quince años*, Katia's family had definitely experienced some generational role reversal. She told me, "Ana makes the major decisions [for the family]. Our parents talk about it, Ana gives her opinion, then they go with what she says." But during the year that it took to prepare and execute her quince, Katia began to recognize her parents as having more authority and ultimate deciding power within their household. She acknowledged that what her mother told me was true: "Toda la preparación es mi sola. Las ideas son más de mi, y mi esposo dice 'okay,' porque él trabaja para pagar" (All of the preparation is me alone. The ideas are mostly mine, and my husband says 'okay,' because he's working to pay [for it]").

Such recognition is important because it better enables immigrant parents to exert authority over their daughters—even as their daughters presumably leave childhood behind and are announced as women. Belinda said:

> Pues, sí. En la misa, [la quinceañera] se convierte a una señorita. No está una niña chicita, pero, sigue siendo una joven. Quince años es la tradición. Pero dieciocho es cuando es una mujer real, porque es responsible para su misma, y sus decisiones son de ella sola.

> ———

> Well, yes. During mass, [the quinceañera] becomes a young lady. She is not a little girl, but she still is a young person. Fifteen years is the tradition. But eighteen is when she is a real woman because she is responsible for herself, and her decisions are her own.

And Angela's mother, Juliet Garza, told me:

I don't think Angela's debut changed her, but it's helping her, so that she knows what she's doing and sees what she really wants. She's more confident of herself, and she's become more mature. But at the age of eighteen, she should only start dating. For women, at twenty-six years old they're ready to marry—twenty-nine years old for the man. When the kids decide to have husbands and wives, then they will stop living with us, and they can be independent.

Here, both mothers suggest that they still see themselves as the principal influences in their daughter's lives—Belinda's statement implied that she planned to remain so at least until Katia turned eighteen, and Juliet's implied that she planned to remain so at least until Angela turned twenty-six. Both women felt that this was their responsibility as mothers, which incidentally helps to strengthen claims that they, and by extension their native cultures, are morally superior. Belinda said, "Madres [latinas] aquí son más responsible, porque es una país más liberal. Tengan enseñar respeto, y tengan mantener comunicación con [sus hijos]" ([Latina] mothers here are more responsible because it's a more liberal country. They have to teach respect, and they have to maintain communication with [their children]). And Juliet said, "Both parents need to help each other in bringing up children; it's not separate parents' responsibilities to teach good moral, spiritual values. But it's the mother who is expected to raise children." And since Katia's and Angela's coming-of-age experiences helped train them to recognize and defer to their parents' expectations and to associate doing so with their new responsibilities as young ladies,[2] Belinda and Juliet might have had better chances at making sure their daughters do not fall victim to America's culture of "too much independence," which Juliet describes as "more dangerous for females because they are the weaker sex."

Prepping

Aside from negotiating numerous decisions for their coming-of-age celebrations with their parents and other adults, the Mexicana and Filipina celebrants in my study typically spent several months to a year prepping, or preparing, to be presented at their quinces or debuts.

Workshops

Such preparation was most extensive and explicit for girls who participated in group cotillions. For example, LRPS required its debutantes to attend monthly Mentorship Workshops throughout the year before their ball.

One or two debutantes-to-be coordinated one workshop during the year, which involved inviting a host and several expert speakers (usually notable Filipino American professionals), securing a venue (usually someone's home), and organizing the workshop's presentations to create an effective three-hour program. These workshops aimed at training debutantes (and their parents) on such topics as cybersafety, fashion, financial investing, and personal etiquette. Missus M explained that she mandated these, along with attendance at other LRPS community events, to expose LRPS debutantes to those "who serve the Filipino community as role models in the fields of business, community services, education, international [work], medicine, government, the military, sciences, arts, and politics," and to prepare them to "project a higher image of the Pilipina onto the Del Sol community, and throughout the nation."

Such activities were effective at helping LRPS debutantes link womanhood with being successful representatives of their Filipino communities. This was partly because of Missus M's clear imperative that her debutantes learn to "preserve and promote Philippine interest and culture in the homes, schools, and communities" and largely because of how LRPS managed to have girls themselves take responsibility for planning and organizing their own workshops. This compelled girls to take ownership of the lessons being shared—to begin understanding the LRPS version of ladyhood as truly their own and not simply one to which Missus M or their mothers were trying to subject them. And it allowed debutantes to tangibly experience "serving the Filipino community" and "projecting a higher image of the Pilipina" before their balls. Former LRPS debutante Ramona Fuentes corroborated this by telling me:

> I mean, you think of the single event of having a ball. But, when you think about it, it's that whole prepping time when you're learning about everything else and being more involved. They used to have the balls in June, and you'd start prepping a year ahead. And during that year, there were certain events, like workshops, luncheons, and things that you'd prep for. You'd always wear like this *balinta*[3] thing, to kind of constitute that you are being made or whatever. We always wore that and never wore makeup, stuff like that. Our hair was always up and in a traditional hairdo. The whole year we were like that. And that was pretty interesting 'cause it didn't seem so much like you were just becoming a debutante. You were learning more about your culture and getting involved—and that was interesting to me.

The fact that Mona and the other LRPS girls were required to be in costume during their workshops and prepping activities also should not be overlooked, since this contributed to how effectual these events were in helping shape girls into dalaga. This imbued these activities with a specialness by forcing girls to physically personify that they were being made into women. Anthropologist Victor Turner might say that it helped further mark the debutantes' prep period as a "liminal" one, a "betwixt-and-between" stage, which allows those undergoing a rite of passage to reflect on how they are being "transform[ed] from one kind of human being into another" and being empowered with "capacities to undertake successfully the tasks of their new office, in this world" (1987: 17).

Dance Rehearsals

Although none of the debutantes and quinceañera celebrants who organized individual celebrations in my study had to enroll in a program similar to the LRPS program, part of prepping for all the girls entailed learning and rehearsing dance performances for their big day. Dance rehearsals with their courts were the most time- and energy-consuming activities required by debutantes, quinceañeras, and their courts during their preparation period. During these weekly (and sometimes daily) occasions, two to three months before the actual events, young quince and debut participants learned and repeatedly practiced the steps required to execute the dance routines that would be performed during their receptions.

This is because, as described in Chapter 2, the grand highlight of a debutante or quinceañera event is almost always the dance performance. In some cases, the dance is as simple as the honoree's "first dance" with her father or escort; however, in most cases, the dance is a choreographed waltz (vals or cotillion) performed by the birthday girl, most often to a European-composed piece like "The Blue Danube" or "La Marcha Triunfal," along with her entire court. *Debutante and Bride Philippines* declares that "if you desire a proper cotillion, the only dance appropriate is the waltz. . . . It's a romance of rhythm and grace, a dance you should enjoy for many, many years after your debut" ("Do the Waltz" 1998: 36). And *Quinceañera! The Essential Guide to Planning the Perfect Sweet Fifteen Celebration* states that "for the kids in the court, the dance is the culmination of weeks of work and dedication. For the guests and family, it's the transforming moment, the moment that turns their little girl into la quinceañera" (Salcedo 1997: 105).

Fittingly, many of my second-generation subjects described practice for their dance performances as both most rewarding and stressful. For the most part, Mexicanas recalled their practices as fun and fairly undemanding. Dalía said that practices were easy—her corte came to her house every week directly after school, and her mother and choreographer managed practices. "It was more time to hang out with my friends," she recollected. Similarly, Lea, another former quinceañera, told me, "I had to show up for rehearsal for the waltz and help out in what I was instructed to do, which was minor. Doria [Lea's quinceañera planner] was so on top of organizing everything that [it] did not leave a lot for me to do."

Alternatively, Lea and Dalía's Filipina counterparts remembered their dance practices as more intense. For instance, when I asked Angela about "the worst part of your debut," without hesitation, she replied:

> I think having to act, like, not really nice to my friends 'cause they got on my nerves! Like, in practice, it was like, "I can't come to your practice because of this and that," and then I'd have to be understanding of that. And sometimes I'd think I'm too nice; then, I was like, "Don't you understand how much I'm stressing?" 'Cause, like, I had to get them drinks and food and this and that and, like, clean—you know, stuff like that. . . . I cried during rehearsals 'cause like my mom would be mad 'cause we had rehearsals every Sunday every week, but some [court members] had work and school, and it would be too hard for them to come to practice. And so my mom would be mad. . . . You know, it put pressure on me. I think that was the hardest part for me, having to deal with everyone's pressure.

At the same time, when I asked her if there was "an absolute favorite part of your debut," she said, "I would say dancing with the court 'cause that was fun. Like, we worked so hard for that, and when it came down to it, we were all having so much fun." Angela also reflected on how the experience of practicing so much with her friends for something so meaningful to her deepened her relationships with many of them: "Their dedication and time means so much to me."

Since I observed Angela's preparation for months before her debut, I also had the opportunity to watch her learn to assert herself as a leader, mediator, and authority figure in various ways. While Angela struggled during earlier rehearsals to maintain her happy disposition and was never able to gather all her twenty-four court members together or to keep those who showed up very focused, by the time they had reached the six-week countdown, she had significantly sharpened her leadership skills. At the start of the count-down, Angela assembled her court for brunch, reminded them of their upcoming timeline and responsibilities (e.g., attending practice and paying for costumes), and required that they submit to her *all* forms of contact information (i.e., e-mail addresses, cell phone numbers, landline numbers—this was before Facebook), as well as their work and school schedules. During practices, she was visibly more assertive—firmly making sure everyone was on task, quizzing dancers on choreography, and taping rehearsals for them to watch over lunch and critique. During critiques, she asked dancers to "spot five things you did wrong," and this noticeably encouraged court members to take their duties—and the debutante—more seriously. While dancers typically flirted, gossiped, and joked with each other in between learning new steps at previous practices, during countdown rehearsals, I noticed them practicing even when Angela had to step away. Once, while Angela was receiving the food that her mother had brought for lunch, I heard a male direct several other court members, "So Angela won't get mad, we should go practice." This showed that over the few weeks leading to her debut, Angela had established herself as someone her peers respected and wanted to satisfy. This is not to suggest that Angela lost her pre-countdown perkiness—ever cheery, she encouraged dancers to laugh at their mistakes and still tried to remind them, "This is fun! Practice is fun!"

Angela's rehearsal experiences, and her metamorphosis into a stronger leader as a result, were characteristic of the individual debutantes in my study. Thus, while both Filipinas and Mexicanas had to rehearse with their courts extensively before their birthday celebrations, this usually called for debutantes to become more skilled at organizing events; managing multiple schedules, personalities, and learning styles; and exercising their authority. Quinceañera celebrants typically simply "had to show up for rehearsal," while adults such as parents, choreographers, and planners took care of arranging their practice space, schedules (usually easier because younger court members were unemployed and either lived nearby or were family members), and refreshments and maintaining order and discipline among dancers. Consequently, dance rehearsals helped train quinceañeras to relate becoming señoritas with assuming increased responsibilities but to continue their reliance on their elders, while cotillion rehearsals trained debutantes to relate becoming dalaga with being more self-reliant but still hospitable and patient.

Los Ensayos
None of this should imply that quinceañeras have an easier preparation process than debutantes, though, especially because all the quinceañeras in my study had the added responsibility of assembling their families, padrinos, and cortes for a minimum of one preparation class with their parish

quinceañera coordinator, and at least one *ensayo*, or rehearsal of the quinceañera mass, at church.

Flora Favino was the no-nonsense director of religious education at
Prince of Peace parish. She had immigrated to Las Querubes from Mexico
twenty years earlier and had more or less shaped the quinceañera curriculum
for her parish as well as several others in Las Querubes (having trained several other coordinators). During our interview in her neat office, Mrs. Favino
recounted:

> When I started, there were no quinceañeras at Prince of Peace be-
> cause the archdiocese said they weren't a religious celebration. But
> I argued that the quinceañera was an important part of Hispanic
> culture, and I convinced them to let me start the program so that
> kids will think that the quinceañera is more than a dress and a party.

A month later, I observed her in the classroom as she helped prepare Katia,
her family, and her padrinos for her upcoming quince mass. Mrs. Favino
conducted the class primarily in Spanish for the benefit of the immigrant
adults present and started by distributing some handouts, featuring a drawing of la Virgen, printed on pink paper. When she asked the room what
they knew about the quinceañera tradition, one chambelán volunteered,
"a Hispanic heritage thing." She vigorously continued:

> El significado es la transición, o pasaje, de niña a mujer. Es cuando
> una niña se ha convertido a una señorita y se ha presentada a la con-
> gregación, a la comunidad de fe. Es una tradición que es durante
> cuatrocientos años. En el pasado, la mujer mexicana tenía una lugar
> especial. Los hombres eran guerreros, y la mujer era algo especial.
> Somos servidores de nuestra comunidad, dueñas de ese mundo.
>
> ———
>
> The meaning is the transition, or passage, of a girl into a woman. It
> is when a girl has changed to a young lady and has been presented to
> the congregation, to the community of faith. It is a tradition that is
> over four hundred years old. In the past, the Mexicana woman had
> a special place. Men were warriors, and the woman was something
> special. We [women] are servants of our community, caretakers of
> this world.

Then, without taking comments or questions, Mrs. Favino transitioned into
a talk about Mexicana women, and she began discussing how

hoy, en ese día, jovenes tienen abortos, embarazos inesperados. Hay la promiscuidad que vemos en la TV, el cine, programas, billboards. Hemos perdido el foco verdadero de la sexualidad femenina. Esto es el razón tenemos esta tradición [la quinceañera]: para recordar que la sexualidad femenina es algo natural y buena, pero es sacra. Es un don de Dios a ser un instrumento de vida. Esta es la razón las quinceañeras van a la iglesia—para ofrecer su juventud y vida a Dios, y porque la Virgen pueda ser un modelo para ellas.

---

nowadays, young women have abortions, unexpected pregnancies. There is promiscuity that we see on TV, the movies, programs, billboards. The true focus of female sexuality has been lost. This is the reason we have this tradition [the quinceañera]: to remember that female sexuality is something natural and good, but it's sacred. It is a gift of God to be an instrument of life. This is the reason quinceañeras go to church—to offer their youth and life to God, and so that the Virgin Mary can be a model for them.

As Mrs. Favino started talking about *"sexualidad,"* Katia seemed to get bored and the young men appeared visibly uncomfortable, stifling laughter and fidgeting in their seats. Noticing this, Mrs. Favino commanded them to "pay attention. Stop playing, or else we're gonna get away from the real meaning."

She then asked all the youth to volunteer what they thought their *"dones"* (gifts from God)[4] were (their responses included "going to school," "being a good big brother," "skating," and "playing video games") to emphasize her point that *"todos tenemos algo, y tenemos compartir ese don"* (we all have something, and we have to share this gift). Then Mrs. Favino spent the final half of the class referring to her handouts and discussing fundamentals of the Catholic faith (with an extended discussion of the Immaculate Conception and the Virgin Mary). Occasionally she checked in and asked the group, "Are you listening?" Once, after she detected a young man starting to joke around, she instructed, "If you're not going to say something intelligent, please don't say anything, *m'ijo* (son)." She closed the class by reminding them to arrive at rehearsal promptly (because *"el tiempo es oro"* [time is gold]) and to "confess a week before la quinceañera so you can participate in communion."

Like other quinceañera ensayos, Katia's took place the day before her celebration in the church where her mass was held. Ensayos are intended to show and explain to participants the rules of conduct in a Catholic church, how the quinceañera mass will be conducted, what everyone's roles are, and

where everyone should be at all times during the ceremony. Those in attendance typically complete a dry run of the entire mass under the direction of
a parish staff member and then are reminded of the date and time of the real
quinceañera event and asked to arrive early.

Mrs. Favino ran Katia's rehearsal as exactingly as she had conducted their
class. She supervised everything from in front of the altar, before the pews,
where everyone sat silently—except for a few boys seated in the back. After
soliciting details about the readings, music, and decorations from Belinda,
Katia's mother, Mrs. Favino began directing everyone to their places for the
mass's opening *marcha*, or processional. When she got to Katia's chambelán
de honor, she unreservedly inquired, "Are you going to cut your hair? I know
it's the style, but—hmm." Her suggestions/criticisms continued throughout
the evening. As they practiced the marcha, she instructed the youth to "stand
straight" and "to separate yourself so it looks nice" once they were seated. She
also ordered them to "sit up straight. Remember you're not in a living room
in your house, and you're going to come out in every picture they take. So,
no hablando, ni chiclet" (no talking, no gum either). When the readers came
to the lectern, she commanded them to speak more loudly and to "sound like
you feel it." When Katia was supposed to offer her parents the sign of peace,
Mrs. Favino said, "Come here. Show some emotion—*un beso, un abrazo*"
(a kiss, a hug). Finally, after everyone had practiced the recessional and el
ensayo was nearly over, Mrs. Favino reminded them all, "This is not a place
to play, or for dancing, either. Be alert." Rehearsal was officially over after
Katia told her chambelanes, readers, and padrinos, "The quinceañera is at
2:00. We have to be here at 1:00, so be at my house at 11:30."

This case helps to illustrate how the ensayos that Mexicanas have to undertake with their cortes and families further bond quinceañeras' emerging
adult femininity to their ethnic identities (e.g., the quinceañera is "an important part of Hispanic culture," "a Hispanic heritage thing," and regular
references to la Virgen). Classes like Mrs. Favino's help stress the fact that
quinceañera celebrants represent their ethnic group by declaring women "servants of our community" who must "share their God-given gifts." Ensayos
also help convey to all participating youth—not just quinceañeras—that
coming of age involves disciplining the body—learning how to sit straight,
look nice, be on time, and, most important, guard female sexuality. Parish
classes and rehearsals also remind Latino youth once again that while their
families and communities recognize that they are rising adults, their immigrant parents and elders are continuing to monitor them and still hold a
reasonable degree of authority over them. Although class and ensayos did not
demand as much time and energy from quinceañera celebrants as their dance

rehearsals, or as some cotillion preparation programs, they were remarkably effective at transmitting all these lessons because they were connected to the powerful institution of the Catholic church and took place in spaces that were designated as sacred. This ascribed the training received there with a privileged and transcendent meaning for participants.

Moreover, like other quinceañera activities, ensayos reflected the experiences of my Mexican American subjects. I have already discussed the significance of first-generation Latino parents demonstrating their authority; here I discuss the emphasis on protecting women's sexuality. Although Filipino parents shared as many concerns over their daughters' sexualities during our interviews, only quinceañera ensayos ever openly addressed this topic. I believe that this is because of the myths and realities surrounding young Latina sexuality. When they are not portrayed in Western media as self-denying women suffering under macho men (see Juarez and Kerl 2003), Latinas are depicted as "hot (hypersexual) and as possessing abhorrently high fertility rates" (Chavez 2008: 80). Sadly, figures for teen Latina pregnancies are just as disturbing. The pregnancy rate for young Latinas (13 percent) is almost three times that of non-Hispanic whites (4.8 percent). In 2008, the National Campaign to Prevent Teen and Unplanned Pregnancy reported that 53 percent of Latina teens become pregnant at least once before age twenty. This is especially troubling, since women who experience unplanned pregnancies are more likely to undergo abortions; suffer greater relationship instability, physical abuse, and depression; and leave school (National Campaign to Prevent Teen and Unplanned Pregnancy 2008a). With more than one out of two of their daughters experiencing a pregnancy before they reach college, this is an understandably major concern for Latino parents. So it is not surprising that Mexican families and communities take advantage of girls' coming-of-age celebrations to candidly address youth about their sexuality and to remind them that "female sexuality is something natural and good *but it's sacred.*" This shows the inventiveness of some Mexican immigrant parents in using quinceañeras not only to recover some generational authority but also to initiate a dialogue with their children about a topic that is difficult for many parents and teenagers to broach.

"Learning More about My Culture"
Quinceañera and debutante preparation also worked inventively by serving as a vehicle for helping second-generation youth learn more about their culture. Mexican parents and coordinators emphasized to their children that quinceañeras are Mexican traditions. Mexican adults often explained that the quince tradition harked back centuries. Recall Mrs. Favino's teaching

Katia and her entourage that the quinceañera "is a tradition that is over four hundred years old." The declarations of Mrs. Favino and other adults were supported by classic how-to guides for quinceañeras. In her "essential guide," Salcedo proclaims that the quinceañera's "beginnings go much further back, thousands of years back, to the indigenous people of our respective cultures" (1997: xi). And Angela Erevia's religious guide for quinceañera masses elaborates that "the custom probably dates back to a custom of the Mayas and the Toltecas. . . . The young lady was . . . presented to the community because she was looked upon as a vital force of the tribe" (1980: 3).

Filipino parents also framed debuts as traditions but specified that they were not widely celebrated by all Filipinos. For instance, when I asked Imelda, "In your opinion, are debuts important in the Philippines?" like most Filipino immigrants I spoke with, she answered, "Only for the rich." And when I asked Rose the same question, she went into a little more detail by saying, "It's the tradition. Mostly—usually, though, you should be someone who can afford it because it's very expensive. But those who can afford it, they still have a debut." Juliet added, "It's a tradition not everybody can afford. But I happen to have a daughter and means to do it. I feel sorry for people who don't because I think everyone wants to do it."

By characterizing debuts and quinceañeras as traditions, Filipino and Mexican Americans create the impression that their association with what these customs convey—noble refinement and wealth—is something deeply, and perhaps even naturally, entrenched in their cultures. Eric Hobsbawm writes that the evocation of tradition "automatically implies continuity with a suitable historic past" (1983: 1). By suggesting that quinces and debuts are customs that date back to a distant Mexican or Filipino past, organizers and participants powerfully challenge notions of Mexicans and Filipinos as being less civilized or well bred than European Americans and imply that they have been all the things that debuts and quinceañeras are meant to portray them as—proper, honorable, dignified, and worthy of enormous respect—*throughout history.*

Characterizing quinces and debuts as Mexican and Filipino traditions also helps normalize the fact that these events are used by immigrants to impart greater knowledge and pride about Mexican and Filipino culture to young people. For example, although the ostensible aim of a quinceañera is to usher a girl into womanhood, no one questioned the fact that Mrs. Favino also used a significant portion of her preparation with quinceañeras and their peers to talk about Mexican history and culture. She shared, "I take advantage of the celebration to work with the youth, to teach them . . . that it is important to celebrate our culture. . . . I would like them to know and recognize that 'I am contributing to the continuation of a beautiful tradition and history.'"

Likewise, Josie of the Ladies' Association admitted that "the girls [debutantes] are made aware that this [their cotillion] is a cultural thing. So that gets them into thinking about where they came from. At least they can know that we are also civilized people and culturally geared people. Most kids don't understand the Philippines. . . . [T]hese kids right now, they don't know about their culture."

To these ends, Mrs. Favino encouraged youth to use Spanish during their classes and their religious ceremonies, lectured on indigenous Mexican history, and actively advocated for youth to understand that they "share the responsibility and privilege" of participating and building their community and church. And the Ladies' Association required debutantes to learn about Maria Clara and the history and choreography of the Filipino dances they performed.

As a result, almost all of the debutantes and quinceañeras I spoke with shared that they became more interested in learning about their culture during and/or after their celebrations. Dalía concisely told me what many of her peers had related—that her quince "reaffirmed my Mexican-ness. I felt that I was still part of an important tradition. And it reinforced the feeling that I was part of a strong community." Nambia, a woman who was in one of my focus groups, also told me that her quinceañera helped her confirm what she had known to a lesser extent before her celebration. She said:

It helped me see more how I like my traditions, the way we [Latinos] do things. [White] Americans like to be more quiet, but we like to party. We have big families, and everyone is really united when we get together. We understand each other more.

While their Mexicana counterparts felt that their coming-of-age preparation reaffirmed what they were already fairly familiar with beforehand, Filipinas talked about how their debutantes opened them to new lessons about their culture. For example, Klara Napolo, a former SCUFA debutante, frankly shared:

In junior high, I would see a white girl in the mirror. I never said it, but I didn't want my culture to be acknowledged as Filipino. I told people I was Filipino even though it didn't sound cool. I wasn't as proud. . . . I never said it, but to me Filipinos weren't as witty or as smart. . . . After the debutante, I felt different. When we were preparing for it [her debutante], Brianna and Eliane [the cotillion organizers] talked about the greatness of it, and they glamorized and romanticized the culture. . . . I started appreciating being Filipino and acknowledging the traditions.

Former LRPS debutante Anabel Currabeg told me that her debut awakened in her a new cultural curiosity as well as a lifelong commitment to discovering more about Filipinos in the United States. She said:

They [LRPS] make you think and really reevaluate who you are as a Filipina American and your family background, so you know the cultural experience here as a Fil-Am in America. That [during her debutante] is when I started asking my dad questions [about being Filipino American]. . . . That is when I realized that I did not know about this and that. . . . It definitely did open the door to learning more about my culture and myself.

When we met, Anabel was serving on a regional executive board for Filipino collegiate organizations, she had already served as an LRPS officer and the president of her high school's Filipino culture club, and she was eagerly looking forward to finding creative ways to continue working with and leading her fellow Filipino Americans.

And former SCUFA debutante Olivia told me:

I didn't realize it right away, but I think that it [her debut] was sort of like the first step to me really starting to like have *pride* in my [Filipino] identity. It's not like I was ashamed before. But I guess I was more like, "It's just what I am; it doesn't really make a difference in my life." Maybe—just being a debutante, being around all these other Filipinos, learning all about the tradition—it made me want to talk to my parents more about where they came from, stuff I just didn't think about before.

This must have pleased her parents, since her father, Ramiro, told me that increasing Olivia's understanding of her Filipino roots was a large motivation for him and his wife to involve her in a cotillion:

We [he and his wife] didn't raise Olivia and Suzy [Olivia's sister] with the [Pilipino] language or the history, because we didn't want them to have any disadvantages in school. . . . We just wanted them to be American kids, because they were going to be in American schools, growing up here in America. . . . But when [Olivia] turned eighteen . . . it was time for her to learn about herself, to learn about her family and where she came from.

All this again helps to show how powerfully debut and quinceañera preparation ties becoming a woman with developing one's ethnic identity. By employing these events to help enhance second-generation participants' cultural knowledge, pride, and sense of community responsibility, immigrants yet again promote the understanding that debuts and quinceañeras transform celebrants into specifically Filipino and Mexican American ladies, and "not just any woman." The learning experiences of my younger subjects also highlight further differences between Mexican and Filipino immigrants' approaches to preparing their children for coming-of-age rituals—how they frame these events as traditions, how young women feel about their ethnic identities before their coming of age, and what these women feel they gain about their culture afterward. I discuss these differences in more detail in the final section of this chapter.

Getting Ready

After months of learning more about their culture, rehearsing their dance(s) and/or religious celebrations, organizing and attending various classes, and negotiating decisions with their parents and other adults, debutantes and quinceañeras' big days inevitably arrive and begin with hours of getting ready: extensively grooming and adorning young women's bodies to physically prepare them for their formal introduction to family and friends as dalaga and señoritas for the first time.

Among those I interviewed and observed, the process of getting ready actually started some time before the big day, with girls heeding beauty tips advising them to "drink water, sleep well, and exercise" (Garcia de Angela 2012), to "start eating right" ("The Big Day" 1998), to "schedule hair, makeup, nail appointments" ("The Ultimate Planning Timeline" 2011), and to conduct "hair and makeup rehearsals" ("The Big Day" 1998) weeks beforehand. The goal, of course, was for girls to achieve "a look" that would appear "timeless and stunning in photographs years from now" and that would allow them to feel like "the star" during their celebrations (Thalia 2011).

Hair and Makeup

Once the day of their parties arrived, hair and makeup were typically the first things to be done. Most of the debutante and quinceañera celebrants I interviewed did not do their own hair; they either had their hair done in a professional salon or had stylists come to their homes. LRPS debutantes were all required to wear their hair pulled back into a bun, "in the style of Maria Clara." Otherwise, hairstyles varied, though "red carpet" looks— curled hair and updos that took at least a half hour to create—were popular. Most girls aimed for hairstyles they felt reflected their personalities ("romantic," "modern," or "simple," for example) and for styles that would serve as suitable settings for their accessories (tiaras, combs with silk flowers or butterflies, ribbons, rhinestones, etc.). The proper hairstyle was so critical that girls dreamed about it, redid it when it didn't turn out as planned, and were haunted by hairstyles they regretted. In a focus group, Lilac related, "I had a dream before my quince: they brought the wrong limo, part of my friends got sick or got hurt or something, and the salon didn't do [my hair] how I wanted. My quince turned out good, but it was such a bad dream." When I asked her what the worst thing about her quinceañera was, Katia recalled, "My hair. The ladies messed up, so they had to redo it. It was a tragedy." And Olivia told me:

> For years, my mom kept putting this huge picture from my debutante up [a professional solo portrait displayed in the house], and I *hated* it. I was always, like, trying to take it down and hide it. . . . I guess what I hate most about it was my hair. I just can't stand to look at it. [*Grimaces.*] Ugh. I tried to curl it in like a modern ponytail, but that turned out unacceptable. So I had to wash it out, which was hard and took a long time to do because there was all this hair spray in it. So by the time it was clean and blow-dried, there was no time left, and I just had to wear it straight and puffy for the shoot. It looks *so* bad. Every time I see it, I wish I could go back in time and just flat-iron it or something, so that I wouldn't have to remember forever how bad it was.

If all hair "tragedies" were averted, then makeup could be applied. Again, somebody else usually did this. In my study, I saw older mothers and sisters enlisted to do makeup for free, MAC[5] teams hired to come to a family's home to apply makeup for the honoree and all her female court members, and everything in between. LRPS debutantes were instructed to keep their cosmetics to a minimum. Otherwise, makeup styles were as varied as the debutantes and quinceañeras themselves. While girls were often eager to mimic the looks of adult celebrities, parents usually tried to discourage them from going overly dramatic. They would agree with quince beauty advisor Thalia, who says, "The goal should be a playful, fun, and fresh look, nothing too sexy. There is plenty of time to look sexy" (2011). At the same time, I did observe a few parents who asked artists to lighten their daughters' makeup to keep them from looking "dark" (though this would mean using a makeup that was shades lighter than the girls' natural pigment). I also overheard a few Filipino parents request makeup that would make their daughters' noses appear "higher," or more European. This reveals how even the ethnicized female beauty ideals of Mexican and Filipino Americans still bear the residue of centuries of European colonialism (and American neocolonialism) in Mexico and the Philippines (for more on Mexican and Filipino beauty ideals, see Nakano-Glenn 2009; Rondilla and Spickard 2007).

The Dress

After makeup, debutantes and quinceañeras were expected to get into their dresses to complete their Big Day preparations. As noted throughout the book, dresses were typically custom-made or custom-altered floor-length gowns. White was the most common dress color for debutantes (it was required for girls in group cotillions), and quinceañera dresses came in all shades of pastels. Girls were encouraged to use special undergarments with their gowns—such as strapless corset bras, panties that offer women "smooth coverage and shape," and nylon stockings (Ana 2010). Olivia lightheartedly recalled:

> I got my first backless, strapless bra for my debutante. Just that alone felt sort of fancy and grown-up! I remember when my mom brought it home one day and was like, "You have to wear this special bra." It was sort of sexy, in that old-fashioned, like, sophisticated kind of way—maybe it was my first lingerie! It made my waist so small; it was like a girdle. And it made me stand so straight. I felt adult just wearing that.

Professionals and parents estimated the dress as the single most expensive purchase[6] in a typical coming-of-age budget. This seemed appropriate, given the heavy symbolism of a coming-of-age dress. In her handbook, Salcedo writes, "The dress transforms la niña beyond a señorita and into a real-life fairy princess" (1997: 135).

LRPS and Ladies' Association debutantes were required to wear Maria Clara gowns, which were actually ensembles of three[7] separates: a square-neck blouse with long bell sleeves, worn with a stiff *pañuelo* wrapped around the shoulders and back of the neck and then tucked into a floor-length skirt traditionally made out of two (but sometimes as many as seven) layers of *piña*.

"Like the heroine," the gown has been described as "delicate and feminine but clearly self-assured in terms of its projected sense of identity" (Moreno 2001). Josie of the Ladies' Association would agree. She told me, "We tell them [debutantes] stories about experiences [in the Philippines], about the clothes, about Maria Clara. Maria Clara is so beautiful, just like the dress. Maria Clara depicts the beautiful womanhood of Filipino women." Missus M of LRPS felt similarly and encouraged her debutantes to avoid extravagant gowns. She said:

> When she's [the debutante] here, she and her parents agree to be team players, minus an attitude, and expect to work hard towards the traditions and goals of LRPS, which doesn't mean, "You know, I have more money than you have money," or "I'm going to make my gown with, ooh, diamonds!" and "Ooh, I want to order my gown, and I know it's gonna cost $1,200 or $1,800." That's an attitude. Our team is about simplicity in elegance. In our gowns, we have no decorations except for the blouse. . . . I say, "You need to keep it simple. You can decorate the blouse any fun way you make it. If you want to make yours a head-turner, it has to be only in white. You want to put diamonds on it? That's your problem."

Quite conversely, most girls holding individual celebrations felt that their gowns should "make a statement"—within the boundaries laid down for them by their parents and other adults. In the written agreement parents had to sign to reserve a private quince mass, St. Anne's parish specified that the "quinceañera and participants must wear MODEST attire (no strapless gowns)." Eliane Dizon, a former SCUFA cotillion coordinator, explained that SCUFA debutantes could choose their own dress designs but that "the attire has to be white, to connote innocence." Written guides also highlighted modesty as important; Salcedo states that quince dresses can come in all colors, with all different embellishments, "but they are all long and feminine, and should have an air of innocence" (1997: 140).

None of this prevented girls from finding or creating dresses that could rival those of a bride or fairy-tale heroine, however. For instance, Dalía's quinceañera dress was an almost exact replica of a bridal gown she and her mother had spotted in a magazine. It had pink bows everywhere and elaborate details throughout the front and skirt. She recalled, "That dress was so heavy. I wanted to just sit because it was so hard to walk in." Klara's gown was an off-the-rack white wedding gown that she had custom-altered to fit her, which featured modest cap sleeves and sparkling ornaments throughout the skirt and bodice. She said that the dress was what ultimately persuaded her to become a debutante:

> I thought it [a debut] would be like those Mexican things [quince-añeras], that I could be a Southern belle. I didn't comprehend what it stood for. I was attracted to the material stuff. . . . The dress was a big deal, and dressing up. . . . The only thing I picked and chose for myself was the dress; my mom chose everything else. It just felt really special. . . . It was my first real dress, my first real dress shopping.

Ethnic Beauties

All this shows that "getting ready" for debutantes and quinceañeras "practically require[s] a woman to make her body and face a 'project'" and frames beautifying oneself as "hard work" that can be "a deeply absorbing and rewarding activity," just as lavish weddings do (Otnes and Pleck 2003: 274). But while wedding preparation is seen as allowing women to satisfy *their own* "intrinsic needs for sociability, creativity, play, and self-definition" (Otnes and Pleck 2003: 274), getting ready for debuts and quinces further coaches Filipinas and Mexicanas to align their desires with those of their parents, their organizers and planners, and other influential adults. Girls even feel pressured to submit to adults like quince photographer Gabriel Ortega, who stipulates during the contract signing with his clients:

> I tell them, "You've got to sleep before your big day; you've got to be at the church on time, at 10:00 [A.M.]." . . . They think they can get their makeup at 9:00. They think, "That's good; it gives me an hour." But what if the girl's late [to her hairstyling appointment]? Then she's not finished until 9:45; she still has to do makeup, and then she has to go home and put on her dress. I tell them, "This is what time you go to sleep. Get your makeup done at 8:00. Be on time."

Moreover, getting ready for a quince or debut continues to bring together the project of becoming a woman with that of developing one's ethnic identity. This was especially evident in the case of group cotillions that called for participants to explicitly emulate Maria Clara's hair and clothing. But it was also apparent in how individual debutantes' and quinceañeras' appearances were similarly framed as representing ethnic ideals of feminine beauty. For example, it was common to hear exclamations of "*Binibining Pilipinas!*" (the title of the winning candidates who represent the Philippines in international beauty pageants each year) and "Oy! Si Maria Clara!" (Hey! It's Maria

Clara!) after debutantes first appeared fully made up and attired for their celebrations. And quinceañera celebrants were constantly referred to as "señoritas" and reminded that they were "not just at another party" but instead "taking part in an important celebration in our culture" as they got ready.

The beauty ideal most individual debutantes and quinceañeras seemed to strive for was "modern-day princess." In a society in which "for girls specifically, being 'cool' means looking hot," this allowed girls to personify characters who "are, by definition, special elevated creatures" (Orenstein 2011: 24, 23) while still allowing parents to see and present their daughters as pure, innocent, and virginal. The latter were always characterized as specifically Mexican or Filipino female traits. For example, Adele, Olivia's mother, said:

> I think Olivia's dress is very pretty—very appropriate for a dalaga. It is in style, but it is still *modest* and very beautiful. It shows that she is now a proper young lady, ready to be introduced to the society. She is a good girl. People can see she has respect for herself, that she is going to accomplish her goals because of the love and support of her parents.

And Selena Gutierrez, a vivacious and expressive *modista*, or seamstress, who has made countless quinceañera dresses, observed:

> The girl will always want something more. "I want my neck down here" [*motions to a low point on her chest*]; "I don't want no sleeves"; "I don't want no back." But she has to listen to her mami, you know? Her mami will tell her, "Girl, this is how we [Mexicans] do it: a young lady has to be covered; she cannot show everything. She is already beautiful; she does not need to show her body like that to be so beautiful."

Getting ready thus "draws attention to the way that gender is constructed, acted and worked upon as a form of social control" in quinceañeras and debuts and how this is similar to how Rebecca King-O'Riain found gender to be used in ethnic beauty pageants (2006: 120). Immigrants' framing of debut and quince beautification as cultural projects (e.g., becoming a Maria Clara, creating an appearance "how we [Mexicans] do it") places daughters under the pressure of representing their respective ethnic communities as ideal Filipino and Mexican American women. This helps further justify the first generation's close supervision of young women's appearance and behavior, since immigrants are understood as cultural experts and authorities. In debuts and quinces, immigrants help groom young women not just to display their femininity but to display and enact particular ethnicized (and middle- or upper-class) gender identities. This is because "it is not only the dress itself" that affects female bodily appearances and movements but the "*knowledge about how to behave in a dress* that is restrictive" (Martin 1998: 498; emphasis added). Wearing Filipino and Mexican hairstyles, accessories, makeup, and gowns visibly, tangibly, and psychologically reminds debutantes and quinceañeras of how and who they "should be": "delicate and feminine but clearly self-assured," as regal as a "real-life fairy princess," and, above all else, sexually *modest*. This, in turn, racializes these traits among Filipino and Mexican Americans and additionally constructs them as morally superior to white Americans.

Performing

To fully understand my subjects' claims to Filipino and Mexican moral superiority and the ways second-generation daughters come to enact ethnicized femininities through debuts and quinces, we must now examine how Filipinas and Mexicanas are introduced and perform as newly initiated dalaga and señoritas during their cotillions.

Posing

The first thing many debutantes and quinceañeras were required to do after getting ready was to pose for formal photos (and/or pose for videographers). Like photos of weddings and other momentous occasions, debut and quince photos were depicted as keepsakes "you and your family will be looking at . . . for years to come" (Thalia 2011). Joyce Fernandez, former editor of *Debutante and Bride Philippines*, even equates the entire enterprise of a cotillion to one big photo shoot when she writes, "In one big night, [the debutante] is making a living scrapbook of her young life" (1998: 15). Accordingly, parents (or sponsors) often paid significantly to have photographers and videographers record their daughters' big days and to help capture them at their finest: successful, proper, unified as a family, and completely at home in their surroundings. Success and propriety were suggested not just by a family's regal attire but by the series of before-and-after photos often taken of girls as they were getting ready, which demonstrated their and their family's victory at physically transforming the honoree from an ordinary girl to a remarkable young lady. Family unity was portrayed in photos of parents with their children (and sometimes extended family members) as well as in numerous shots of the debutante or quinceañera celebrant with her mother. In addition to taking conventional photographs of the two women, photographers often posed mothers to look like they were putting the final touches on their daughters' hair, makeup, and/or attire. This produced a set of photos that made it appear as if mothers were primarily responsible for their daughters' physical transformations. Missus M explained that this rendered visible an important lesson that she wanted LRPS debutantes to take with them as they came of age:

> When you look at our souvenir program, you will see a page of mother-daughter [a two-page spread of professional portraits of each debutante with her mother], to show that those who commit [to becoming an LRPS debutante] commit to strong mother-daughter relationships from the beginning. . . . This is because the bottom line is your best friend is your mother. You got her, whether you hate her now, because in the long run, you know, when you get to be my age, you look back, and she's your best friend. You have to understand and respect Filipino families that way.

This demonstrates that debut and quince photographs of family unity do not just hold sentimental value for the celebrant and her family, but are also intended to reinforce the notion of Filipinos and Mexicans as morally superior because of the close bond they promote between parents and children, especially between mothers and daughters. This was particularly evident in how, while discussing the LRPS mother-daughter photos, Missus M reflected, "You have to understand and respect Filipino families that way."

Pre-event photos were taken at home as well as at local landmarks. In my study, photo sites included landscaped parks and gardens, wineries, amusement parks, reception venues' opulent lobbies, and other (sometimes internationally) recognizable locations. These photos fostered an image of the immigrant families in them as flourishing and completely adjusted to their new homes in America. Quince mother Catalina told me, "My family from Mexico, they say, 'Beautiful! Very beautiful.' Because some of them never saw this [as lavish a quinceañera as her daughter's]. They're thinking we're [her family] in heaven [in America]."

And Olivia's mother, Adele, told me:

> When our relatives in the Philippines see Olivia's debutante, they are so impressed. They think that we are living like *artista* [celebrities] in the States. Our life here is simple, but they think that it's something, like, rich. They think we are rich and very happy in America. This is our

home now because this is where Olivia and Suzy [Olivia's sister] were born. They are American children—Americans with Filipino blood.

Thus, debut and quince photos served not just to prove that immigrant families were respectable, financially well off, and cohesive but to also communicate that they rightfully belonged in the United States. This helps show how immigrant critiques of (white) American morality and people are aimed not at locating immigrant families *outside* U.S. culture but, rather, at helping immigrant families establish their suitability for full cultural citizenship within the United States.

Posing for photos during the big day could take hours, and photographers usually remained with the family afterward to document the rest of the day's events. As a result, debutantes and quinceañera celebrants were sent the message that there was a reward for the time and labor invested in negotiating, preparing, and physically transforming themselves: being in the spotlight. Girls recalled this with mixed feelings. Dalía expressed most girls' ambivalence over such attention best when she told me:

Being in the spotlight . . . was the best and the worst thing. I felt all self-conscious and awkward with all the attention. I just felt like I had to be poised. I mean, the attention was nice, but there was this camera crew following me everywhere. And everyone was watching me—I couldn't do anything!

So posing for photos brought quinceañera celebrants and debutantes the pleasure of being admired and appreciated while reinforcing the notion that their womanhood would be closely patrolled by adults and conveying the idea that their personal successes as ladies would be understood as a reflection of their parents' and their families' successes in America. Like photos of other formal occasions, debut and quince photos also provided girls and their families with a way of "retaining and reliving special memories" (Otnes and Pleck 2003: 16), but I reserve my discussion of photographs and memories for my discussion of ritual memories (see Chapter 6).

Mass
The first time a debutante or quinceañera celebrant appeared before her guests was usually after posing for photos, and this was often dramatic. Quinceañeras typically did this much earlier than their Filipina counterparts because of their mass. While some Filipinas attended a mass for their

eighteenth birthdays, only the quinceañeras in my study had personal masses celebrated for them.

Katia's mass was characteristic of the masses I observed. Fresh from being photographed and video-recorded, she arrived fifteen minutes before her service at Prince of Peace in a stretch white Ford Expedition limousine. With the help of her mother and Mrs. Favino, Katia and her entourage—her family, corte, padrinos, readers, and younger attendants (some of her parents' friends' young children carried the items Katia would have blessed during the mass as part of her marcha)—were all in the church foyer five minutes before mass was scheduled to begin. Here, as the photographer snapped away, the chambelánes were reminded by Mrs. Favino to "walk up like gentlemen." Seconds before two o'clock, Mrs. Favino placed her hand on the doors that would open into the church and said, "The minute I open up the door, everybody be quiet. Then walk beautiful and slowly." As the church bells rang on the hour, piano music started to fill the space, Mrs. Favino slowly pulled the doors open, and Katia's marcha proceeded into the church. Katia came in last. As she moved from the back of the church, necks craned and smiles broadened as she self-consciously made her way down the aisle in a white gown, with a crown of flowers atop her head and a bouquet in her hands. After her court was seated and she took her place at a kneeler before the center of the altar, the priest remarked, "What a sharp-looking group."

The priest, Father George, commenced the mass in English and spoke about how the congregation (there were about thirty guests at mass—a far cry from the more than two hundred who would show up for the reception) was there to celebrate Katia's growing "maturity." He also made use of a prayer printed in Sr. Erevia's manual:

> Guide [the quinceañera's] way through life, as you guided your favorite daughter, the Virgin Mary; so may this young lady be always pleasing to you and inspire others to know, love, and serve you through the Christian life she lives fully. (1980: 15)

The first reading was then recited in Spanish, the second in English, and the Gospel in Spanish. This was followed by an English homily, or sermon that seemed directed at only Katia, since Father George stood directly before her and seemed to address only her.

The homily began with Father George saying, "Today you come here to tell God you want him to be part of your life. Congratulations to your parents, and to everyone who supports you." He continued with "It will be hard sometimes, especially here in Las Querubes. But you have support—you are not alone. You have Mary as a model of faith, who followed the teachings of the Lord."

About five minutes later, he concluded by saying, "I want you to remember this today: Put God first and love everybody." Father George's homily again emphasized the idea that Katia's successful transition to womanhood was a by-product of her parents' good upbringing.

After Katia renewed her baptismal vows and had her *regalos* (gifts) blessed, she was directed to offer her *ramo* (bouquet) to a statue of la Virgen, to the right of the altar. Here, she quietly recited the following prayer:

> *Oh, María, Madre mia . . .* be my model of a valiant woman, my strength and my guide. You have the power to change hearts; take my heart then, and make me a worthy daughter of yours. . . . I dedicate myself to you, *María, Madre de Jesus.* You . . . are my model of faith. From you, may I continually learn what it is to be a woman and a Christian. (Erevia 1980)

Afterward, Prayers of the Faithful[8] were recited in Spanish, the Eucharist was shared, the congregation greeted each other in peace, and Father George gave a final blessing and then invited those gathered to applaud Katia. Since this mass, like most, required those in attendance to be hushed and reserved, the visible and audible enthusiasm that followed seemed extraordinary.

For most quinceañeras, the mass, more than any other event related to their *quince años*, induced them to seriously consider la Virgen, a Mexican incarnation of the mother of God, as a model of femininity. This is because of how forcefully the space and activities of mass help ritualize and sanctify a Mexicana's coming of age. The words and actions during a quinceañera mass are so strongly set apart from ordinary activities and actors that they are endowed with greater power and experienced as having more profound meaning for participants. This is why Dalía felt that her prayer at la Virgen's altar was the most powerful moment of her quinceañera. She said:

> I got all emotional then. I don't know why. I think I prayed la Virgen would help me be a loving, responsible daughter. I started thinking about how I was supposed to be thankful for my life, and I almost began to cry. I was putting the flowers there, and I was getting all choked up.

This is how the message that becoming a "worthy daughter" involves carrying oneself properly ("walk beautiful and slowly"), pleasing others, having courage in the face of uncertainty ("be my model of a valiant woman"), and striking a harmonious balance between being Latina and American (as reflected by the bilingual mass) came to be internalized so deeply by some.

Presentation
A reception at a separate location typically followed a quinceañera mass; it was usually the grand event for both Mexicanas and Filipinas.

All of the receptions I observed and heard about officially commenced with some kind of grand presentation. After guests were seated, an emcee usually called everyone to attention to announce that the entourage would soon be entering. The order in which people were introduced varied; however, as a general rule, parents and/or grandparents entered first, followed by padrinos (at a quince), Candles and Roses (at debutantes), the court (in couples, if there were an equal number of males and females), and then the honoree, accompanied by her escort of honor. A young lady's grand entrance inevitably garnered vigorous applause and oohs and aahs from those seeing her for the first time that day. After the debutante or quinceañera took her place (e.g., at a special table with her family and/or court, standing in the middle of a dance floor for all to see), a prayer was usually said. Then the emcee often announced something like what Dino Manuel said at Janice's debut:

> It's our pleasure to present to you our debutante as she faces a whole new world of challenges, ready, with confidence to face the future. Congratulations to [her parents] and the rest of the family on helping raise her from a little girl to a mature young adult.

At group cotillions, debutantes almost always individually processed into their events, in an order determined by the organizing association, escorted either by their parents or their escorts. After entering the ballroom, debutantes usually walked around the dance floor or slowly across it. As each debutante paraded before guests, an emcee might share some biographical information (e.g., who her parents are, her parents' hometowns in the Philippines, where the debutante was born, and where she lived and went to school). Later, the young lady's notable accomplishments and goals (usually provided in advance by parents or daughters themselves) might be announced. At some point, the debutante typically made a formal curtsy to her guests. And after all the debs were introduced, emcees such as SCUFA's Willis Santos characteristically asked everyone to "give the lovely debutantes another round of applause," adding:

Tonight we all have been invited to take part in the Filipino custom of watching our most outstanding young ladies be presented to society by their loving parents. As you have just listened to, tonight's debutantes have already achieved very much. We know that with their exceptional personalities, devotion to God, family, and their Filipino culture, this is just the beginning.

The ceremonious opening for most debutante receptions reflects both the fact that this was the Filipinas' first and only entrance (in contrast to Mexicanas, who made notable arrivals at mass *and* their *salón*) and the distinctive ways Filipino immigrants desired to present their daughters. At individual debuts, the fact that honorees often entered last seemed to convey that a dalaga must be patient, willing to let others go before her, and conscious that her appearance and deportment are under close scrutiny from members of their community. The curtsy suggested that the proper response to being in the spotlight and being recognized as a lady is modesty, gratitude, and continued respect toward those who have supported her.[9] And announcing parents' biographical information before debutantes' accomplishments and goals emphasized that a dalaga was the by-product of, and representative of, her parents and family. It gave the impression that becoming a dalaga did not necessarily mean becoming a fully independent adult but rather a qualified family ambassador. It also made the debutante more aware of how closely her community would continue to monitor her development. Angela hinted at this when she said:

I think the main thing I got out of it [her debut] is that there are people in my life who care about me. And I don't want to disappoint them. And that should help me do the best that I can do, so, like, all those people who were there, who watched me grow up, won't be like, "What happened to her?" To me, having the people I care about the most feel disappointed in me—I could not stand that. Like, it would break my heart.

Dancing

At both Filipino and Mexican coming-of-age celebrations, dance performances usually followed shortly after the grand entrance (along with dinner). The first dance was often a father-daughter piece. These were usually not highly choreographed performances—sometimes they were completely improvised on the dance floor. In my study, the most popular quinceañera father-daughter song was Julio Iglesias's "De Niña a Mujer" (1981); Al Martino's "Daddy's Little Girl" (1967) was considered most appropriate for debutantes and their dads. Iglesias croons about memories of when his young daughter used to make believe she was grown ("*jugabas a ser mujer*") and about how time has betrayed him by allowing her to change into a woman ("Pensando que no debería crecer / Pero el tiempo me estaba engañando. / Mi niña se hacía mujer"). Martino likens his daughter to every imaginable treasure, concluding, "You're the treasure I cherish so sparkling and bright; / You were touched by the holy and beautiful light."

This dance often afforded fathers an intimate moment to convey a personal message to their daughters. Nambia reminisced, "I cried when I was dancing with my dad. He was talking, giving me advice, like, 'You're a grown woman; you have to take care of yourself.'" Guests found these dances touching, but the dances everyone anticipated most were usually the waltz and native Filipino or Mexican dances, such as *ballet folklorico* (Mexican folk dances) or *tinikling*.[10]

Since these dances were "the culmination of . . . work and dedication" (Salcedo 1997: 105), guests read the quality of these group routines as evidence of young women's ability to successfully train their bodies to move as dalaga and señoritas—with elegance, modesty (physical contact with their male partners was limited to that which was carefully choreographed), and poise. These performances were also seen as indicative of the investment parents had made in their daughters' dance and social training, of the ability of immigrants to gracefully discipline and control their children, and of the ability of families to create and/or call on their networks to gather together sufficient dancers. And all these things, of course, were understood as marks of the ascendancy of Mexican and Filipino families, values, and culture. Josie of the Ladies' Association reflected: "When the whole dance floor is filled up with those kids . . . you feel like you are showing off what you have, your kids, to the whole community. . . . It makes families so happy to see them dancing the Maria Clara dance, [to know] that their kids understand the [Filipino] culture."

Youth were highly aware of how much rested on the successful execution of their group dances. Subsequently, the moments before their performance and their two to three minutes on the dance floor were often the most nerve-racking and rewarding of their entire day. Nambia recalled, "It was fun and stressful. Everybody's looking at you; you have to dance your best. But it goes by quick. And once you're there, you wish it could happen again." Janice said:

I hated thinking about how the dance was such a difficult thing. So much is expected of the debutante—how could you deal with that? It was tense before we were on the dance floor; everybody [the dancers] got really pressured. . . . But all the dancers were my friends, and everyone was cheering me on, so it really worked out.

More recent debutante and quinceañera events frequently featured more relaxed "modern" routines after the waltz or native dances.[11] These were usually performed to uptempo music such as hip-hop, salsa, or swing. Sometimes the honoree was included in these performances; at other times, these were presented as "surprises" by the honorees' court. While waltzes were often carried out self-consciously, dancers seemed to genuinely enjoy their modern numbers—they moved more naturally and easily in less formal costumes, and they smiled broadly and sincerely throughout their performances. Although one might expect adults to find such dances inappropriate at such formal occasions, most seemed truly impressed. After watching a modern performance, one mother told me, "I guess young people always want to do something different to the old traditions. It's nice to see their other talent." This serves as a reminder that debuts and quinceañeras also allow immigrant parents to reflect on their children's experiences in the United States, something I discuss further in Chapter 5.

Debut and Quinceañera Performances as Mini-dramas

In a scene from the film *Quinceañera*, a group of girls are gathered to view their friend's quinceañera video. The video begins with a few notes of synthesized music. Then as the words *Mis Quince Años* appear, white petals descend from the top of the screen. As they watch, one girl observes, "It looks like one of those openings for one of those bad *novelas*."[12] This is fitting because the typical coming-of-age reception program ultimately serves as a mini-drama, encapsulating the honoree's social transition.[13] It captures how girls are first brought into the world as cherished members of a family and community with the grand presentation and then kept close to their parents through the father-daughter dance. Then it emulates how debutantes and quinceañeras are expected to take on more responsibility as they gain (some) freedom from their parents' supervision during the waltz, and, finally, how they can look forward to an enjoyable and exciting future if they continue to honor their family and "understand their culture," which is represented in the modern dance. And like a *novela*, debuts and quinceañeras are charged with intense sentiment and emotion all the way through.

This demonstrates the crux of a debut or quince's power: it does not simply signify a girl's coming of age; it requires young women to ritualistically, bodily *enact* becoming dalaga and señoritas. Collective-memory scholar Paul Connerton writes, "Our bodies . . . keep the past . . . in an entirely effective form in their continuing ability to perform certain skilled actions" (1989: 72). And anthropologist Catherine Bell maintains that ritualization brings about "an internalization of [cultural] schemes with which [actors] are capable of reinterpreting reality in such a way as to afford perceptions and experiences of a redemptive hegemonic order" (1992: 141). Taken together, these theories suggest that debut and quinceañera performances inscribe codes and values onto young women's bodies that become unconsciously reproduced and remembered as "habit-memories" (Connerton 1989: 84) and that teach debutantes and quinceañeras to reflexively regulate themselves to behave as proper young ladies. As a result, debuts and quinces—more effectively than any words and images—compel young women to form profound commitments to their emergent selves and all that entails: being seen as beautiful, morally decent, and dutiful; serving as a family and cultural ambassadors; and pursuing adult success not just for their own sakes but for the good of their communities.

Espejo, Salamin

Now that I have illustrated how debutantes and quinceañeras mark and facilitate the passage of Filipino and Mexican American girls into "not just any women," but rather dalaga and señoritas, I turn my attention to how variations in Mexican and Filipino approaches to training coming-of-age daughters mirror[14] the distinctive ways many Mexican and Filipino immigrant families are experiencing life in the United States. I advance that these strategies reflect, and are outcomes of, a concentration of Mexican American immigrants in the working class and a relative majority of Filipino American immigrants in the middle and upper classes, as well as Mexican immigrant families' experiences of dissonant acculturation and perceived hypervisibility and Filipino immigrant families' experiences of consonant acculturation and perceived invisibility. As a result, working-class Mexicans (and Filipinos) generally employ their daughters' coming-of-age rituals to help *challenge* demeaning racial representations and frame these events as ways to *prevent* their daughters from experiencing downward assimilation in the United States, while middle- and upper-class Filipinos (and Mexicans) typically use these events to *assert* and *enhance* their cultural identities, and to *prepare* their daughters for bicultural social ascension in U.S. society. I visually condense this argument in Figure 4.2.

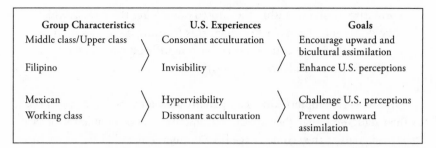

Group Characteristics	U.S. Experiences	Goals
Middle class/Upper class	Consonant acculturation	Encourage upward and bicultural assimilation
Filipino	Invisibility	Enhance U.S. perceptions
Mexican	Hypervisibility	Challenge U.S. perceptions
Working class	Dissonant acculturation	Prevent downward assimilation

Figure 4.2 Relationships between ethnicity, class, and debut and quinceañera goals.

Parental Authority and Acculturation

The first notable difference in how Mexican and Filipino American girls are shaped into ethnicized young women through their coming-of-age events is the extent to which their parents exercise influence and control over them during the preparation period. During the run-up to their events, debutantes were somewhat more willing to discuss and negotiate differences with their parents and were given more responsibility for managing rehearsals and their entourages, while quinceañeras were more acquiescent. While Mexicanas like Dalía relinquished almost all control during their event planning to adults ("What could I do?"), Filipinas were almost always expected to direct and manage the preparation with their peers and occasionally demanded more say in their planning. Recall how Angela, for instance, learned to assert herself as an organizer, mediator, and authority by managing her twenty-four court members and occasionally tried to verbally reason with her parents over debut-related decisions. Weeks after her debut, Angela reflected, "There was a bunch of fights and stuff, but I think after [her debut] they [her parents] realized—they finally realized—that I'm not a little girl anymore. My mom sometimes treats me like I'm a little girl, but I tell her, 'You know what, Mom, I'm eighteen. I didn't turn twelve; I turned eighteen.' And she's like, 'All right, all right.'"

While these variations are probably due, in part, to the age differences between seventeen-year-old debutantes-to-be and their fourteen-year-old Mexicana counterparts, I also believe that they reflect Mexican immigrant families' generally *dissonant* rates of acculturation between generations, and Filipino immigrant families' generally *consonant* rates of acculturation. Alejandro Portes and Rubén Rumbaut write:

The process of acculturation is the first step toward assimilation, as both immigrant parents and children learn the new language and normative lifestyles [within the United States]. Yet the rates at which they do so and the extent to which this learning combines with retention of the home culture varies, with significant consequences for second-generation adaptation. (2001b: 53)

Middle-class Filipino American parents are better positioned to impart to their daughters that they should become more accountable for meeting their own goals as they come of age because they generally have experienced consonant acculturation with their offspring: "This situation is most common when immigrant parents possess enough human capital to accompany the cultural evolution of their children and monitor it" (Portes and Rumbaut 2001b: 54). More Filipino Americans hold professional occupations (39.7 percent) and college degrees (47.9 percent) than Mexican Americans and even white Americans (American Community Survey 2007a). This indicates that they have high levels of human capital and supports the idea that Filipino parents and their children are acculturating to mainstream U.S. culture at parallel rates.

Meanwhile, the 2000 census indicates that more than three-quarters of the Mexican American population speaks a language other than English at home; that most hold occupations in service, construction, or production; and that 47.6 percent (age twenty-five and older) have less than a high school degree (American Community Survey 2007b). Not surprisingly, many working-class Mexican American parents and their children are experiencing dissonant acculturation, which can occur "when children's learning of the English language and American ways and simultaneous loss of the immigrant culture outstrip their parents'" (Portes and Rumbaut 2001b: 54). Dissonant acculturation can lead to generational role reversal, which is perilous, since preservation of parental authority helps minimize the risk of *downward* assimilation[15] for the second-generation. So it is in Mexican American parents' interests to condition their daughters to question parental authority *less* and to teach them that their successful coming of age is extremely reliant on their parents' knowledge, goodwill, and resources.

On the other hand, Filipino American parents' consonant acculturation with their children makes conceding some power to their daughters less threatening. I also believe this is why first-generation Filipino Americans seem more disposed to cultivating their daughters' leadership skills by letting them take charge of significant parts of their preparation (e.g., rehearsals and workshops) and by publicly announcing their education and career "goals" during their celebrations. Josie explained that the Ladies' Association aimed to form debutantes who "want to *achieve*—not just go and get married and do nothing."

Gendered Immigration and Female Autonomy

This interest in nurturing Filipinas' achievement additionally reflects distinct gender immigration patterns and related gender mores between Filipino and Mexican Americans. Since the early twentieth century, immigration from Mexico has been primarily male. Between the 1940s and 1960s, the *bracero* program was geared at importing only male guest workers from Mexico for agricultural and railroad work in United States. Although the *bracero* program ended in 1964, "the United States did not stop employing Mexican workers; it simply shifted . . . to a de facto policy of passive labor acceptance, combining modest legal immigration with massive undocumented entry" (Durand, Massey, and Parrado 1999: 519). And because the demand for cheap manual labor in the United States never diminished, and twenty-two years of the *bracero* program's implementation have helped make it culturally acceptable for males to leave their wives and children in Mexico "for short or long periods of time in order to provide income" (Rodriguez-Scott 2002), immigration from Mexico has stayed predominately male.[16] Conversely, while early-twentieth-century migration from the Philippines was also primarily male (to fulfill the same manual labor needs as Mexican migrants), the passage of the 1965 Immigration Act and "the growth of female-intensive industries in the United States, particularly in the service, microelectronics, apparel manufacturing, and health-care industries" has produced what Espiritu describes as a "female-first migration of highly educated and professional women" from the Philippines to the United States (2003: 145–146).

The increased feminization of Philippine migration reflects, and has reinforced, mores of greater female autonomy, educational attainment, and achievement among Filipina women (Oishi 2002: 12–14). Josie from the Ladies' Association alluded to this when she remarked, "The Philippines is a matriarchal society. It's the woman who is usually strong, the mother who is the head of the family, and the ones who plan." Meanwhile, the ongoing masculinization of migration from Mexico has upheld Mexican cultural beliefs, which support that if possible, "male[s] work . . . to provide financial support and . . . women [are] left behind to run the household and family" (Rodriguez-Scott 2002). Such divergences in ideas about women's capacities and responsibilities are even apparent in differences between la Virgen and Maria Clara. While la Virgen completely surrendered her life to bear God's son, Maria Clara ultimately chose her own fate and is still considered an anticolonial figure by many Filipinos (Lim 2005: 129).

Because the aforementioned ideas have contributed to immigrant Filipino parents' trying to promote more self-sufficiency in their daughters, debutante mothers like Juliet can acknowledge that a girl's coming of age marks "the time of becoming an independent person" (although you will recall that Juliet also said she anticipates being the primary influence in her daughter's life until her daughter's marriage). And although almost all the second-generation adults I spoke with were college graduates, leaders, and activists, Filipinas most frequently associated their adult achievements with having been a debutante. Ramona shared a particularly impressive example. Before becoming a debutante, she was "very shy." She explained, "A lot of verbal communication, to me, was very difficult." But while "prepping" to become a deb, she said, "My self-confidence boosted. I did speech, I did debate, mock trial. I did student government. I mean that was like total change, transition time for me." Years after, Ramona served as president of LRPS. Then, in college, she founded the first chapter of an all-Asian sorority at the oldest and largest university in Del Sol. Reflecting on all this, she divulged, "I attribute my changes to two different things: one is Leonor Rivera and the second is my speech debate coach." And Missus M made clear that Ramona wasn't an exception. She reported that over the years, LRPS has "produced teachers, businesswomen, doctors, engineers, military officers, and students in science, research, legal, political sciences, and ethnic studies, on campuses across the country."

Tradition and Visibility

Besides exercising different degrees of authority over their daughters, Filipino and Mexican parents in my study also stressed the "tradition" aspect of their daughters' celebrations in divergent ways. Mexican immigrants portrayed quinces as deeply entrenched traditions dating back centuries to *challenge* unfavorable U.S. perceptions of their community, while Filipinos described debuts as traditions, "only for the rich," to *assert* and *enhance* their community's image as upwardly mobile and cultured. These divergent strategies reflect the generally distinct ways Mexicans and Filipinos in the United States feel they are (or are not) perceived.

Mexicans I spoke with felt that their race made them almost too visible—as poor, uneducated, and undesirable citizens. Alternatively, Filipinos felt practically overlooked. For example, Rose, like many other Filipino immigrants I interviewed, felt that most Americans were unaware of Filipino culture. She reflected, "Most people don't know too much about Filipinos." Fellow immigrant Ramiro observed that this invisibility seemed to subject Filipinos to second-rate consideration in the United States, in spite of their success:

> To some extent there's always some discrimination. Most of the Filipinos are sort of successful, though; they're called the silent minority. They don't really complain that much because they're able to hold on their own. But they still have discrimination on the job; sometimes they don't get promotions and that kind of thing.

Mexican immigrants were more reluctant to share encounters with racism but shared more degrading experiences when they did. For example, when I asked, "Is life in the United States what you imagined it would be like before you came?" Catalina emphatically told me, "No. For the first ten years here, I was crying. I had no family. I was so young. I didn't know English." When I asked if she had ever experienced discrimination as a Mexicana, Catalina paused for a long while and finally told me, "I forgot a lot of stuff because I don't want to remember, maybe." Then, later, she related this traumatic experience:

> I remember like five years ago, or a little bit more, my husband was in the car. And I was in an accident. . . . And then the police came. . . . The two police . . . thought my husband was driving, and [they were] thinking my husband was driving very fast. I was panicked and was talking in Spanish, 'cause I thought my husband was going to die. But they tried to tell [accuse] him. Then I said, "You think I'm Hispanic, so I'm stupid, and I'm giving him the chance to drive? No! I have a family waiting for us!" They [the police] said I'm keeping these things [deliberately concealing the truth]. They accused [us of] these things. But asking [about what really happened]? Never. No. Because I'm Mexican, and I sound Mexican.

Selena, one of the few immigrants who talked openly about discrimination toward Mexicans in the United States, told me, "Some people, they think, 'There's too many Mexicans [in the United States].' They think, 'You [Mexicans] don't know how to speak English. You are so poor. You did not go to school. You do not belong here.' Not everybody [every American] thinks this. But there are some people [who do]."

This all suggests that while Filipino immigrants desired greater recognition (in response to being seen as "the silent minority" and others "not knowing too much about Filipinos"), their Mexican counterparts sought to be seen differently (to counter being seen as part of a population of "too many," or being racially profiled like Catalina). By framing quinceañeras as widely celebrated and long-standing traditions, working-class Mexican parents are able to challenge "the castelike status of being Mexican" (López and Stanton-Salazar 2001: 73), by implying that Mexicans share a hundreds-of-years-old (even thousands-of-years-old) history of civility and respectability. And by framing debuts as upper-class traditions, middle-class Filipino parents are able to draw some attention to how their accomplishments in the United States have enabled them to offer their daughters what "only the rich" can enjoy in the Philippines.

Cultural Socialization and Biculturalism

Related to this, most Filipino parents felt a greater need to educate their children about Filipino culture. This is because while Mexicans have maintained the highest rate of language and cultural retention among U.S. ethnic groups (López and Stanton-Salazar 2001: 66, 71), "there is a lack of active cultural socialization—the deliberate teaching and practicing of the languages, traditions, and history of the Philippines—in Filipino American homes" (Espiritu and Wolf 2001: 175). This is also why most debutantes dramatically spoke about how their debuts "opened their eyes" to being Filipina, while most quinceañeras spoke about their quinces as simply reaffirming their ethnic identities. The more pressing desire of Filipino parents to teach their kids about their culture reveals how consonant acculturation has contributed to some "abandonment of home language and culture" within Filipino American families (Portes and Rumbaut 2001b: 54) and how Filipino immigrants are attempting to use debuts as a way to offset this and to encourage the *upward and bicultural* assimilation—that is, upward mobility with at least "partial retention and the parents' home language and norms" (Portes and Rumbaut 2001b: 54)—of their children.

The Politics of Ethnic Female Beauty

In spite of divergent, almost opposite, motivations and aims for organizing debutantes and quinceañeras, the work of constructing ethnicized femininities still demonstrates that both Mexicans and Filipinos use their daughters' coming-of-age rituals creatively and politically. By effectively shaping and showcasing their daughters as chaste, dutiful, and self-sacrificing dalaga and señoritas, Filipino and Mexican immigrants are able to claim that they (and their respective cultures) are morally superior to "wild," out-of-control, and selfish American women (and mainstream American culture). This demonstrates that they are not mere victims of the differential inclusion of people of color in the United States and that they are also actively constructing white Americans for themselves and choosing what parts of American culture they want to adopt—and to reject. By framing quinceañeras and debuts as traditions, Mexicans and Filipinos counter notions of themselves as less civilized or well bred than European Americans, and by using these events to display their financial and social success, Mexican and Filipino immigrants also challenge the impression that they are not here to stay and further assert their full cultural belonging in America. Finally, the process of training girls to embrace identities as dalaga and señoritas enables Filipino immigrants to contest their invisibility in U.S. society and to promote their children's upward mobility and retention of Filipino culture while making it possible for Mexican immigrants to contest degrading images of themselves in U.S. culture, to restore parental authority, and to try to avert their children's downward assimilation.

In short, the molding of dalaga and señoritas makes irrefutably clear the fact that Filipino American debuts and Mexican American quinceañeras are *political*—that they are resourcefully and strategically deployed by immigrants to gain and use power within their families, their communities, and the larger U.S. society. It also shows the complex and sometimes contradictory nature of such politics—denouncing the morality of a culture that one aspires to participate in fully. This suggests, of course, that the road to Mexican and Filipino American womanhood is at least a little bumpier (and less serious) than rendered in this chapter. In Chapter 5, therefore, I focus on the messier, more playful moments of organizing and participating in debuts and quinceañeras.

❦

CHAPTER 5

Traviesos/Troublemakers

There's a scene in the film *Quinceañera* when Carlos, brother of recent quinceañera Eileen and cousin of soon-to-be quinceañera Magdalena, is being seduced by the couple who own the backyard cottage he and his uncle rent. Buzzed on beers, Carlos mutters, "I'm so fucked up" as he falls backward onto the couple's bed. Noticing something underneath Carlos's tank top, one partner asks, "Is that a tattoo?" Carlos murmurs, "Yeah," as the other partner lifts the tank top, to reveal the Spanish word *travieso* stained in an arch over Carlos's navel. "What's that mean?" someone asks. "Troublemaker," Carlos replies.

So far, the portrait I've painted of Filipino American debutantes and Mexican American quinceañeras has only hinted at the fact that there is more to these events than hardworking immigrants, real-life princesses, supportive communities, and minor squabbles over cake flavors and coordinating court member schedules. But like almost any major family occasion, these events typically have their fair share of drama. Hence, I devote this chapter to traviesos and to investigating what the troubles they stir up tell us about Filipino and Mexican immigrant families' lives in the United States. More specifically, I look at Control Freaks, Big Spenders, Party Poopers, Party Crashers, and Scene Stealers.

Because of my self-selected sample and the fact that many of these characters are usually forced into the background by girls and families who want to preserve the impression that their debutantes and quinceañeras are "perfect," I did not come across many traviesos personally. However, these troublemakers were mentioned so regularly during my fieldwork that I finally realized that their experiences cannot simply be overlooked—as many of their families wish they could be. There is value in bringing their experiences to the forefront because they are brazen rule breakers in the minidramas that are debuts and quinceañeras. Thus, they highlight the ways that producing ethnicized femininities are inevitably contentious, contradictory, unstable, and sometimes critical of not only mainstream U.S. culture but also Mexican and Filipino American responses to it. Therefore, I take a quasi-case-study approach to considering the quince and debut traviesos I heard about (mine is probably by no means an exhaustive list of them), their motivations, and their effects.

American sociologist C. Wright Mills defines "the sociological imagination," the distinguishing approach used by sociologists to view and conceive of the world, as the capacity to discern relationships "between 'the personal troubles of milieu' and 'the public social issues of social structure'" (1959: 8). He explains that although personal troubles are often thought of as "private matters," sociologists understand that they are inextricably linked to "issues," "public matters" that usually concern "some value cherished by publics" and perceived of as under threat because of "a crisis in institutional arrangements" (Mills 1959: 8, 9). In examining actors' individual troubles, we can, therefore, better understand the social conditions that structure their lives, as well as how such structures are informed by the behaviors of individuals.

Taking a look at debut and quince troubles, and troublemakers specifically, reveals that quinceañeras and debutantes are not simply carbon copies, reproducing a singular, uncontested version of gender and/or ethnicity. Joshua Gamson and Laura Grindstaff conjecture that gender performances, though often seen as strictly one or the other, are usually both "inside" (i.e., "gender conformist") and "outside" (i.e., "gender transgressive"). They write:

> Understanding the inside-outside dynamics—the relative strengths of the traditional and transgressive aspects of the performance [helps] to illustrate . . . gender performances as sites of tension between conformity and non-conformity—ultimately, sites of tension between accepting or challenging prevailing power arrangements (2010: 254–255).

Traviesos draw attention to the ways that U.S. debuts and quinces challenge the gender and ethnic conformity that these events try to impose, and they help refine and complicate understandings of how these events shape what it means to be a good Mexican, a good Filipino, a Mexican American female (or Mexican American male), or a Filipino American female (or

Filipino American male). Looking at their "troublemaking" sheds more light on prevailing power arrangements both inside and outside the communities that organize quinceañeras and debuts and how these have influenced both resistance and receptivity to transformations in the ethnic and gender identities of Mexican and Filipino Americans.

Control Freaks

I use the term *Control Freaks* to describe one of the most frequently alluded-to troublemakers among my subjects: mothers who overregulate the planning and performance of their daughters' debuts and quinceañeras. In truth, although almost all the girls I interviewed shared a few complaints about how their mothers imposed choices and limits on them, only one daughter viewed her mother as having crossed the line between taking charge and taking over.

Cassandra, the second daughter of Gabby and Sharon Dobrado, was born in Las Querubes; moved to the Philippines with her mother three years later; was reunited with her father and older sister, Kristina, in Maui before she started school; and then was transplanted with the rest of her nuclear family back to Las Querubes when she started ninth grade. By the time we met, it was clear that Cassandra had successfully transitioned from "new girl" to a popular and successful student in the four years since she and her family had returned to Las Querubes. Having heard about some of her high school accomplishments—student officer, cheerleader, recent admission to a reputable private four-year university—from my earlier interview with her outspoken mother, I expected Cassandra to be just as gregarious, animated, and even perky. To my surprise, I found her to be soft-spoken and self-described as "quiet. I'm shy, but it's like, later, I get a little blabbery." Only later did I recall Sharon telling me, "Cassandra, she's the shy type. Like, I had to push her to become a cheerleader, 'cause she was gaining weight. I told her I don't want her to be like me. I had my hangups in high school, so I really push them [her children] to do whatever they want to do." Cassandra agreed that Sharon (and Gabby) could be a little pushy. She confided, "They don't understand. They think they're right all the time. They don't hear me out."

Cassandra's debut brought some of her and Sharon's differences to the surface. First, Cassandra said that her debut had been predetermined long before she was close to coming of age. She said:

> I didn't really decide to have one. I just knew it was coming because
> my sister didn't want one, and my mom really wanted one of us to

have one, 'cause she loves to party, planning things. She likes being in charge of stuff. So I just went with it.

Sharon explained:

> When I was growing up, it got crazy before my debut. My father died. He was shot three months before I had my debut. But we were planning it [before her father's death]. . . . Because I didn't have one, I was planning on it with Kristina. And then Kristina fell in love and ran away. It ruined everything. So, it was Cassandra.

The opportunity to finally organize a debut, after decades of dreaming, brought out a zeal in Sharon that was unsurpassed by any other mother I spoke with. When we met, one of the first things Sharon did was to invite me to peruse her methodically ordered planning folder. Although Cassandra told me that Sharon had persuaded her to have a debut less than a year away from her eighteenth birthday, Sharon said that she had been planning Cassandra's celebration for at least one and a half years. Accordingly, her folder was thick with budget worksheets, to-do lists, drafts of seating charts, business cards, and neatly scrapbooked pages of samples and "souvenirs" from her months of preparation.

As she allowed me to examine her records, she enthusiastically recollected the planning process. And her pleasure at giving her daughter something so beautiful and meticulously prepared was evident. She recalled with amusement how she made spaghetti, hot dogs with bacon, and sandwiches "every Sunday [for] three months before," while Cassandra and her cotillion practiced their dance at the Dobrado home; how she chose Cassandra's debut invitations, program, and colors; how she designed and redesigned seating arrangements "because some relatives [were] not talking to each other"; and how she ordered her own decorations, costumes, and giveaway souvenirs—all without going into debt:

> I didn't loan. I didn't charge credit card. . . . I paid all of it by check and cash. That's better, so you don't have to charge anything, you don't have to borrow, you don't have to ask anybody, "Can you answer for this?" "Can you pay for the video?" I didn't do that.

In the end, Sharon's hard work really produced an extravaganza: a three-hundred-guest affair held in a large dance studio, with Cassandra standing out as a dazzling jewel with her thirty-six-person entourage and serenaded with surprise performances throughout the evening. "I'm really proud," Sharon reflected, though she still seemed a little puzzled. She said:

> It wasn't hard [the preparation]. But there was so much *drama* because [Cassandra] said, "I want it my way," and she, of course, wants it her way. She gave me a long letter. She said that I hurt her feelings. I was surprised to see the letter, telling me, explaining to me that it's her debut. I can let you read this if you like.

With that, Sharon allowed me to read the candid letter Cassandra left in one of her planning notebooks. It read, in part:

> I appreciate EVERYTHING you're doing but I want it my way too. I want to plan it along with you. . . . I'm not saying that I don't want you to do anything, but I was just hoping to actually be involved in something that's FOR ME. . . . Please Mom, just ask me what I think. I don't want to sound spoiled but I just want something big like this to be special.

When I told Cassandra that Sharon had shown me her note, Cassandra told me she had written it after months of frustrated attempts to speak to her mother about her debutante planning. "I wrote that midway into it [planning for her debut], 'cause . . . when I talked, she didn't really listen that well. So I figured, if I could write it, then maybe she would read it better." To illustrate her lack of say, Cassandra told me that she had not picked out her debut gown because it was a gift from the manager of the bridal store where Sharon worked; that Sharon had determined several of the people in her court ("She was making me pick this girl that I wasn't really close to at all, and I had another closer friend"); and that her mother had "invited all the people she wanted, and she kinda forgot that I have friends to invite" (250 of Cassandra's guests were Sharon's family and associates, by Sharon's count). Cassandra said, "When I wrote that [note], she got a little better after," but it didn't really change the fact that Sharon is "like the head of the family—she's the boss."

Cassandra and Sharon's stories demonstrate that preparation for a debut (or quince) is not always trouble-free, particularly if and when mothers tyrannically seek to mold the event and their daughters into something their daughters feel they have no say in. Without minimizing the distress such extreme control brings daughters like Cassandra, it is important to note that female immigrants of color sometimes face exceptional circumstances that are the basis of such forceful parenting. A closer look at Sharon's biography, for example, reveals how little control she has felt over much of her life. Aside from her father being murdered and her elder daughter running away from home, Sharon was raised by her grandfather, a former U.S. Marine, in the Philippines as a child. She explained:

> I was only seven months when he got me, when he retired from the Marines. I asked him about that—why did he get me? He said he was asking my mom that [to take her] 'cause he was gonna be bored. Since I was the only girl, he took me. But it was just like four blocks from my village.

And though Sharon recalled childhood with her grandfather fondly, she also remembered feeling restricted and associated this with her unexpected first pregnancy. She recollected, "With me, my parents were so strict. So we had to hide [dating]. That's why I got pregnant." And this happened just when Sharon was starting a new life: "I immigrated here [to the United States] in July. I got my green card in October, I think, then [went] home [to the Philippines] in November. Then I married." Because her first pregnancy was tied to her marriage, Sharon now characterizes all marriages as beyond control. "Marriage just comes. You cannot predict when, cannot *plano*. Maybe, to some people, they can plan it. I don't know. Once they get pregnant, though, they have to get married." Even Cassandra was aware of the impact an unintended pregnancy and marriage had on her mother. She said, "My family is crazy in a way. Like my parents weren't really ready to be parents when they gave birth to my sister."

Then, despite how much Sharon loved life in the Philippines, her grandfather's death meant that she could not stay. "I like it there," Sharon said. "If only I'm rich, I will stay there. But it's hard living there. When my grandpa died, he who was supporting us, no one [other family members] could take care of us. They hardly kn[e]w us."

Now, Sharon feels that her own children seem beyond her control:

> Everything we [Filipinos in the Philippines] do, like the way we grew up, I'm doing that to my kids. But they're not doing it [submitting to their parents]. They won't be scared. They don't care. You know, you cannot scare them—they follow whatever they want. . . . It's like you don't have any more rights with your kids. . . . That's always the concern with Filipinos; like, you want to know where your kids are all the time.

Kristina's running away heightened Sharon's insecurities as a mother. "That's one of the reasons we moved [from Maui to California]—because we felt so bad there. We were not good parents. It's like, 'No. Why did it happen like that?' [Kristina] ran away [though] she was a very good student." So, even after nearly two decades in the United States, Sharon still longs to return to the Philippines. She told me, "I still miss it. I wanna live there, if I have the money. I don't like it here."

The major events that have contributed to Sharon's perceived lack of control have to do with how her life has been shaped by the United States and the fact that she is a woman. Her adoption by her grandfather was shaped by his U.S. military service. As an American Filipino in the Philippines, he could exercise power over Sharon's mother, and he asked her to surrender her last child to keep him from getting bored during retirement. Living on a U.S. military pension there, he also had enough resources to raise another child and to possibly make it impossible for Sharon's mother to refuse to let him. She was probably already indebted to him, after all, for helping to provide for their family during his military career. The strictness with which Sharon was brought up was no doubt in some part because of her being a woman. And she definitely experienced her unintended pregnancy and urgency to marry differently than she would have if she had been male. For example, had she been a man, it might have been acceptable for her to leave her family behind (as her grandfather had) or to never marry at all. Finally, Sharon's sense of "not having any more rights with your kids" is a common one among immigrant parents (see Chapter 4), who are often bewildered at the relative autonomy young people are able to exercise in America.

All of this in combination with Sharon's strong personality contributed to her desire to shape Cassandra's debut into her own, rather than her daughter's, celebration. Although Sharon's is an extreme case, it helps illustrate how debuts and quinceañeras offer immigrant planners—whose experiences with migration, racism, sexism, blocked mobility, and/or generational role reversal can leave them feeling powerless, invisible, and/or degraded—an exceptional form of self-expression that enables them to take full charge of the image they want to project to themselves, their families, and their communities. Beautiful and extraordinary quinceañeras and debuts afford immigrants an opportunity to fashion themselves domains of creativity where, under the pretext of "following cultural tradition," they are able to freely experience and enjoy a feeling of agency to help them better deal with the frequently disinterested (if not hostile) environments they face in the United States. Artist Julia Cameron reminds social scientists that such self-expression helps free people from feeling "stuck," that "the imagination at play" allows us to "call to our deepest selves," and "achieve a sense of safety and hope" (2002: 49). Psychologists and behavioral scientists affirm that such "play" is essential for everybody. They argue that without creative and recreational outlets— extraordinary luxuries for many immigrants—we deplete our abilities to efficiently problem-solve, communicate, and be productive (National Institute for Play 2003). And poststructural theorist Maria Lugones (1987) argues that play helps produce change, that stepping outside rigid "game" rules to understand oneself and the world from different vantage points enables people to imagine new possibilities for themselves and the world.

Control Freaks are usually mothers who undertake such play at the cost of their daughters' sense of agency and self-expression. Like Sharon, they are often trying so desperately to compensate for their own thwarted ambitions and feelings of helplessness that they do not realize that their actions may diminish their children's sense of pleasure and dignity. Fortunately in the Dobrados' case, Cassandra was not so diminished that she could not challenge her mother's overbearing personality. In fact, Cassandra's response shows how debuts (and quinces) actually offer members of the second generation opportunities to introduce and explain to immigrants their points of view regarding culture, race, and gender in the United States. But this is not always the case, and this is one reason debuts and quinceañeras have been criticized as being unhealthy for girls.

Big Spenders

By far, the most pervasive criticism thrown at debuts and quinceañeras is that they are wastes of time and money (rather than wise investments) that promote frivolity and materialism (rather than industriousness and prudent spending). A feature article on debutante balls incited one reader to write, "I cannot think of a worse way to blow thousands of dollars" (Pastor 2004), and an article in the popular national magazine *Latina* suggested that contemporary quinceañeras have turned "what used to be a rite of passage marked with a modest celebration" into "a budget-busting extravaganza" ("Quinceañera" 2004). Gabriel Ortega, who earns his living photographing quinceañeras and other special occasions, confided:

> They [families organizing quinceañeras] will throw the house out the window for their daughter's fifteen. . . . If I could get one quinceañera to get that money together and go to college—if I could get them to ask their uncles, "Okay, you buy my books; you buy this class; you buy this class"—that would be the greatest thing I could do.

Such claims are not without merit. While there are certainly modest, at-home debuts and quinces like the "small and cautious" events described in Chapter 3, the mention of a debut or quince more often summons up images of an opulent, weddinglike gala with a girl bedecked in a princess gown and tiara, waited on by a court of best friends, whisked around town in a Hummer limo, and hosting a reception for hundreds of guests. The price tag for such an event ranges from $5,000 to $15,000 (Mabalon 2004; Tierney 2006). And while these costs are sometimes slightly offset by padrinos and other family members who sponsor, or pay for, specific quinceañera or debut expenses, by members of a girl's court who buy or rent their own costumes, and by hookups (discounts) from vendors who know a girl's family, the debutante or quinceañera's family is almost always responsible for most expenses, which also include "hidden costs" such as feeding a small army of teenagers during weekly dance rehearsals or hosting out-of-town guests. Gabriel told me that he's even seen families undertake home remodels during a quinceañera to impress and accommodate visitors.

The celebrations in my study typically cost between $12,000 and $13,000, but the price tag for the most expensive events topped $25,000 (all before any hidden costs). This is considerable when we take into account that at the time of my study, the cost of full-time undergraduate attendance at a public university ranged from $10,000 to more than $23,000 per year (California Department of Finance 2005); the average price of a car started at $12,500 ("Car Prices Top $30,000" 2004; Reed and DiPietro 2001); the average wedding budget was $20,000 ("Bridal Industry Statistics" 2005); and while a few of my subjects were comfortably upper class and middle class, most were lower working class or working class.[1]

The parents I interviewed were too modest to ever disclose exactly how much they had saved and given up to organize their daughters' debuts and quinceañeras, but their daughters spoke to me of the costs and sacrifices made for their special day. Patrisia, a former quinceañera and the current quince coordinator at Saint Brigid parish in Las Querubes told me, "I know now [as an adult] how much it cost them. Now I look back and say, 'They could have bought a house.'" And Marabel, a former debutante, shared:

My sister was working at the bank at the time, so she took out a $2,000 loan. . . . Even though we cut corners, there was still so much drama over money. . . . We still went into debt. I'm not sure how long, but I know it took my mom a while to pay off. Three years maybe?

U.S. culture promotes saving over spending and accumulating wealth over merely consuming wealth, so it is not surprising that when working-class families spend tens of thousands of dollars on their teenage daughters' birthdays, it causes some raised eyebrows. Seen from a strictly economic viewpoint, debuts and quinces are not just irrational—they are potentially ruinous. But the experiences of those in my study suggest that some immigrants use conspicuous consumption as a way of challenging their differential inclusion in U.S. society.

Debutantes and quinceañeras make it possible for Filipino and Mexican immigrants and their families to challenge their differential inclusion in the United States because these events offer them highly visible opportunities to simultaneously participate in America's consumerist culture and to defy it. Lavish spending on quinceañeras and debuts violates capitalist society's unwritten "consumption rules for different social classes" (Otnes and Pleck 2003: 10). These conventions maintain that the wealthy can justify spending on nonessential luxuries but that people of more modest means should spend their money on only what society approves of (e.g., a wedding) and/or sees as necessary (e.g., college). By breaking these rules, debut and quinceañera organizers and participants call attention not just to the fact that they can afford certain luxuries but also to how, despite their hard work, they have been granted only partial access to the goods and services that would enable them to enjoy the lifestyle to which they aspire.

At the same time, debut and quince spending enables immigrant families to assert that they should be included as full legal and cultural citizens of the United States. Full participation in America's democracy has always been coupled with race, gender, and the ability to acquire and own goods. Until 1850, only white propertied males had the right to vote in the United States. African American men were classified by the Constitution as three-fifths of a person and were not granted franchise until 1865, and American women did not win suffrage until 1920, with the passage of the Nineteenth Amendment. After World War II, with the U.S. shift from an industrial society to a consumer service economy, women and racial minorities began to strategically use conspicuous consumption to "show their modernity, prove their cultural citizenship, and thus lessen racial prejudice and further equality" (Lim 2005: 89). Second-generation Japanese Americans in the 1940s strategically chose not to patronize issei entrepreneurships in order to avoid sending other Americans the message of Japanese insularity and unassimilability (Kurashige 2002). In the 1960s, U.S. civil rights workers fought for "racial desegregation through . . . the desegregation of Woolworth's lunch

counters, of buses, and of schools" because they understood that one way racial equality is signified (and presumably achieved) is through equal, multi-
racial participation in the U.S. consumption culture (Lim 2005: 88). And
today, the economic contributions (or the perceived lack thereof) of immigrant workers is still at the crux of the U.S. debate on immigration—a debate
that is essentially about who is deserving of being in the United States and of
its rights and protections. Immigration advocates have defended contemporary immigration by demonstrating that "immigrants fuel the U.S. economy
through their hard work and entrepreneurship" (National Immigration Law
Center 2006). They cite multiple studies of various U.S. southern border city
economies (e.g., Burge 2011; Pavlakovich-Kochi and Charney 2008; Rivard
2010) that have established that "for all the debate about Mexican nationals
here illegally . . . the more important truth is that . . . [w]ithout the presence and spending power of Mexican nationals here, it is safe to say, the . . .
retail economy would be reeling" (Rivard 2010). Meanwhile, immigration
opponents such as Lou Dobbs justify their support of discriminatory policies
toward undocumented immigrants by arguing that "illegal immigrants are a
burden to the taxpayer, unequivocally" (Carter and Steinberg 2006).

Ramiro Hernandez explained how his daughter's cotillion allowed him
both to challenge the notion that middle-class families should avoid material
frivolities and to use spending on his daughter's debut to help make a strong
declaration about his family's material and moral worth:

> We work to give what we can to our kids. You can't take your money
> with you [after death]; you cannot enjoy your money from the grave.
> So we give it to our children because they are our priority. . . . It's
> something [special] to be able to show people you can do it, to let
> them see that the children have their material needs and that they are
> great kids with the right values.

And with more than a decade of hindsight, Dalía, a former quinceañera,
could distinguish that her mother likely had similar motivations. She
told me:

> All that debt took her [Dalía's mother] years to pay off. . . . I know
> how much she struggled afterwards. . . . But I think she wanted to
> make a statement, to show her family and everybody else that she
> could do this, that she was a good mom, and that she could bring
> everyone together and give me something nice.

So when some immigrant families spend large amounts of money on quinceañeras and debuts, they are not just proving that they have the means to do so; they are using "the language of liberal-democratic consumer citizenship" (Lim 2005) to convey that they should be eligible for full legal and cultural citizenship in this country. They are attempting to demonstrate, through the power of their pocketbooks, that they are capable of being true Americans and deserving of all the rights and privileges that accompany such status.[2] Consider how Ramiro viewed his daughter's debut as an opportunity to show others that he and his wife have not only met their children's "material needs" but also raised them "with the right values"—fit for full civic participation. Others in my study also articulated an understanding of how debuts and quinces could help establish their virtue, decency, and financial qualifications for full legal and cultural citizenship. Helen Martines, LRPS president, told me:

> All LRPS wants to do is show only the good side of ordinary Filipinos, and maybe that's why the *City Tribune* [Del Sol's local newspaper] presents us all the time. . . . We do not want to hurt anybody, only to promote the good of our people through education and through social activities . . . to show that we have a history here.

And an aspiring quinceañera told me:

> One thing about being a Mexican is we're disadvantaged at a lot of things. But I think when there's a quinceañera, people maybe think that we [Mexicans] must have some money, that we can do nice things that other Americans do—sometimes, even better!

The perception that Mexican Americans have more to prove in terms of being able to "do nice things," acquire wealth, and successfully assimilate may explain why quinceañeras seem to be exploding in popularity, while Filipino group cotillions have all but disappeared, and fewer and fewer middle-class Filipina daughters are electing to have individual debuts. The surging popularity in quinceañeras could be the result of Mexican Americans feeling greater urgency to express their suitability as full cultural citizens in the United States, while declining popularity in debuts could be the outcome of more Filipinos joining the ranks of the U.S. middle class since the 1980s. Since more Filipino Americans can now afford to display their U.S. cultural membership through white-collar careers, home ownership, intermarriage,

and the like, perhaps Filipino families (and families who have already organized a quinceañera) feel less compelled to use their daughters' coming-of-
age to prove that they can and should be accepted as good citizens. On the
other hand, while many Mexican Americans are still concentrated in low-
wage labor and continue to be seen as "slow to fit in" (Schulte 2008), perhaps
quinceañeras offer one of the few autonomous, effective means for them to
publicly assert that they can and do belong in the United States.[3]

Hence, conspicuous consumption for debuts and quinces should be
understood not only as reckless materialism and showboating. While there
are certainly far cheaper ways to observe a daughter's coming of age (and to
"make a statement" about one's suitability for full citizenship), spending for
quinceañeras and debuts gives Mexican and Filipino American immigrant
families a matchless opportunity to call attention to the injustice of their differential inclusion, to profoundly insert themselves into America's consumer
culture, and to powerfully declare that they are deserving of and prepared for
the rights and responsibilities that come with full membership in U.S. society.

Party Poopers

Even the most head-turning quince or debut cannot convince *everyone* of
these events' value or prudence, however. I use the term *Party Pooper* to describe those who reject debuts and quinces. And I place in this category of
troublemakers daughters who resolve not to participate in these rituals and
churches that refuse to commemorate quinceañeras. Because I had a self-
selected sample of individuals, families, and institutions who *did* participate
in debuts and quinces, I draw on anecdotal conversations, some focus group
members, and stories shared by my primary respondents to discuss these
traviesos.

Poopy Daughters

Most girls who choose not to mark their coming of age with a debut or
quince are not troublemakers. In fact, some parents welcome the decision,
realizing that it will save them money. When his youngest daughter, Suzy,
declined the opportunity to have one, Ramiro said, "We asked her [if she
wanted to be part of a cotillion], but she didn't want it. Maybe it would've
been nice, to present her. But she went to a private school [university], so it
was good that we could save the money."

Juana said that her parents were likewise all right with her decision not
to have a quince:

I didn't have one because I wasn't really into that because of the way I was raised. My parents want me to be economic[ally], mental[ly], and physical[ly] stable, so I think they thought it was a good choice. I think I probably made them happy not having to stress over a party—all the planning and money for one day.

The trouble comes when parents are determined to give one to their daughters, but their daughters repudiate the offer. When this happens, it starkly exposes how debutantes and quinceañeras are just as much for immigrant parents as they are for the young women they celebrate. Take Klara's recollection of the distress of her mother, Linet, when Destinee, the youngest female sibling in the family, declined to participate in a cotillion: "When Destinee didn't have one, my mom was upset. I guess because she [Linet] felt, 'This is what a "lady" does,' so she was upset. Maybe it was a little vicarious for her because she went through the sweet-sixteen birthday, with the [photo] album and the band, but she never really had a cotillion."

And take the reply to a young woman who posted the following inquiry (reproduced here exactly as written) to an online message board:

> i really really really don't want a quinceanera but my family is gonna make me have one. they know i don't want one but they make decisions. i tell them i don't want one but they don't listen to me. what should i do?!

> Best Answer: A "quinceanera" is more for the "family" then [*sic*] it is for the girl. Even if you don't want to participate then do it for your family. Sometimes in life we do things for others because it makes them happy. These people, your family are the ones who have loved you, fed you and stuck by you in good and bad times. They are just asking that for one day you give them the benefit of the doubt and let them "celebrate" one of the biggest days of your life thus far. If you have tried talking to them and it has failed then go along with them and have as much fun as possible. Do it for your parents, your grandparents and those you love. (Yahoo! Answers 2009)

Like Cassandra and other young women who seriously dissented from overregulating Control Freak parents, daughters who disregard their parents' strong wishes for them to have a debut or quinceañera reveal that Filipino and Mexican immigrant families are composed of individuals with distinct—and sometimes contradictory—motivations, needs, and concerns.

Destinee helped illuminate this when I casually asked her why she did not succumb to Linet's desire to have her follow the examples of Klara and her next-eldest sister, Nansee, by taking part in the annual South Cove Union of Filipino Americans (SCUFA) cotillion. She told me:

> I just had other interests. . . . I remember watching my sisters' rehearsals, and enjoying watching them. Members of the Fil-Am community would look at me and say, "You are next." In my head, I knew this would never happen. I think I saw it as my sisters' interest, not mine. . . . I think Nansee enjoys having the spotlight. . . . I'm not sure why Klara wanted to do it. . . . I was different because I had different interests than them. I listened to different music, had different friends, and had a different style from my sisters.

Girls who outright refuse a quince or debutante (not for material reasons) are far more vulnerable to charges of cultural inauthenticity, though. For example, Linet seemed to suggest that Destinee was less Filipina than her other daughters when she said:

> I don't think it's [a debutante] really important to her [Destinee]. . . . I think it's because the way I raise her up. For Klara and Nansee, they have limited number of friends at that time. Destinee has more freedom. So she is around more of the American influence: she stands up to fight [i.e., expresses her opinions to her parents], goes out of the house; she had a boyfriend already. Klara and Nansee are more like the Filipino way when they were growing up.

Yen Le Espiritu writes:

> As self-appointed guardians of "authentic" cultural memory, immigrant parents can attempt to regulate their daughters' independent choices by linking them to cultural ignorance or betrayal. . . . Young women who disobey . . . parental strictures [a]re often branded "non-ethnic," "untraditional," "radical," "selfish," and not "caring about the family." (2003: 173)

She argues, "To second-generation daughters, these charges are stinging" (Espiritu 2003: 174); therefore, immigrant parents find tying children's behavior to cultural authenticity "a source of power." While I certainly found this to be the case for parents who successfully persuaded their daughters to have a debut or quince and/or be good señoritas or dalaga, under the pretense of "keeping tradition," I also found that daughters who defied their parents' debut or quince dreams were not necessarily hurt by being labeled as "more American" and did not inevitably feel less Mexican or Filipino because of this. Destinee explained that although she considered herself different from her sisters, she still felt secure in her ethnic identity:

> You could say that my interests growing up were non-typically Fili-pino. I was interested in British pop music at the time, and my friends were multicultural. That is not to say that there weren't other Filipi-nos that were interested in the same music. In fact, my boyfriend was Filipino and listened to the same music I did.

Some girls even consider declining to hold a debut or quince because they feel these events are not Filipino or Mexican *enough*. They see such events as symptomatic of Filipinos' and Mexicans' ongoing colonial mentali-ties, or idealization of their former colonizers' cultures and beliefs, and view such practices as elite, outdated, nonnative customs that sway today's Filipi-nos and Mexicans into essentially trying to emulate and buy the social status of their past conquerors. Olivia, a former SCUFA debutante, explained some of her initial reluctance to take part in a debut:

> It seemed so old-fashioned, and so unlike me. At the time, I was re-ally involved in all these things—I was a school leader, applying for college, blah, blah, blah. And a debutante just seemed so girly and backwards—like, "Be demure and pretty, and come in on the arm of this guy in your poufy white dress." . . . There was a part of me that was also like, "Hmm. Isn't this what the Filipinos who, like, bleach their skin and always claim, 'I'm Spanish' do?" I just never saw my family like those Filipinos.

Reflections and experiences like those of Olivia and Destinee demon-strate that accusations of cultural betrayal are not always sufficient means of influencing the behavior of second-generation women and that the first generation cannot lay sole claim to what or who is Filipino or Mexican. They help underscore the heterogeneity of Filipino and Mexican American families and communities, the dynamic nature of ethnicity and culture in the United States, and the second generation's contribution to shaping how *Mexican, Filipino, good girl,* and even *American* are understood.

Poopy Parishes

The other Party Pooper I came across during my research was the church. The church's ambivalence over quinceañeras first became evident to me as I fumbled through my initial months of fieldwork, cold-calling parish after parish in Las Querubes in search of willing subjects, only to find that for every five churches I called, three did "not do quinceañeras." Most offices did not offer an explanation, although one parish did take the time to clarify: "Quinceañeras are not a sacrament."

The history of the church's various views on these rites of passage offers more clues as to why some parishes decline to perform quinceañera masses. In a brief review of the discourse around quinceañeras in Chicago between 1971 and 1991, Karen Mary Davalos reported that while some churches defended quinceañeras by referring to "papal decrees that promote popular religiosity and cultural diversity within the Catholic Church" and to the pragmatic fact that quinceañeras help entice Mexican immigrants and young people to attend and stay committed to the church (immigrants have been vital to the durability and growth of the U.S. Catholic church), other clergy and laypeople found "worshippers who celebrate the quinceañera [as] misguided" (Davalos 1996: 108). Davalos elaborated, "Clergy argue that worshippers can be misguided in two ways: first, they are overly concerned with money and social prestige, and second, with sex" (1996: 108).

To illustrate, Davalos cited a Catholic pastor who disapproved of quinceañeras because "the families that throw these often go into tremendous debt . . . [and] I have a problem with the message of the ceremony: 'Here's the girl and she's ripe for the picking'" (1996: 109).

Critics like this clergyperson call into question the *morality* of quinceañeras. They view lavish spending not just as stealing from a college trust fund or future wedding budget but also as promoting the kind of worldly materialism that detracts people from service for and with their communities. When framed as sexualizing young girls and elevating the self-interested pursuit (and ostentatious display) of material wealth, quinceañeras can be seen as morally objectionable because they play a role in depriving families and communities of valuable current and future resources. Overconcern with gaining money and social status distracts individuals from doing work that could help meet people's basic needs and help build and improve communities. And overconcern with sex sidetracks young people from being able to make and achieve educational goals and to become healthy contributors to society.

However, churches such as Saint Brigid, where Patrisia Valdes served as quince coordinator, feel that offering quinceañeras helps them meaningfully, effectively address the same problems. Patrisia explained:

Girls at this age are seen as troublemakers. The teenage age group is really a challenge because this is when you could lose them. . . . I use the quinceañera as a teaching opportunity, to tell girls, "You don't have to leave your Catholic faith." . . . I don't give up on them. . . . They think they know a lot, and they face a lot of peer pressure. This [religious education for quinceañera preparation] is an opportunity to teach them to hang in there. . . . I teach them to concentrate on entering service, so they won't get in trouble. I tell them they should have respect for themselves because abstinence is a gift.

This shows how, despite their different ideas about what quinceañeras epitomize, both parishes that refuse to celebrate quinceañeras and those that promote them feel that young-adult Latinas are at risk for leaving the church, dropping out of school, and not accepting the responsibility to "enter service" and contribute to society. This is in response to startling realities for Latinas in the United States: "At 21 percent, the national Latino high school dropout rate is more than twice the national average at 10 percent" (Pew Hispanic Center 2004), and "The reasons Latina girls leave high school before graduation are many. One major factor is pregnancy. . . . Other factors . . . are marriage, gender roles, stereotyping, family demands and economic status" (Vives 2001). This, in turn, calls our attention to how American institutions are being forced to reevaluate and reconsider their practices in response to the growth of immigrant communities in the United States.

Party Crashers

While Party Poopers refused to take part in debuts and quinces, the other traviesos in my study, Party Crashers, refused be kept out. Although none of my primary, secondary, or focus group respondents admitted to ever crashing, or joining a debut or quince without invitation, party crashers are so routine at these events that both the films *Quinceañera* and *The Debut* feature crashers as significant characters.

In *Quinceañera*, the audience is introduced to the film's first party crasher, Carlos, the brother of the celebrant, as he swaggers down a nighttime street, to a hard-hitting *cumbia*.[4] He is the image of a stereotypical L.A. *cholo* (Chicano slang for "gangster"): tan, shaved head, muscular, and humorless. He wears a bulky black jacket over an unbuttoned checked shirt and a white tank top, with sagging black pants and running shoes. On the back of his neck, a tattoo reads *213*, the area code for Echo Park, the (rapidly gentrifying) working-class Los Angeles Latino community where he lives. As Carlos passes a sidewalk flower stand, he deftly plucks a long-stemmed rose out of a tub and then sprints down the block. The flower vendor chasing after him, an older man, does not stand a chance.

Soon after, Carlos is shown creeping up behind his sister, Eileen, to present her with the rose he has just taken. Even before he completes the sentence, "Happy Birthday, *hermanita* [little sister]; I got that for you," a worried Eileen instructs her brother, "You better get out of here," and their father, Walter, starts charging from his table toward them. Over the blaring music, Walter shouts at Carlos, "What are you doing here? You're trying to embarrass me. I told you not to be around this family—you have no place in this family. You're not my son anymore! I don't want you around here anymore! Get out!"

In response, Carlos spits out a contemptuous "Fuck you, man; it's my sister's birthday, you asshole," as he forcefully pushes Walter back with both hands. When Walter throws a punch in return, the room suddenly seems to go quiet, except for Eileen's cry, "No, Daddy, no!"

The men in the room then work together to thrust Carlos out of the *salón* as everyone watches in horror. As one particularly burly guest throws Carlos out the double doors, he cautions, "Don't do it, Carlos. Don't ruin your sister's special day." After Carlos leaves, the next shot shows the deejay mechanically talking into the mic to a nearly cleared-out reception hall, comically conveying how disruptive Carlos's party crashing has been.

In *The Debut*, the Party Crasher technically is not a person but the unwelcome object brought to the debut by Augusto, the son of the debutante's family friends. Like Carlos, Augusto's shaved head, baggy clothes, and severe attitude epitomize a community "bad boy." Augusto is also the ex-boyfriend of Annabelle, the debutante's best friend, so when Augusto finds Annabelle alone with Ben, the debutante's brother, in a hallway outside the gym where the debut is taking place, a hostile confrontation ensues.

"Got it hard for my girl, punk?" Augusto barks, as he brings his angry face inches away from Ben's. When Ben replies by stepping back and saying, "Look, I don't want any trouble, okay, Augusto?" Augusto responds by grabbing Ben's collar with both hands, shoving him strongly several times, and then grabbing Ben's face and pushing it away as he mocks, "Fucking coconut."[5] At this, Ben punches Augusto; Augusto reacts by running toward Ben and ramming him into a wall; then the two begin to fight on the ground. During the scrabble, Annabelle escapes to summon help, and after a lengthy minute, Ben's father, Roland, and uncle, Lenny, run in with about a dozen other family members and guests to break up the fight. Uncle Lenny picks up Ben and pulls him away, and Roland grabs Augusto. As Augusto struggles to get away, Roland is forced to shift and tighten his hold on him. In the midst of all the chaos, Roland discovers that Augusto has been hiding a gun in his pants. Infuriated, Roland puts Augusto in a headlock and demands, "Who do you think you are? You think you can come here? Are you trying to use it, hah?" When Augusto's mother finally breaks through the crowd and realizes what her son has done, she tells Augusto, "*Tama na! Bastos ka!* What are you doing? [*Sobs and slaps him.*] You're such a rude boy! *Anong nangyari sa iyo?*" [Stop it! You are so obscene![6] . . . Whatever happened to you?]

The final Party Crasher I came across (albeit cinematically), like Augusto's gun, was actually something brought to the party by an "official" invitee: a teen pregnancy. In *Quinceañera*, the protagonist, Magdalena, who is planning to celebrate her "special day" in just months, becomes pregnant, though she and her boyfriend have never had full intercourse.[7] When she first tries to explain to her father that she could not be pregnant because she has not had sex, he angrily rebukes her, shouting:

> Ve te . . . después de la verguenza que has traido a esta casa. Y no solo eso—a nuestra iglesia. "Él que fornica contra su propio cuerpo peca." . . . Estás tan llena de pecado que no quieres admitir la verdad. Cuando tu maldar está allí en frente de tus ojos, y todo el mundo! . . . Ve te; ve te—no te quiero ver.
>
> ———
>
> Go away . . . after the shame you've brought on this house. And not just here—to our church. "He who commits fornication sins against his own body." . . . You are so full of sin that you can't admit the truth. With your wickedness in front of your eyes, and the whole world! . . . Go away; get out. I don't want to see you.

After this confrontation, Magdalena leaves her family home to live with her *tío* Tomás, who has already taken in the family's other black sheep, her defiant cousin, Carlos.

People who crash debuts and quinceañeras are usually deliberately not invited. For example, Sharon told me that Cassandra's unexpected guests were not asked to attend because they were quarreling with other guests. Dalía told me that the teenage boys who arrived at her reception without invitations had not been invited because they were boys her mom was unfamiliar with. Although Augusto had been invited to Rose's debut with his parents, Roland's father, Lolo Carlos, later reproached his son for doing so. He admonished, "Hindi ka nag-iisip! Iresponsable! At ba't ka nag-iimbita ng mga barumbadong tao dito? Pinabayaan mo lang ang mga hoodlums na 'yon!" (You don't think! So irresponsible! And how could you invite those kinds of people here? You let those hoodlums in like that!) Magdalena was essentially disinvited from her own quinceañera because of the "shame" and "sin" her pregnancy brought on to her family and community. And it turns out that Carlos had been forbidden to attend his sister's quinceañera after his father discovered he was gay.

By highlighting what (and who) immigrant families are trying to keep out of their debuts and quinceañeras, Party Crashers help us further discern what kind of image organizers desire to project of themselves, their families, and their communities, and the challenges they face in managing this image. Attempts to hide anything that implies female vice—such as Magdalena's pregnancy and male strangers like those who crashed Dalía's quinceañera— demonstrate how significant it is for immigrant families to render their daughters as protected and well supervised. And efforts to keep young men like Augusto and Carlos out of sight show that it is also important to these families to come across as bringing up motivated, disciplined sons.

Fundamentally, Party Crashers reveal the priority that debut and quince organizers place on presenting their families as portraits of integrity and discord-free solidarity. As discussed throughout this book and particularly in Chapter 4, this is because many Filipino and Mexican immigrant families are invested in presenting an idealized image of themselves and their communities, "to present an unblemished, if not morally superior, public face to . . . locate themselves above the dominant group" (Espiritu 2003: 177). Like other mothers I have discussed, debutante mother Linet suggested as much when she talked about the strict policing of her family:

> I tend to be strict. . . . I let them [her children] go [i.e., leave home] once in a while, but it's in a way that's "Okay, where are you going?" I need to find out. It's not like, you know, I have to lock them up, you know. But I need to know: "Where are you going?" and "How long are you gonna be out?" Those things, like in the Philippines, I just can't get out [of her system]. . . . I'm not like American parents. They are permissive too much. Too much of everything. Sometimes, they forget they are the parents already. Sometimes they're being over-powered by the children. Sometimes that's how it is, I think. . . . But I came from another country.

Squabbling members, daughters who associate with strange men (or worse, have sex), and "hoodlum" sons threaten the image of parents who want to communicate that they can still keep their sons and daughters in line and that they have not been "overpowered by the children." Excluding such characters from important family occasions like debuts and quinces symboli-cally "erases" them from their families and communities, so that families can "uphold the narrative" that they are more virtuous, decent, and respectable than other groups (Espiritu 2003: 166–167).

This helps explain why the reactions to Carlos and Magdalena were ex-ceptionally harsh. As a *cholo*, Carlos already sent others the message that he was beyond the influence of his parents, and that worse, he was a menace to his community. This put into question his and his entire family's suitability for legal and cultural citizenship in the United States. But his homosexuality definitively laid that question to rest. At least for his father, being gay marked Carlos as monstrous, morally depraved, and unfit for membership in society. And Magdalena's illegitimate pregnancy did the same for her. Since their "wicked" children seemed so obviously beyond rehabilitation, their fathers' attempts to protect their families from such indecency was to banish them. Magdalena's father kicked her out of his home, and Walter publicly declared that Carlos had "no place in this family" and was "not my son anymore."

Carlos's tale and the fact that Magdalena was the only female Crasher I came across also indicate significant gender-related differences among mem-bers of the second generation. The types of male Party Crashers I have de-scribed help point out that second-generation men experience pressure from the first generation to be "good boys": honest (rather than secretive), ambi-tious (rather than aimless), and productive (rather than destructive). It also suggests that second-generation males both are given more freedom from parental supervision and are more susceptible to external obstacles to their upward assimilation—partly because parents do not feel they can police their sons in the same manner that they do their daughters. More specifi-cally, I think that male traviesos reveal that while Mexican American and Filipino American females are expected to serve as "keepers of [homeland] culture," their male counterparts are expected to help advance their families' acceptance as new Americans. Writers have found this true for the children of other immigrants as well: "Women are expected to perform the work of sustaining the private, ethnic essence of community identity in the United States while . . . men [are designated] as participants in the public or main-stream sphere of capitalist enterprise and state policy" (Maira 2002: 181, summarizing A. Bhattacharjee [1992]). This is why immigrants are unable to effectively level charges of cultural inauthenticity against young men who refuse to conform to their "good son" ideals as they do with their daughters.[8]

Party Crashers help elucidate Portes and Rumbaut's observation regard-ing outcomes for the children of immigrants, that "gender enters the pic-ture in an important way because of the different roles that boys and girls occupy during adolescence and the different ways in which they are socialized" (Portes and Rumbaut 2001b: 64). It also lends modest support to the idea that immigrant ethnicity facilitates the upward mobility of immigrants, while second-generation children's "Americanization" "tends to inhibit upward mobility by fostering an oppositional stance toward mainstream institutions, education, and work" (R. Smith 2002: 111). This has been used to help explain why females in immigrant families have been able to attain higher levels of education, occupational prestige, and even incomes than their male counterparts (for contemporary research and reviews of past research on this topic, see Kiang et al. 2011; Qin-Hilliard 2003; R. Smith 2002).

For some second-generation sons and daughters, it is probably supremely ironic that girls' lack of freedom and perceived obligation to represent their families' moral superiority has been linked to females' greater academic and professional achievement. Regardless, Party Crashers compel immigrant communities to acknowledge and grapple with intragroup conflicts, diversity, and challenges.

Scene Stealers

Scene Stealers, traviesos who have completely reappropriated debutantes and quinceañeras to spotlight the ways they boldly do not conform, take their troublemaking one step further. They go beyond calling attention to intragroup issues and conflicts and are helping deliberately reshape their families' and communities' gender and ethnic ideals. During this study, I had the good fortune to come across three Scene Stealers: Sean Taleza, a gay teenager planning his debut; Andrew Tan, a gay Filipino who organized a *treintañera* for his thirtieth birthday; and Ariel Campos, a woman who held a *cincuentañera* when she turned fifty years old.

I met Sean when he was seventeen years old and living with his divorced mother and younger brother in an apartment in a working-class neighborhood of Las Querubes. He was born in the Philippines and had been living in the United States for only five years, but he did not seem much different from many of his American-born peers. He spoke English like many native speakers, was academically successful (he was enrolled in advanced-placement classes in high school and was admitted to a nationally top-ranked university shortly after I interviewed him), and seemed to have developed a solid peer network (he was "really active in all gay and lesbian associations in school and the Filipino organizations" and made the cheerleading team some time after we met). He self-identified as "homosexual" and told me that he had been open about his sexuality since he was two years old. He explained:

I've always been open—ever since I was like two. I knew then that I wanted to play Barbie instead of Legos. . . . My grandma knew, too. She will buy me like a Barbies [*sic*] collection. In the Philippines, it costs a fortune to buy a single Barbie, you know? And she will still buy me *three*. And before, my mom really—my mom thought that she could still change me. That's why she tried to keep those girly things away for a moment, just to see if I will change. But my grandma cannot handle that. . . . Finally, she convinced my mom, when I was eight, to actually buy me Barbie. She knew all I want was like gay and Barbies. And she [Sean's mother] was okay with it.

By the time I talked to Sean, his mother was comfortable enough with his sexuality to live in an apartment decorated with numerous eight-by-ten headshots of Sean in full (and convincing) drag.

Describing the debut he had been envisioning for himself for a year, Sean told me:

It's either gonna be a big one, or I'm just not having any. . . . I want to walk on an aisle of petals, pink petals . . . and have some butter-flies. . . . And I would surely enjoy the party if I wear a pink, long dress. I figure . . . we use the stairs, put some net on it, with flowers, but-terflies, a pink light. I can walk down from up there, down the stairs. . . . I'm going to turn from upstairs, and I'll be barefoot. I'll go downstairs with my mom. . . . Then, when I reach the bottom of the stairs . . . my mom will give the bouquet, and I will put on leather heels. . . . My court will be waiting outside the gate for me—it's gonna be nine guys and nine girls. And my grandma will be the queen. And then I'll give the roses to my mom, and my mom will give them to my grandma. It's kind of a metaphor for, you know, three generations of ladies.

Sean also said, "Basically, it's a family thing and friend thing. I will invite my closest friends; that's it." But then he added, "Oh my goodness! I will totally invite my enemies and slap it in their faces: 'I told you, I'm the princess, so you all gonna recognize.'"

Sean's remarks demonstrate how some young gay Filipinos have begun to imagine debutantes as rituals that offer them a vehicle for presenting them-selves publicly as gay, devoted to their families, *and* Filipino. In doing so, boys like Sean are able to affirm (and force others to "recognize") that such identities can coexist and need not be opposing. Sean proudly embraced his sexual and ethnic identities, though he was aware of the fact that many Filipinos condemn homosexuality and that there is racism in the U.S. gay community. He declared several times during our interview, "I feel really strongly about my homosexuality and my being a Filipino." But he also said, "American society is kinda like open to a lot of stuff that Filipino society is not—for example, my homosexuality. . . . Sexual epithets were just constantly thrown at me growing up [in the Philippines]." At the same time, he shared:

> Periodically I have some grudges against white people. I love them, but I hate them. Most of them I love just because they're nice to me, and they know—you know, like 60 percent of the gay population are whites[9]—so they kinda know what I'm going through. But on the other hand, it's kinda like, most of them are also homophobes.

Regrettably, I never found out if Sean's grand debut fantasies ever materialized. I do know that his mother, though supremely supportive and proud of her son, did not share his enthusiasm for the idea. This was because of the anticipated cost of sending him to college and because of her own ideas about what debuts should signify. She told me:

> You know, I don't have any plan for this plan [Sean's debut]. I was just talking about it; I did not know he was serious about it. Because normally we don't give debutantes to the man. A debutante is always a lady. . . . It's kind of weird, you know? Did you ever hear somebody like a boy having [something] like that? So I was just thinking [to celebrate Sean's eighteenth birthday], maybe a party—just a party with food and dancing. That's it.

And interestingly, in spite of Sean's remarkable imagination, he seemed unable to conceive of debutantes as truly masculine spaces. Recall all of the traditionally feminine elements that Sean envisioned as part of his debut (e.g., petals, butterflies, a dress, a bouquet, and heels) and how he characterized himself being introduced to society as "a lady." And when I asked Sean if he ever imagined his younger brother holding a debut, he laughed as he told me, "No, no! Hopefully he doesn't want a debut because it's hard to be gay. Maybe like a rave party, big strip-club party, but not—not a debut like mine."

By the time Andrew, who was about a decade Sean's senior, decided to throw himself a *treintañera*, he seemed better able to not just challenge the idea that *gay* and *good Filipino son* were inevitably discrete but also confront the notion that one cannot be both gay and masculine. Months before turning thirty, Andrew realized:

> A lot of my female friends fondly recall their debuts and quinces. Since I was turning thirty, I wanted to celebrate in a big way. . . . I spent a lot of time thinking about this. I thought that if turning fifteen was a significant milestone, then turning thirty was twice as special. I coined the term *treintañera*—I had never seen it previously.

For the event itself, he donned a G-Star shirt, vest, and jeans;[10] rented out the private upstairs lounge of a restaurant in a fashionable part of Las Querubes; assembled more than a hundred people from "several of [his] circles" from throughout the nation to help him "welcome [his] third decade in style and in good company"; brought in a deejay to spin "seventies funk/disco/ soul, eighties freestyle/R&B, nineties hip-hop, house, [and] dancehall"; and financed the whole event himself. In doing so, he deliberately projected the image of a Filipino man who was stylish, strong, well supported by a dense and strong network, financially secure, *and* gay. He reflected, "It was empowering because I felt like I was creating a tradition, as if I was taking part in creating and defining what it meant to be gay—the way I want to."

Throughout his life, Andrew had been the "perfect" Filipino eldest son: devoutly Catholic, high school valedictorian, JROTC[11] battalion commander, and an altogether sound role model for his younger brother. But he did not choose to come out until after his first year of college. After that, he continued to be involved in the Filipino and Asian American communities on campus, and he also became an outspoken member of the LGBT[12] community. Even after graduating from college, Andrew continued working with all these communities, both as an activist and a professional. His *treintañera* Evite (reproduced here exactly as written) helped remind guests of how far he had come before he turned thirty:

> we braved the winters of alaska together. we hung out . . . after the game together. we took the F train to brooklyn together. we protested on campus and in the streets together. we did the walk of shame together. we climbed the corporate ladder together. we drank sake and sang karaoke all-night together. we hit the open road with my civic and my mini together. we probably did a [Pilipino Culture Night performance]. . . . we swam the waters of hawaii and bahamas together. we watched bjork in the desert together. we became overeducated in the ivory towers together.

Both Andrew's adult life and thirtieth birthday party—a sophisticated celebration that buzzed for hours with bass-thumping music and the merry-making of people of all races, sexual orientations, occupations, geographic regions, and the like—reflected Andrew's willingness and ability to bring together his multiple identities and declare them inseparable. Andrew contemplated, "I guess I realized [and] reconfirmed that because I have chosen a different path—coming out—that I . . . need to let go of straight paradigms and start defining my life based on my own desires and goals." In doing this, Andrew showed how he and men like him are contesting restraining ideas about their ethnicity, gender, and sexuality, and, in the process, helping to rework what it means to be Filipino (or Mexican), male, and gay in the United States.

Straight second-generation females are also refusing to be fastened into cultural and gender straitjackets and participating in the construction of fresh understandings of what it means to be Mexican (or Filipino) in America. Ariel Campos, for example, did this by choosing to commemorate her fiftieth birthday with a *cincuentañera*, which another self-identified Chicana has described as "kind of like a Mexican *quinceañera* but without going to church and having to listen to a priest go on and on about how I should live my life post-fifties. ¡Ay no!" ("I Want You to Say" 2007). Ariel is a single Mexican American woman who was raised in the Mountain West region of the United States, earned her doctorate degree, and has now lived and worked in California for several decades. As an independent, highly educated, divorced mother and professional, Ariel challenges the idea that the most admirable Latina women have to be married, entirely maternal, and bound strictly to home and family.

As she was reaching fifty, she realized that she wanted to

> celebrate coming of age as an older woman, to embrace that process, instead of being afraid to get old as most women feel in the American culture. In our Mexican culture, elders are respected and sought out by the family and community, and I was hoping to affirm us as women in our life journey.

Thus, although she had never heard of other women organizing such an event,[13] Ariel invented her own *cincuentañera* by "kind of tailor[ing it] after the quinceañera in terms of making it a family and friends event with dinner and dancing." Instead of a mass, she designed a "spiritual ceremony" to commence her celebration, which consisted of "prayer to the four directions, and prayer and *palabras* [words] about wisdom of entering the stage of second half of life and being an elder." Rather than a pastel ball gown, Ariel wore a red dress and asked those playing a part in her event to dress in "black with red accessories to complement my red dress." During a catered, "sit-down dinner," Ariel sat at "a head table" with her daughter, parents, brother, and sister-in-law. Finally, in place of a corte and vals, Ariel "had a circle of *comadres*, women who were my closest friends . . . speak to words I gave each one. I chose the words as they were and are important to me, such as 'passion,' 'community,' 'power.'" Then, she said, "I had the deejay, my old friend, start the music with 'We Are Family.' My *comadres* and I danced at first; then we each grabbed one of my family members to dance. Then it was a great dancing party into the evening."

By adapting the quince tradition to celebrate her fiftieth birthday with a *cincuentañera*, Ariel highlighted and celebrated the fact that she is a successful Mexicana—who also happens to be a single woman, and a professional who holds personal passions, besides *familia*. This helps further call into question and reinvent what it means to be a "good" Mexicana woman in the United States—even while it continues to construct Mexican culture as somewhat distinct from American culture (recall how Ariel explained that rather than "being afraid to get old as most women feel in this American culture," Mexicanos embrace aging and respect elders). This shows again how Scene Stealers, more so than other traviesos, help challenge "static, singular conception of [ethnic groups] in America" and "highlight . . . the *process* of identity as an unfolding set of contradictions and possibilities, rather than the fixed *structure of identity to be (re)presented*" (Gonzalves 1997: 170, 180).[14]

Rear View

Throughout this book, I have likened debutantes and quinceañeras to *ventanas* into Filipino and Mexican immigrant family life in the United States. And at the start of this chapter, I mention that Carlos, the male travieso in the film *Quinceañera*, lived in a backyard rental with his uncle (where Magdalena, the female traviesa, ultimately also found refuge). In this chapter, I have taken readers from a vantage point by the main house, to observe the same home from the hidden *casita* in the rear. In doing so, I have exposed and discussed how the production of ethnicized femininities is contended and unstable and, often unintentionally, helps provoke the construction of new ways of being Mexican or Filipino women and men.

I have done this by employing a sociological imagination and closely examining the traviesos I came across during my study. Control Freaks are mothers who overregulate their daughters and their daughters' coming-of-age events. Control Freaks, though extreme, help highlight how debutantes and quinceañeras afford female parents a rare opportunity for creativity and self-expression. They also illustrate how "immigrants . . . commonly see fulfillment of their ambitions not in their own achievement but in those of their offspring" (Portes and Rumbaut 2001b: 62), especially because of the ways in which they have been personally and systematically prevented from satisfying many of their dreams. Big Spenders have been accused of spending their time and money unwisely and even risking their children's ability to afford and attend college. A closer look at their experiences, though, reveals that for some parents, conspicuous consumption is one way to challenge their differential inclusion and to try to demonstrate that they are qualified, economically and culturally, for full legal and cultural citizenship in the United States. Party Poopers, or individuals and institutions who refuse to participate in debuts and quinces, call attention to how immigrants use charges of cultural inauthenticity to police their daughters' behaviors, and how American social organizations and communities are being forced to reconsider their rules and regulations in response to the growth of U.S. immigrant populations. Party Crashers, the ubiquitous uninvited guests who refuse to be kept out at debuts and quinces, help expose "troubles" that contemporary immigrant families and communities are dealing with but are trying to hide: squabbling relations, out-of-control sons, sexually active and/or gay family members, and others who threaten to shatter the carefully managed impression of immigrant families as unified and conflict-free. They underscore how important it is for immigrant families to portray themselves as morally superior to whites, in response to the ways they have otherwise been positioned as "less than" within American society. Party Crashers also illustrate how boys and girls are socialized, and how they experience their ethnicities, in distinct ways. Finally, Scene Stealers illuminate how the most daring nonconforming members of the second generation are resourcefully using quinceañeras and debuts to help expand and reshape what it means to be a Filipino or Mexican man or woman in the United States. All these traviesos highlight how within Mexican and Filipino communities, there exist an array of "nonethnic based differences" that offer us "occasion to critique the tendency toward essentialist currents in ethnic-based narratives and disciplines" (Takagi 2000: 557).

In writing about nonconformist teenagers finding ways to "resist the traditional trappings" of another conventional, youth-centered, American event, the high school prom, Amy Best points out how youth who protest proms both "reinscribe the event's cultural significance" and intentionally and unintentionally politicize the social spaces of this event (2000: 142–159). This chapter has aimed to illustrate that traviesos similarly politicize and underscore the cultural significance of debuts and quinceañeras for the immigrant families and communities that organize them. Traviesos show how certain individuals are forced to the fringes, even within already differentially included/excluded communities. And their troublemaking exemplifies how these doubly disenfranchised individuals attempt to confront, undermine, and reconfigure practices and beliefs within their communities that overlook and ostracize those who do not adhere to conventional ways of being "good" Mexican or Filipino American males or females. They also remind us of the exceptional power that debuts and quinces have to present and help solidify new identities, because they are rituals. In Chapter 6, I look more closely at the enduring power of these events by examining how they generate "memories that last a lifetime."

꧁꩜꧂

CHAPTER 6

Pagalaala Na/Just a Remembrance: The Work of Making Memories

The morning of her debut, Lauren Aquino's family home bustled with the barely contained energy of a beehive preparing to gather nectar for its queen. While a dozen teenage girls fluttered between rooms in their pajamas taking turns having their hair styled, their makeup applied, and their costumes fitted one last time by a seamstress stationed in the garage, a group of aunties hovered in the kitchen. Lauren's mother issued firm but giddy orders to her husband and son. In the meantime, Lauren's father, Nate, and the crew of photographers and videographers he was scuttling through the house seemed to be everywhere at once—so that they could be well positioned to "capture the best memories," as one photographer put it.

Two hours after the first women started getting their hair and makeup done, all the girls were finally dressed and coiffed. So Nate began moving Lauren and her entourage into the backyard, where a first round of formal photos was to be taken. Amid the chaos of everyone getting assembled, however, Lauren observed, "Two of the guys are missing, so they're screwing everything up." Another entourage member then asked, "So do you just want the girls to take photos?" To which Lauren rejoined, with a mixture of disappointment and annoyance, "Um, that's not how I want to remember today." Echoing Lauren's sentiment, one of her "ladies" then remarked, "It's your day; we want you to have the best memories!" Meanwhile, away from the deliberating debutante, Nate whispered to his sister, Laura's aunt, "I can't wait until this is over—I'm exhausted." Without hesitation, she replied, "It's worth it. Lauren will remember her debut for her whole life."

Lauren, her family, her friends, and her vendors were not alone in invoking "memories" as a vital goal and outcome of girls' coming-of-age celebrations—in fact, nearly every magazine and book I read and every person who spoke with me about debuts and quinceañeras declared memories the ultimate justification and reward of organizing and/or participating in one. Parents stressed the importance of the memories that quinceañeras and debutantes generate. For example, when I asked why she wanted to throw quinces for her two daughters, Belinda Santiago shared, "Para mi, es importante para los padres a regalar a sus hijas un recuerdo" (For me, it's important for parents to give their children a memory). Cam Maldivas, a Filipina mother, dramatically underscored Belinda's point when she told me, "Now if I die tomorrow, at least I'll know I made my daughter happy. That she had that moment, her special day. No one can take the memories away." And Alex Moreno, a Mexican father less inclined to hyperbole, described a quinceañera as "a beautiful day for the father to introduce his daughter as a young lady. The girl will always remember it."

Youth echoed the first generation's association between coming-of-age parties and the production of invaluable memories. Daniel, a former chambelán, described the experience of participating in a quinceañera as an honor: "It's like you're being asked to be in someone's memory, to be included in someone's memory. After, when they're looking back at the pictures, they'll remember that you were a part of their special party." And like many of her female peers, Abby explained that memories are the primary rationale for a quinceañera: "You have it for the memories. For Mexican people it's a big deal. Don't you want to have that memory of everyone getting to see you become a woman?" Here Abby not only invoked quinceañera memories to defend their practice; she specifically identified their significance as related to having others publicly witness a personal transformation and claimed that such recollections are of particular importance to her ethnic group.

In this chapter I critically explore the ubiquitous claims that "memories" are a compelling reason for considering and organizing quinceañeras and debuts. I describe how such events produce powerful memories because they are collective as well as personal, and constructed as extraordinary "once-in-a-lifetime" occasions marked by an array of special symbols and displays of emotion that are carefully edited and preserved for posterity in photographs, souvenirs, and videos. As Abby suggested, such memories are especially essential to first- and second-generation celebrants and participants because they provide an array of shared and documented images of Mexican and Filipino Americans as cultivated, cohesive, and capable. This reveals again how quinceañeras and debutantes are employed to contest cultural representations of Mexicans and Filipinos as uncivilized, fragmented, and incapable. Furthermore, it illuminates how ritual memories can produce what I call "emotional operating capital," a potent psychic resource that can be drawn on to help holders realize their goals, even in the face of difficult times.

In the business world, *operating capital* is defined as assets used for daily operations in a company. Operating capital cannot technically be exchanged for other goods or invested for the purpose of accumulating profit, but it is essential to a company's survival because without it, it could not function to do either. Taking from this notion, I conceive of *emotional operating capital* as the affective assets required by actors to accumulate other kinds of capital. Emotional operating capital is related to Randall Collins's concept of "high emotional energy," which he describes as the long-term, positive feelings that are one outcome of successful rituals (2004). However, while Collins defines high emotional energy as what motivates people toward affirmative social encounters, emotional operating capital conveys how positive emotional legacies can also *facilitate* social advancement. This is because emotional operating capital provides actors with the resilience and self-assurance needed to effectively navigate barriers to acquiring, building, and activating the benefits of human, social, and cultural capital. Human capital is composed of personal knowledge, skills, and competencies, and social capital is composed of personal connections and relationships between contacts. Pierre Bourdieu first defined cultural capital as knowledge that "function[s] below the level of consciousness and language" and that helps us to recognize "a 'sense of one's place,'" so that we can perform accordingly in given social environments and therefore be granted (or excluded from) access to certain social groups (1984: 471). All of these forms of capital improve one's opportunities for socioeconomic mobility and status. So understanding how ritual memories can produce emotional operating capital to obtain all these resources again illuminates the value and work entailed in debuts and quinceañeras.

Making Collective Memories

Debutantes and quinceañeras generate both remembrances of people, places, and moments that were personally experienced, as well as what sociologists call "collective memory," recollections shared by a group that "emerge . . . when those without firsthand experience of an event identify with those who have such experience" (Saito 2010: 629). Often this "memory work" starts long before a debutante or quinceañera even begins planning a celebration.

For years, Dalía's mother, Astrud, regaled her with stories of quinceañeras. When she was fourteen, Dalía finally allowed her mother to convince her that she should have one. "My mom helped me decide [to have a quince-añera] because she really wanted me to have one, and she never had one." When I asked Dalía if there was anything her mom specifically said to "help her decide," Dalía replied, "About the tradition. Everyone has one—it's, like, the norm. My mom's family didn't have a lot of money, so they couldn't afford to give her a quinceañera. But it's a part of the Mexican culture or ethnicity to give one to a girl when she turns fifteen." Lea, another former quinceañera, was similarly inspired to have a quinceañera by seeing and hear-ing renderings of quinces as "something Mexicans do." Contemplating why she chose to have a quince, she told me, "The idea to have a quinceañera was mine, based on other quinceañeras I had seen. I saw how the fiesta is a spe-cial rite of passage for Mexicana girls. I did not consider any other option [to commemorate her fifteenth birthday]. A quinceañera was under the wings of tradition, so I wanted to experience that." Lea's older sister and event planner reinforced this idea by telling her:

> Otros razones para tener la quinceañera: para seguir sus costumbres, y si vive con una familia muy tradicionalistas, llegados, y católicos. Cuando vive en ese ambiente, es que pasa cuando una muchacha pasa de la niñez a ser una joven adolescente.
>
> ———
>
> Other reasons to have a quinceañera: to follow customs, and if you live with a very traditionalist, distinguished, and Catholic family. When you live in an environment like this, it's what happens when a girl passes from childhood to become a young adolescent.

The fact that Lea's planner taught Lea that la quinceañera was a "cus-tom" for distinguished and Catholic families, and that Astrud successfully conveyed to Dalía that "everyone" who is part of "the Mexican culture" has a quinceañera—though Astrud had not had a quince herself—exemplifies how the ritual has been constructed as a collective memory, an experience shared by all members of a social group (e.g., Mexicans, Catholics, and "dis-tinguished" families), even when some or many individuals in the group have not directly taken part.

Filipina girls did not as consistently report hearing about others' collec-tive memories of debutantes before their own. However, among those who did, analogous to their Mexicana counterparts, they characterized debuts as coming-of-age events that *all* "Filipinos do." Rose was one of the few Filipina mothers who invoked collective memories (although she did not have a debu-tante herself) to persuade her daughter Rosadina to have a debut:

My friends, my sisters, they started inquiring, "Rosadina is going to be eighteen next year! Aren't you going to have a debut for her?" They kept on telling me, "Hey, you start planning now." And I start to think so—it's our tradition. Rosadina didn't go for that. She'd rather get the money. But we convinced her. She doesn't want a big one. So we convinced her, "Just us, then—a family cotillion. But you have to do it because it's our way, the Filipino way," of presenting her to society.

Erika, a lively college student, who punctuated her rapid storytelling with deep, elongated vowels when trying to make a point, was one of the few Filipina daughters whose decision to have a debut was shaped by collective memory: "I went to my first cotillion, my cousin's, when I was five. Since then, I dreamed of having my own." Erika shared that when she started high school, she actually began documenting who she wanted in her court, what her colors would be, and different themes for the reception. When she turned seventeen, Erika's mom asked her if she was really serious about having a debut, and Erika explained, "Obviously, of course! I already had my lists [of details she wanted to include in her celebration]!" When I asked what about her cousin's debut inspired Erika's "dream," she exclaimed, "It was so beautiful! It was like this fairy-tale thing Filipinos do to show everyone you're an adult."

Although Filipinas seemed less privy to others' collective memories of coming-of-age celebrations before their own, by the time they were in the real planning stages of their debuts, it was clear that they had been exposed. More significantly, both Filipinas and Mexicanas had plainly started to take ownership in such memories by then and to invite others to identify with them, too. During a rehearsal, for instance, I overheard a chambelán jokingly ask Katia, the quinceañera, "Why are we doing this again?" To which she pronounced in a clear, sure voice, "Because the best thing of being a Mexican is that we have traditions. And the quince is one of the most special because it's for us to show respect when a girl, like me, supposedly starts being mature." Janice, a Filipina debutante, was more soft-spoken than many of her peers but still commanded the deference of her friends, who were impressed with her organization and written instructions for nearly everything related to her debut. Two weeks before her celebration, she wrote a script for her emcee to read during her ceremony, which "everyone started telling me about when I found out my parents wanted to give me one [a debut]" and which she later corroborated by doing online research: "A debut is a cultural tradition of the Filipino people that comes from Spanish history. It is a ceremony that Filipino families do, to celebrate a girl's eighteenth birthday, when she takes the big step of going from a girl to a woman."

Experiences like these demonstrate how during the debut and quinceañera processes, collective memories are evoked as well as constructed. These memories invite actors to understand Filipinos and Mexicans as having the tradition of distinguished, virtuous (Catholic, family-centered), and idyllic ("fairy-tale") histories and people. And although these memories usually originate as the stories of parents and old-timers, during preparation for a debut or quince, they start to become something celebrants own as part of their *personal* pasts, as well. Hiro Saito, drawing on Maurice Halbwachs (1992), would say that this shows how debuts and quinceañeras, like other rituals, "transform historical knowledge into collective memory, making emotionally charged interpretation of past events integral to people's social identities as they shift from a subject position of audience/observers to actors/participants" (Saito 2010: 630). The kinds of collective memories that are conjured and crafted through debutantes and quinceañeras help constitute Mexican and Filipino Americans as truly sharing a noble identity and past with Mexicans and Filipinos across generations and national borders.[1]

Other ennobling stories of their cultures do not as effectively induce young Mexican Americans and Filipino Americans to imagine themselves as genuinely sharing histories and identities with Mexicans and Filipinos outside the United States or with those who are not their immediate contemporaries. Rose observed, for example, "The kids are comparing; they don't know much [about Filipino culture] until now [after her daughter's debut]. I remember, we are talking a lot [about] Filipinos before. But they don't know anything about the Philippines. We are telling them about our tradition, our culture, but they're not interested until now." Debuts and quinceañeras are rituals that are highly affective and require participants to represent and embody what it means to be a Filipina or a Mexicana woman. Therefore, they are more successful at promoting "imagination of secondhand knowledge as shared living memory" and at "help[ing] participants feel authentic about autobiographical narratives of their purportedly shared past" (Saito 2010: 630).

Differences in how exposed some second-generation Mexican and Filipino Americans are to collective memories of quinces and debuts *before* they have one suggest that they have different needs for these, which are reflective of their and their families' social positions and experiences in the United States. Among the families in my study, those who identified as working class were more likely to provide idealized images of debutantes and quinceañeras before their daughters' coming of age, and their daughters were more likely to expect that those in their social network already shared the same notions. For example, Dalía and Erika, who were both told that a special party was their ethnic community's way of commemorating a girl's coming of age, also both related that their parents were financially "strapped." Erika's mother took out a cash advance from American Express to help pay for her daughter's cotillion; later, Erika reimbursed her with cash she had received as gifts. Dalía told me, "I think my mom was also making a statement that she could do this for me. At the time [of her quinceañera], we were having financial problems, and I think my mom wanted to give me a big party . . . to show that she could do it." Neither of these girls ever formally incorporated teaching their courts or their guests about what a debut or quinceañera[2] is—the assumption was that doing so was unnecessary, since these were customs "everyone" knew.

On the other hand, those who were more comfortably middle or upper middle class usually assumed that most people in their social network did not know about debuts or quinceañeras, so they more frequently provided formal explanations and descriptions for others. For example, Janice, the woman who prepared a script for her emcee to read during her ceremony, was solidly middle class. Her family lived comfortably in a quiet suburb in a large, well-furnished tract home, with a long, private driveway and a pool that Janice often made available to her court members after practice. And Lauren, whose parents flew her photographers and videographers out from the Philippines, had her emcee explain to her guests that "the cotillion comes from the Spanish influence. It is when a Filipino girl becomes a mature young adult and is presented to society."

Such patterns indicate that working-class Filipino and Mexican Americans are more likely to have more homogeneous co-ethnic social networks, while their middle-class counterparts have fewer co-ethnic connections (henceforth, I describe this as *cultural isolation*). This means the latter group experiences less frequent contact with Filipino or Mexican culture. These patterns also suggest that more culturally isolated Mexican and Filipino American families seek to generate collective memories to help their children form stronger ethnic identities, while Mexicans and Filipinos who may feel that their ethnicity is associated with being lower class want to activate collective memories to challenge such associations. Most of the people in my study who had plentiful co-ethnic networks were of Mexican descent, while most who were culturally isolated were Filipino, but this simply reflects the relatively larger proportion of working-class households among the Mexican population in the United States and the relatively sizable proportion of middle- and upper-middle-class Filipino American households.

My argument that more culturally removed families seek collective memories to strengthen their children's ethnic identities is supported by my finding that the daughters of such families were more likely to use collective memories of and from their birthday celebrations as catalysts for learning more about Mexican or Filipino history, culture, and practices. Olivia, who had "never really heard about" Filipino debuts before she signed up to be part of the South Cove Union of Filipino Americans (SCUFA) annual group cotillion, provides a moving example of this. In a letter she gave her parents after her debut, she wrote:

> I want to thank you for giving me the chance to be a debutante. . . . I feel like before [her cotillion], I did not know much about the Philippines and our culture. Now, I want to learn more about the culture, to know more about the beautiful traditions, music, dancing, and history, and where we come from.

Furthermore, my argument that collective memories are one vehicle used by those who want to break associations between their ethnicity and being lower class is supported by my finding that girls who already knew about quinces or debuts before having their own often mentioned that they were motivated to have a celebration, in part, to "make a statement." Recall how Dalía's mother wanted to "show that she could do it." Dalía elaborated, "I think that [growing up poor] played a part in my mom wanting to give me a quinceañera because they [her mother's parents] could've never had that. . . . So I think my mom giving me a quinceañera was kind of like showing that we've come this far." Similarly, Marabel, a self-assured Filipina graduate student who said she "always knew I would have a large party for my eighteenth birthday," said that her family took out a loan to "put my debut together" and endured "so much drama" to organize it, largely "to redeem" themselves and to show that they could afford "the luxury of having one."

By evoking and producing collective memories for their participants, debuts and quinceañeras demonstrate the unique value of remembrances from these events. Debut and quinceañera memories are powerful because, by virtue of their ritual nature, they generate "collective effervescence" (Durkheim [1912] 1965), which brings participants a strong sense of identification and membership in a group. Collective memories of debuts and quinces help girls who have not been exposed to much Filipino culture to see such exposure as something worthwhile, they help those who perceive the downgrading of their ethnicity in U.S. society to believe that they can challenge undesirable representations, and they often help *all* celebrants to develop a greater sense of kinship with and respect for not only their parents and other immigrants but also their ethnic counterparts elsewhere in the world. This is momentous for Filipino and Mexican immigrants because of their histories of colonization and displacement and the subsequent wide-ranging, often compulsory, sometimes violent, and still-enduring erasures of their national histories and identities. Ramiro Hernandez, a former debutante's father, eloquently expressed the importance of collective memories when he told me:

> Well, it's important to us [Filipinos]. Like if you go for your citizenship, you're giving up your identity. The only thing your American citizenship can't take are your memories of your identity and your culture. For kids, it's important so they can remember you, so they can pass it on. Some of the kids, they don't want it. But they are part of the culture, and that's their Filipino identity.

As Ramiro pointed out, collective memories are also significant for immigrants' children because they bequeath them with a true sense of belonging to the same communities as their parents, which allows them to begin imagining how they can and do shape what it means to be Mexican or Filipino.

Making Personal Memories

But while collective memories encourage quinceañeras and debutantes to better conceive of themselves as Mexicana or Filipina, *personal* memories from their events are what give them the psychic fortitude they need to become successful representatives of their ethnic groups. Personal memories are the "mnemonic schemas and objects" that are the outcomes of experiencing an event oneself (Saito 2010: 630). Those produced by debutantes and quinceañeras are often characterized as "once in a lifetime" and encapsulated in lasting keepsakes such as portraits, photo albums, videos, and DVDs.

Like weddings, debuts and quinceañeras have been conferred the status of once-in-a-lifetime events. Nowhere is this more evident than in numerous guides and vendor advertisements targeted at debutantes-to-be. For example, an article from a statewide newspaper with a special section titled "What Goes On in a Debut?" states:

> Though extravagance is what debuts are known for . . . less expensive debuts are not unheard of. In Hawai'i, however, many families appear to go all-out for their daughters' debuts . . . since "the person can only turn 18 once." (Downes 2005)

And the mission statement of the most widely read periodical on quinceañeras reads:

We, at *Quinceañeras Magazine* believe in the fantasy created around a *quinceañera* celebration, for us [it] is the most important event in a woman's life because a *quinceañera* happens once in a lifetime, a *quinceañera* is a unique event for the *quinceañera* girl and her family. ("About Us" 2010)

Parents contributed the notion of debuts and quinces as unparalleled, one-shot occasions. In response to my question about why people think it's important to have debuts for their daughters, Rose told me, "So she will have confidence. So also she will have a memory, memories. It's only one time to become eighteen. Once in her life." Daughters internalized this view. Explaining why she ultimately chose to mark her fifteenth birthday with a quinceañera, Dalía said, "Well, I thought I wanted to travel. But you can always travel; you can only have your quinceañera once." Rosadina told me her parents persuaded her to have a debut by telling her that "it's important for my life and that I'll remember it. They said, 'It will make you happy,' 'It's once in a lifetime,' and 'Other people regret not having a debut.'" When I interviewed her months after her debut, during her first semester of college, Rosadina reflected, "I am happy that I did it. They [her parents] were right: I have no regrets, and I have good memories."

As a result of the construction of coming-of-age celebrations as invaluable events "you can only have once," organizers are expected to spare nothing to make sure such affairs will be ones they "remember forever." Without exception, every debutante and quinceañera in my study prioritized having a photographer at their event. Many devoted at least 10 percent of their event budget to hiring a professional; some even put aside another 7 percent to 10 percent to have a professional videographer record their day and then burn a DVD. Even those who planned small parties designated a responsible friend or family member to take ample photos of their big day.

Because of her family's comfortable socioeconomic position, Lauren was able to document her debut as exhaustively as most girls only wish they could. Every aspect of her debut, including moments with her entourage weeks before their performance, was seemingly captured on film. The formal invitation to her event was an impressive trio of iridescent cardstock pages bound with silver cords that required invitees to open a third of the invitation to the left and a third to the right and then to unfold a quarter of each third to the left and right to see all the information contained inside. The act of doing so gave one the sense of opening several sets of French doors and then entering multiple, dizzying gardens of full-colored images of Lauren (twenty-three in all) and her friends, smiling and laughing at the camera. As described at the opening of this chapter, a team of photographers and videographers followed her for two hours the morning of her debut, as she prepared her hair, makeup, and wardrobe. Then they shot posed photos of her and her family and entourage at home before leaving with her for the city in a limo-bus (this made it easier for them to take plenty of candids during the journey) that took them not directly to the hotel where Lauren's debut would be but rather to two famous parks, where they snapped more photos of everyone. Once at the hotel, to enter the ballroom, everyone had to walk down a "receiving line" of easeled portraits of the debutante—one depicting her during every year of her life—which ended with a full-color, life-size cardboard cutout of Lauren in a gown and a tiara, beckoning everyone inside. During the debut itself, guests were provided with printed programs containing thirty-seven images of the debutante and her court. And in between different dance numbers, everyone watched professionally made videos projected onto the ballroom's movie screen: one that narrated Lauren's life story and three "music videos" starring her and the members of her entourage. After only three dances and two videos, a guest at my table remarked, "I'm burned out with the entertainment now," to which another guest quipped, "I guess none of us will ever forget when Lauren turned eighteen!"

Lest that happen before Lauren started college two months later, within weeks, her photographer sent her the link to a website where she and her family could view some of their photos online. Lauren's debut pictures had been Photoshopped and arranged "chronologically" in an electronic album. Every set of photos was preceded by a two-page spread of just the shoot location and a caption, followed by a couple of pages of solo shots of Lauren and then another couple of pages of her with her court. The set of photographs from the ballroom was the most extensive—additional pages were devoted to detailed close-ups of items such as her guestbook, centerpieces, food, and cake; posed shots of special guests; each part of her program, including her entrance and that of her entourage; dining at the head tables; the multiple dance routines, including her waltz; Lauren's Candles and Roses; and the cutting of her cake. The final page was not actually taken at the end of the evening but was a fitting image of the debutante smiling over her left shoulder. It seemed appropriate, considering how her father justified the expense and extravagance of Lauren's photos and videos by telling me, "It's worth it, I think, for her to have something to look back on to remember we [her family] care."

Although no one else in my study documented the preparation and execution of their celebration as exhaustively as Lauren, like her parents, they did all express that the purpose of collecting so many mementos was to be able to "look back" and "remember" the *emotions* their coming-of-age parties conjured—and not necessarily to maintain an accurate record of every detail of their events. This is why most of the time, their albums and videos were ultimately edited to contain only those moments that helped narrate and preserve their birthday celebrations as "perfect"—flawless, problem-free, and exuding family bliss. Dalía comedically pointed out what a different reality her photographer had attempted to create while we were going through her quinceañera album and passed a picture of her mom awkwardly playing with the flowers in Dalía's hair. "Oh my God! You know, I don't even know why he [the photographer] made us do that! I think he wanted to make it look like my mom fixed my hair, even though she didn't!" Dalía was probably able to recall how artificial that particular photo had been partly because, while most photographers more or less edit out any photos showing evidence of unhappiness from their clients' albums, there was at least one photo in Dalía's album, from before her mass, of her mother looking grimly into a mirror. "Yeah," Dalía explained, "my mom hated how the girl fixed her hair, so she had to wash it out and fix it when we got home, by herself, before we went to church. She was mad."

Memories as Emotional Operating Capital

The previous discussions could leave one with the impression that memories generated through debutantes and quinceañeras are unduly invested in; perhaps, more egregiously, false; and as a result, possibly worthless. But my subjects' experiences demonstrate that, paradoxically, this could not be further from the truth.

Cele Otnes and Elizabeth Pleck assert that "whitewashed memories, while inaccurate, create an emotional connection between the past and the present and are intended to provide a ballast to offset hard times" (2003: 17). Feminist scholar Gayle Greene writes that "memory is especially important to anyone who cares about change" because "memory may look back in order to move forward and transform disabling fictions to enabling fictions, altering our relation to present and future" (1991: 291, 298). I bring together both these ideas by showing that personal memories of one's quince or debut help former celebrants both tolerate and move *beyond* hard times by acting as emotional operating capital. While commemorating collective memories induces a sense of belonging in a social group and generates "emotional energy," which has been described as "a feeling of exhilaration, achievement and enthusiasm which induces initiative" (Baehr and Collins 2005), I advance that ritualized personal memories generate a reservoir of positive self-images and feelings that can be accessed by holders to help surmount times of personal crisis and successfully secure and mobilize human, social, and cultural capital to their advantage.

Immigrants frequently related an understanding of memories as a resource they hoped daughters would draw on later, to remind them of their worth, especially in the face of adversity. When I asked Ramiro Hernandez why he thought memories of his daughter's group cotillion were important, he was silent for a while before he movingly stated, "Maligaya sa kanila, iyun ang mga alaala" (It brings happiness to them; that is what memories are). Then he elaborated, "It has like a pride. *Pagpatunay*. It's like a testimony, the truth: that their culture is with them, and no matter what happens, that's with them."

Catalina Valdes also talked about memories as a kind of bequest. Though petite and gentle-looking, she rousingly recounted how she talked her eldest daughter, Patrisia, into having a quince:

> I said to Patrisia, "You need this [a quinceañera]. I want you to have it. I want to leave you something to remember of when you change from the girl, from childhood, to a woman." And Patrisia say, "I don't want it. . . . You want it for you." I said, "But I think it's good for you because I know sometimes you are lonely. And maybe this [can be] something special in your life. The rest of your life you can say, 'Oh, I was somebody! This is me: beautiful! Beautiful party, beautiful waltz, beautiful dress—like a princess.' You [will] know you can go to a lot of friends. That you have nothing? No!"

Leonor Rivera Pilipina Society (LRPS) president Helen Martines likened cotillion memories to legacies from one generation to the next. While we flipped through her personal archive of souvenir programs from previous balls, she elucidated why she continues to organize the LRPS Annual Debutante Ball:

> What we [LRPS] are trying to do is give them [debutantes] a legacy. . . . We took these pictures of the ball because I want them to see their [own] quality. It's a wonderful thing because, you know, when the girls have this experience [the cotillion] on their own, they will know throughout the years that they are quality, and they aren't ever without a support system.

Like other immigrants in my study, Ramiro, Catalina, and Helen describe personal memories produced by coming-of-age rituals as immeasurably valuable, as "precious gifts." In part, this was because those days captured their daughters at their finest and most brilliant, emanating the quality of their upbringing "like a princess." This again is why only selected events, those that help frame debuts and quinces as "perfect," are usually chosen to be preserved in albums, videos, and other souvenirs. Immigrants also pointed out their understanding of debut and quince memories as emotional operating capital, a source of mental strength they could draw on, especially when faced with calamities such as feeling "lonely" or like they "have nothing."

It is interesting to note that many parents, like Ramiro, described their daughters' memories as "with them . . . no matter what happens," and as possessions that "no one can ever take . . . away," since this is the same language they all used to talk about the other "precious gift" they wanted to impart to their children: their education. This suggests that immigrants view memories similarly to how they view education—as priceless tools that typically require investments of time, energy, and money, and that can enable their children to advance in life. But while education is viewed as supplying knowledge and skills, I believe that memories are viewed as providing the emotional wherewithal to parlay one's education, skills, networks, and cultural capital successfully in society.

Daughters indicated that they have drawn and do indeed draw on their coming-of-age memories to reassure them of their beauty, wealth, and support systems,[3] especially in pursuit of educational, career, and political goals. The oldest former celebrants in my study illustrated this best. I interviewed Ramona, a college graduate and accountant in the spacious house she shared with her husband and young son in a desirable middle-class suburb outside Las Querubes. Reminiscing about how her involvement with the Leonor Rivera Pilipina Society got started, she told me, "My mom always got on me about different things, since I was really shy when I was a kid. She always was like, you know. She just wanted me to participate in a lot of things, experience a lot of things, so Leonor Rivera was part of it." Mona also explained that looking back on what she learned as a debutante had both immediate and long-term effects for her after her cotillion:

> When I did Leonor Rivera, I was way—like I didn't know what I was doing with myself. I was in Catholic school for so long, so when I got to high school, I didn't know what I was doing. And then I did Leonor Rivera [and] my self-confidence boosted. . . . You learn a lot about being a Filipina from Leonor Rivera. After that [her debut], I definitely talked more; I did public speeches; I even founded a sorority. . . . Yeah, being a debutante helped with that.

I definitely would say that when I had to do a public speech, or try for an achievement, I would look back on what I learned about myself that year, and I would remember, "I have it in me [to meet a goal]." Then I'd go for it!

Lea, who had just completed her undergraduate degree at a prestigious state university and was enrolled in an Ivy League graduate program at the time of our interview, eloquently shared these thoughts on how remembrances of her quinceañera shaped her adult life:

Ten or eleven years have passed since my quinceañera, and I would never have imagined that I am where I am at in terms of school and work (at [an Ivy League university]), family (far away from them), culture (more appreciative of culture than before), and life in general. . . . When I look back on my quinceañera, I realize it did help me meet the goals I have met. Because it provided me with a healthy and beautiful experience that made me feel loved, and gave me the energy to spread love and trust my dreams. Of course, had I not had a quinceañera, I still would have felt loved and trusted my dreams, but what the quinceañera did for me was provide wonderful experiences before the event, and afterwards, which impressed upon me feelings of confidence that have lasted to this day.

Lea calls attention to the fact that women who do not have quinces and debuts certainly have other personal memories of their parents' love and their friends' support; however, the personal memories of debuts and quinces are far more potent than ordinary memories. This is because they are generated through rituals, which designates those memories as sacred and infuses the preponderance of physical objects with which they are associated with greater meaning. Thus when accessed, these memories are not just "feel-good" images; they are motivating and enabling recollections of self, family, and community.

The fact that personal ritual memories are enabling and not just motivating is why I distinguish emotional operating capital from Collins's concept of high emotional energy. While high emotional energy has been described as providing drive, it has not been specified as providing a *means* for actors to meet their goals. However, those who have shared their coming-of-age experiences with me say that their personal memories of debuts and quinceañeras did not just inspire them. They also helped them meet their goals by supplying them with powerful and tangible images of themselves, their families, and their cultures as worthy and capable. This in turn allowed them to "trust their dreams," "make good choices," and "go for it"—mobilize all their emotional, cultural, social, and human resources to get themselves where they wanted to be. This affirms Paul Connerton's observation that "our past history is an important source of our conception of ourselves; our self-knowledge, our conception of our own potentialities" (1989: 38), and it explains why other sociologists have found that "a positive perception of oneself and one's family can engender . . . a sense of hopefulness and deservedness" that can play a part in "enabling or restricting mobility" (Bettie 2003: 154).

Few of the former debutantes and quinceañeras who spoke with me have not experienced some upward mobility since coming of age, which could be a by-product of my sample having been self-selected, though still noteworthy. In all likelihood, this is not the case for every woman who has had a cotillion or quince. So it is worth considering why the emotional operating capital generated by some debuts and quinces helps propel some women forward in society, but not others. I advance that this is because like other kinds of reserves we draw from, emotional operating capital must be periodically replenished and wisely invested. But if women live in environments that do not provide subsequent reinforcement of the positive self-images generated by their debutantes or quinceañeras, and/or in environments that necessitate frequent employment of their emotional operating capital as "a ballast to offset hard times," rather than serve as a resource for accumulating and activating other social resources, their reserves can diminish quickly.[4]

This brings up the point that for emotional operating capital to help girls raise their social position, they also need good advising and to be prepared to listen to it. However, maturity, personality, and circumstances can make good advising unavailable and/or girls less receptive to it. I also posit that just as there are forms of cultural capital that are not effectual for securing admission into higher cultural milieu, it is also possible that some forms of emotional operating capital are not useful for facilitating upward mobility. For example, if personal memories from one's debut or quinceañera emphasize a girl's appearance (rather than, say, her support network) or outward performance (rather than achievement) as what make her capable and valued, that could, in effect, encourage her to invest her emotional operating capital imprudently. Peggy Orenstein writes, "According to the American Psychological Association . . . emphasis on beauty and . . . sexiness can increase girls' vulnerability to the pitfalls that most concern parents [of daughters]: depression, eating disorders, distorted body image, risky sexual behavior." She also points out that "a ream of studies shows that teenage girls and college students who hold conventional beliefs about femininity—especially those that emphasize beauty and pleasing behavior—are less ambitious . . . than their peers" (2011: 6, 16). Finally, some girls may never experience their debuts and quinceañeras as personally meaningful. In this event, their rituals may never have generated emotional operating capital in the first place.

Any number of these reasons could have contributed to Lorena's being the only girl who had celebrated her coming of age more than five years before our interview and who had not yet appeared to have experienced some upward mobility. After Lorena's quinceañera, she enrolled in a selective private four-year university but subsequently had to drop out when she found out she was pregnant. She recalled her quinceañera as something "I didn't choose" and "like a pageant." And although she described quinceañeras in general as "a day that we keep close to our hearts, [because of] this extreme idea that we're becoming a woman," she confided that during her quince, "I felt like a little girl. I'm the baby of the house, so after my quince everyone still treated me like a baby. I only felt like an adult when I left home to go to college." Her mother, Catalina, reflected:

> I worked very fast and hard. Ten hours of work everyday: cleaning, cooking, everything. And I don't want it to get back. I give everything [to her children] to show, to [have her children] see that "I grow up. I need to study." When Lorena told me she's having a baby, I scream[ed], and I said a lot of things. "Why you do these things? Is it easy for you?" I say, "I send you to [a] good school. Now, you can't finish the school, so you could have a baby. Why don't you want to finish? You can have a lot of friends. You can have everything. You had everything, Lorena . . . then you got a boyfriend. This is what I teach you? You have a chance to choose, and now you lose it. You don't know." Excuse me for a minute. [*Collects herself.*] I cry. I cry a lot. I said, "I don't want to help you no more." It's hard.

Although she did not tell me so, Lorena may have been unable to turn her emotional operating capital into an effective resource because she was too young at the time of her quince, because her mother was not available to guide her more closely (because she was working ten-hour days), because she found it more pleasing to be sexy and beautiful rather than ambitious, or because her quinceañera did not leave as enduring an impression as others' quinces leave for them. Although I cannot be certain, and hers was the exception in my study, her experience still indicates the important role that the emotional operating capital generated by personal debut or quince memories can play in shaping a young woman's life.

Memories as Work

The experiences of all the families in my study demonstrate that making and utilizing memories requires fastidious thought, planning, and effort. In other words, they are *work*. Gayle Greene writes, "Memory revises, reorders, refigures, resignifies; it includes or omits, embellishes or represses, decorates or drops, according to imperatives of its own"; she defines the aim of "memory work" as "stepping back into the past . . . to understand the processes that make us what we are and so to change what we are" (1991: 294, 300). This chapter has shown the various forms of "memory work" that quinceañera and debutante organizers do. Even before some debut and quinceañera organizers make the decision to commemorate a coming of age, they engage in memory work that connects their present lives to an elegant and aristocratic Filipino or Mexican past. During preparation for a debut or quinceañera, members of the second generation begin to own the first generation's stories of Filipino and Mexican distinction, morality, and gentility as parts of their personal histories, and they begin to more authentically identify as members of Filipino or Mexican culture. Through the ritual of a quinceañera or debut, Mexicans and Filipinos produce and preserve an array of deliberately stylized, affect-laden images of themselves, their families, and their communities at their finest. Afterward, children and parents summon these special memories to provide them with emotional operating capital that helps them offset difficult times and to successfully mobilize their resources to attain their goals. They do not experience mere nostalgia, or a longing to return to the past, which critics say breeds complacency. For they are unmistakably working to "revise, reorder, refigure, resignify," and otherwise excavate the past "to construct alternatives *for the future*" (Greene 1991: 301; emphasis added). It may perplex some to conceive of remembering as an act of transforming the future; however, feminists point out that when remembering highlights "a view of the past not as fixed and finished, but as . . . ever-changing and open to revision," it helps reveal that the "self, present, future, and even environment" are likewise subject to "re-interpretation" (Greene 1991: 312).

Recognizing the production and deployment of memories as work enables us to again distinguish the value of debuts and quinceañeras because it allows us to understand that they require significant labor and generate significant outcomes. As detailed earlier, the memory work that organizers do before, during, and after debuts and quinceañeras contributes to the construction of collective identities to counter and contest demeaning, controlling images of Filipinos and Mexicans in the United States. As Ramiro

Hernandez told me, "The memory of a debutante. . . . It's something like *taas na ulo*. That means something like, 'Raise your head.' It has like a pride. You can raise your head because you know the truth [about Filipino] culture." Additionally, the emotional operating capital generated by memories of debuts and quinceañeras can help organizers endure difficult moments. A poignant example of this was when Belinda Santiago told me why she kept quinceañera portraits of her daughters in a prominent place in their home (their living room, at the center of their apartment, and where they spent most of their time as a family and entertained their guests):

> Son tan especiales. Me recuerdan como yo lloré en las misas. El padre, se dijo sermosillos, sobre cómo están creciendo, y están entrando en otra vida. Cuando estoy trabajando tanto y soy tan cansada, miro estos, y recuerdo: Les estoy dando el amor propio. Creo que es para su vida, y soy así que feliz les lo doy.
>
> ———
>
> They are so special. They remind me how I cried during their masses. The priest delivered such beautiful homilies, about how they are growing, and they are coming into another life. When I am working so much and I am so tired, I look at these, and I remember: I am giving them self-esteem. I believe it is for their life, and I am so happy I give it to them.

Emotional operating capital from quince and debut memories even helps some celebrants experience personal social advancement as discussed earlier and as Josie Espalda, former organizer of the Pilipina Ladies' Association of Southern California's annual cotillion, implied when she told me, "It's memorable when, you know, you are presented to the public. . . . I notice that most of the kids who have gone through this debutante ball, now they are whatever they said they wanted to be [during their cotillion]."

Acknowledging memories as work also provides more insights into how immigrant Mexican and Filipino American families are experiencing U.S. society. First, it points to the existence of a lopsided division of labor in immigrant families with regard to memory work and generation of emotional operating capital, which again highlights the invisible work females do to facilitate upward mobility of their families in the United States. Although some fathers shared in storytelling about Filipino and Mexican culture and coordinated and collected relics of their daughters' debuts and quinces, this work was most often performed by mothers, aunts, sisters, and the celebrants themselves. Closely examining memory work in debutantes and quinces also reveals a gendered distribution of the major outcomes of memory work, emotional energy, and emotional operating capital within families. Since quinceañeras and debutantes are rituals for girls, they offer young women at least one more grand opportunity than young men to accrue the psychic resources that have been shown to motivate and enable actors to overcome obstacles and, thus, one more opportunity to experience upward mobility. Like daughters, sons also participate in other "once-in-a-lifetime" rituals that can generate potent collective and personal memories—events such as first communions, graduation parties, and confirmations. But none of these occasions place individual boys front and center, showering them with the kind of exclusive and extensive attention, time, and resources that quinces and debuts grant girls. This might be one reason why second-generation males seem to be more susceptible to "the looming threat of gangs, drugs, and other forms of downward assimilation" (Portes and Rumbaut 2001b: 62). At the same time, this might also be why career and financial success is still seen as insufficient for the complete success of second-generation women. Women still carry the expectation of "keeping culture" and of trying to make sure their families have sufficient emotional energy and capital—while earning a college degree and finding a good career.

Vale la Pena

All the people in my study—whether they were female or male, parent or child, family member or vendor, former debutantes or debutantes-to-be— told me that quinceañeras and debuts are "once-in-a-lifetime" events that *valen toda la pena* ("are worth all the pain") "for the memories." To this point, they went to extraordinary lengths to capture their coming-of-age rituals in photos, videos, and other keepsakes, and afterward, they looked back on these events for the wherewithal to survive and succeed as adults. Although this is in no way a linear relationship or process, I try to visually represent these observations in Figure 6.1.

To summarize, debuts and quinces produce both collective and personal memories. This strengthens cultural studies scholar Lisa Lowe's argument that culture is "the site through which the past returns and is remembered, however fragmented, imperfect, or disavowed" (1996: x). Collective memories describe recollections shared by a group, although some group members have not had firsthand experience on the subject of memory. These memories grant their holders a sense of belonging in a group and therefore solidify that belonging as an authentic identity for individual group members. I found that debutantes and quinceañeras with greater co-ethnic social

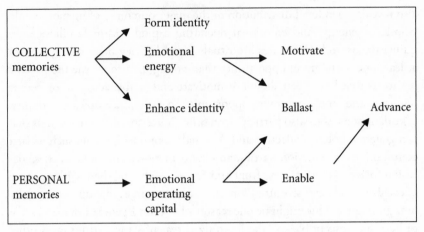

Figure 6.1 Ritual memories and outcomes.

networks were usually working class and that they more often used collective memories to challenge associations between their ethnicity and being lower class (to enhance their collective identities). Meanwhile, more culturally isolated Mexican and Filipino Americans were typically middle or upper middle class and sought to use collective memories to help develop stronger ethnic identities. All debutantes and quinceañeras, however, generated a high degree of emotional energy because they were rituals and were therefore heavily emotionally laden. Emotional energy, according to theorists, induces actors to move toward their goals.

All debutantes and quinceañeras likewise produce personal memories, remembrances of events directly experienced by holders. Personal memories of debuts and quinces provide a reserve of powerful, positive, idealized, and accessible (tangibly and psychically) images of self, family, and community, and of what one is capable and worthy of. I call this reserve *emotional operating capital*, and I argue that unlike emotional energy, which simply motivates, emotional operating capital also enables—that is, emotional operating capital is employed as a real tool that allows possessors to mobilize their social, cultural, and human capital—and therefore helps facilitate social advancement.

Understanding all of this allows us to recognize that making and deploying memories requires and involves a tremendous amount of time, energy, and effort, or "memory work." Such work aims to "look back in order to move forward" and is effective, in part because it illuminates the malleability of the future by pointing out the dynamic nature of the past. Memory work involving debuts and quinceañeras demonstrates that females are disproportionately responsible for generating memories and emotional operating capital; they are emotional energy and capital's primary beneficiaries, and they carry higher expectations to "carry culture" and manage whatever collective reserves of emotional operating capital a family or community shares.

This helps fill in some of the blanks that remain in contemporary theories regarding first- and second-generation outcomes in the United States. With regard to prevailing theories of immigrant and second-generation incorporation in the United States that relate "parental factors, including modes of incorporation, family contexts, and intergenerational acculturation, to the ways in which children of immigrants confront . . . barriers [to upward assimilation]" (Portes and Rumbaut 2001b: 62–63), this sheds light on how ritual, memory, and emotional operating capital also affect how American-born children of immigrants fare. This restores agency to immigrants and their children by showing one way they "deliberately and strategically memorialize and represent the[ir] 'original' culture as a form of resistance to places and practices in the host country that are patently anti-immigrant" (Espiritu 2010: 663–664). It also reveals that one reason "gender differences . . . affect important adaptation outcomes such as language acculturation, aspirations, and academic achievement" (Portes and Rumbaut 2001a: 64) is the gendered allocation of memory work and emotional operating capital among immigrants and their children. Finally, it underscores again how debuts and quinceañeras are not simply recreational distractions on the path to assimilation. Rather, for their first- and second-generation organizers, these rituals are extraordinary vehicles for a critical "re-membering" of their pasts, their presents, and, of course, their futures.

CHAPTER 7

❧

Conclusion: The After-Party

During the course of my research for this book, the many individuals, families, and communities I set out to learn about were generous enough to take me from my perch at their *ventanas* to welcome me into the warmth of their homes. When I asked only to quietly watch their debut and quince preparations, or to hear their family stories, or to observe their parties from some out-of-sight corner, they flung the doors to their dwellings wide open and invited me into their lives and events. Once inside, what I saw and heard was far more impressive, surprising, and exciting than any single debutante or quinceañera gown, limo, court, or ballroom in my study. This book is my best attempt to capture and share some of the most remarkable of what I have witnessed. In this concluding chapter, I recap what I have found, clarify how my findings contribute to what we know about gender and ethnicity in immigrant families, and consider the practical implications of my research for social scientists and for U.S. immigrants, their children, and their communities.

Mirrors into Immigrant Lives

As family rituals, quinceañeras and debuts are expressions of Mexican and Filipino Americans' aspirations and present needs and therefore offer us exceptional outlooks for observing and studying how these communities understand themselves and their surroundings. My deep examination of these events has clarified how the ethnic and socioeconomic backgrounds and experiences of the immigrants I studied affected the type of event they organized and their aims. The few lower-working-class Mexican and working-class Filipino families in my study arranged small celebrations honoring one girl to restrict their personal networks and thereby reduce strain on their limited resources and lessen their risks of downward assimilation. The primarily Mexican working-class families in my study were more likely to throw large celebrations for individual celebrants and to use their events to help challenge demeaning racial representations and inhibit downward mobility. Working-class Filipinos have occasionally joined middle-class Filipinos to participate in large group cotillions that have helped enhance perceptions of Filipinos in larger U.S. society, widen their social networks, and increase their opportunities for upward and bicultural assimilation. But upper-class Filipinos are increasingly turning away from participating in group cotillions and instead are holding large, individual events that help reinforce their existing social connections and status.

Intersections of class and ethnicity have also shaped the approaches the immigrant parents I studied took to preparing their daughters' transitions *de niñas a mujeres*. Working-class Mexican American immigrants took advantage of quinceañeras to restore lost generational authority within their households by teaching their children that their successful coming of age was reliant on immigrants' knowledge, goodwill, and resources. Meanwhile, mostly middle-class Filipino parents were able to confer on their daughters greater responsibility and influence for their celebrations, since Filipino immigrants have generally been able to maintain greater generational authority over their offspring. Furthermore, during their celebrations, middle- and upper-class families emphasized generating memories that could help them develop stronger ethnic identities, while their working-class counterparts emphasized the construction of memories that could help them challenge associations between their ethnicities and being unsophisticated or "low class."

All this draws attention to the concentration of Mexican American families in the working class, the greater range of socioeconomic statuses among Filipino Americans, and Filipino Americans' clustering in the middle class. National statistics bear this out. They show that while the adult Filipino American population is largely college educated, professional, and fluent in English, most adult Mexican Americans have less than a high school degree, work in blue-collar occupations, and speak a language other than English at home. This has created a Mexican American immigrant population with considerably less human, cultural, and financial capital than its Filipino American counterpart, which helps explain the greater dissonance in acculturation that Mexican immigrants have experienced with their children and the increased anxiety Mexicans have concerning their children's risk for downward assimilation.

These demographic realities highlight historic and contemporary differences in migration from Mexico and the Philippines. While early twentieth-century immigration policies brought in primarily male manual laborers from both Mexico and the Philippines to help meet the agricultural and industrial labor needs of the United States, the passage of the 1965 Immigration Act severely limited legal working-class immigration from both countries, essentially forcing the still much-needed flow of working-class Mexican immigration underground and restricting most immigration from the Philippines to (mostly female) college-educated professionals and their families.

The Value of Women's Bodies and Women's Work

My examination of Filipino American debuts and Mexican American quinceañeras makes clear how central women's bodies and women's work are to sustaining and advancing U.S. immigrant communities. First, immigrant families have chosen to invest in and employ young women's rituals and bodies to contest derogatory images of their ethnic groups, to project themselves as morally (and financially) fit for legal and cultural citizenship, and to manage possible obstacles to their progress in the United States. Because of how "women's space, like women's time, continues to be at the disposal of the family in a way that men's time and space are not" (Gillis 1997: 235), organizers of these celebrations in the United States have been able to frame debuts and quinceañeras as "homeland traditions" and to compel young women, who have already been designated as "keepers of culture," to embrace and embody these practices. For the same reasons, organizers have been able to use these events as powerful instruments for fashioning their daughters into virtuous, dutiful, and respectable señoritas and dalaga to help them construct themselves and their communities as more disciplined, caring, and decent than white Americans. This has enabled Mexican and Filipino Americans to counter racist characterizations of their groups as unrefined, disloyal, and otherwise unqualified to fully be included in the civil and moral order of the United States.

Racial discrimination is only one external obstacle that these young women's rituals help address, however. As I allude to earlier in this chapter and show throughout this book, quinceañeras and debutantes also furnish immigrant families with opportunities for building social capital and reinstating parental control over the second generation by constructing parents as important vessels of cultural knowledge. This, in turn, serves as a safeguard against the allure of U.S. countercultures such as gangs and drug subcultures, which promote second-generation hostility toward mainstream institutions, including school. Quinces and debuts also improve children's (and parents') access to people and opportunities that support and enable their successful adaptation to U.S. society and that curtail abandonment of parents' home languages and cultures.

Women's bodies and labor make it possible for immigrant communities to do all this again because of how families and communities are able to lay claim to young women's bodies, socialization, and rituals in ways they cannot do with young men. In addition, first-generation women usually take on the primary responsibility for organizing debutantes and quinceañeras because such labor is considered "kin work," having to do with "the conception, maintenance, and ritual celebration of cross-household kin ties" (Leonardo 1987: 442). And such work has principally and historically been delegated to females.

The fact that these events (and the work they entail) are commonly overlooked as frivolous and inconsequential reminds us that they take place within chauvinistic cultures that privilege economic rationality, males, and the public sphere and that define what is feminine as frivolous "and that which is frivolous as . . . feminine" (Best 2000: 36). This suggests disturbingly that one reason debuts and quinceañeras have been subject to such strong criticisms (as irresponsible and potentially ruinous) by those within and outside Filipino and Mexican American communities is because they are *family* occasions organized primarily by *women* for *girls*.

The Ongoing Differential Inclusion of Filipino Americans and Mexican Americans

The various anticipated and unanticipated motivations, outcomes, and even criticisms of Filipino American debuts and Mexican American quinceañeras underscore how, in spite of the formal independence of the Philippines in 1946, the formal end of the *bracero* program in 1964, and the closure of the last U.S. military bases in the Philippines in 1992, Filipinos and Mexicans both in and outside the United States continue to be deemed simultaneously vital, different, and inferior to America. The fact that Filipino and Mexican immigrants are still coming to the United States in such large numbers speaks to how powerfully early-twentieth-century differential inclusion continues to shape the economies and cultures of the Philippines and Mexico. U.S. colonialism left immense differentials between wages and job prospects in both countries, compelling Mexicans and Filipinos to seek opportunities away from home. And America's history with and within Mexico and the Philippines continues to construct the United States as their preferred destination. Yen Le Espiritu draws on Filipino cultural critic E. San Juan, Jr., to describe how the institution of "English as the imposed language of education, and eventually of government and commerce" in the Philippines, along with more than a century of "exposure to US lifestyles, cultural practices, and consumption patterns," have, in effect, "thoroughly prepared" Filipinos for migration to the United States (Espiritu 2003: 72). One of my subjects, Astrud Azua, related how she was likewise "prepared" for migration to America from Mexico when she told me:

> [Living in Mexico] was like part of living here [the United States]. We listened to the same music—back then, the radio stations were American music, then Mexican music. We were listening to Elvis Presley. The Americans were a big *influencia*. We were also dancing American dances. In the [Mexican] stores, you could buy candies from here. Most of the things we were buying in the stores were bought here. . . . Now . . . we live in a[n American] neighborhood with a lot of Mexicans, and we're so close to the border. We can go to the clinic here, we can go to the stores here and there, and we can speak with everyone just like in Mexico.

The fact that Mexican and Filipino Americans still desire for their children to successfully integrate into U.S. society also reveals the view that most members of the second generation are not fully integrated, in spite of having been born here. And it explains immigrants' efforts to utilize debuts and quinceañeras to address their children's vulnerability to downward assimilation in the United States by strategically managing their families' social capital, restoring parental control, challenging racist representations, and exposing their children to homeland compatriots, languages, and practices. Finally, these communities' remarkable attempts to use quinceañeras and debuts as vehicles for constructing and projecting themselves as portraits of family solidarity, and therefore fit for full legal and cultural membership in U.S. society, disclose a major way that immigrant families are responding to the persistent ways they have been economically, socially, politically, and legally differentially included in the United States.

Mexican Americans and Filipino Americans as Players

The ways that debuts and quinceañeras help construct and reconstruct daughters into dalaga and señoritas, immigrants as exclusive conduits to homeland culture, and Filipino Americans and Mexican Americans as morally and culturally advanced demonstrate that immigrant families' cultural identities are not simply either derivatives of the original cultures they left behind or identities imposed on them by mainstream U.S. culture. In fact, quinceañeras and debuts exhibit how immigrants are purposefully, strategically, and creatively constructing culture to represent themselves, their communities, and white Americans in ways that socially advantage them. This complicates how we conceive of immigrant families' paths toward successful, bicultural assimilation in the United States by clarifying that moving toward such an outcome encompasses more than selectively acculturating to U.S. culture, but also broadening what *American* means. This draws attention to immigrant families' resourcefulness, inventiveness, and agency by illustrating that "immigrants do not merely insert or incorporate themselves into existing spaces in a given host society; they also transform these spaces and create new ones" (Espiritu 2010: 664). And it shows again how immigrants as well as nonimmigrants participate in essentializing cultures, in constructing *Mexican, Filipino, female, male, American*, and so on as identities that are fixed, unchanging, and indisputable.

In spite of how debuts and quinceañeras endeavor to constitute the families and communities that organize them as univocal entities, unified against outside forces that seek to hold them back, they also help expose differences and contradictions within and among them, and offer spaces (usually unintentionally) for considering, debating, and addressing *intra*group divergences, conflicts, and inequalities. In Chapter 5, I discuss how party and community traviesos highlight some of the ways that Filipino and Mexican Americans have tried to suppress those who deviate from the ideals they have constructed for mothers, daughters, and sons, and how some of these "troublemakers"—assertive daughters, playful consumers, noncompliant children, gays and unmarried women—are challenging their own families and communities to enlarge what it means to be "good" Mexican or Filipino women or men. This indicates how quinceañeras and debuts both reinscribe and dispute traditional ways of performing ethnicity/race, gender, and class, and underscores again the significant spaces these events provide for the assertion of cultural identities.

Theoretical Implications

These findings enrich understandings of how ethnic and gender identities are produced, of how immigrants and their offspring actively shape how they are perceived and integrated into the United States, and of how cultures are transformed.

To begin with, the findings refine how we currently understand immigrant and second-generation incorporation. While the prevailing theory of *segmented* assimilation is an improvement on the earlier master concept of assimilation that presumed that all immigrant families eventually followed the same path—shedding their "old world" ways—to the same destination of absorbing modern, American culture over time, it still characterizes immigrant and second-generation trajectories as the inevitable (though assorted) outcomes of immigrants' fixed sets of resources, and of how they have been "received" into American society. According to these theories, "depending on the timing of their arrival and context of reception," immigrants are still said to "find themselves" located on specified tracks to specified outcomes. And their children are still "slated for" smooth or bumpy transitions into mainstream U.S. society, contingent on whether they experience ethnicity as a source of strength, a convenient option, or a mark of subordination (Portes and Rumbaut 2001b: 45). My examination of debutantes, quinceañeras, and the families who organize them calls attention to the fact that immigrants can and do acquire, build, and protect *new* skills, networks, knowledge, and psychic resources. It also shows that although they and their children might initially experience one type of acculturation, this too can be modified through their own efforts to shift and/or share power within their households. And it distinguishes how socioeconomic background shapes the aims and approaches of these efforts, which in turn makes clear that class is not simply an end result for immigrants and their children but a factor that influences the entire adaptation experience.

My research has also shed light on how immigrant families manage, and do not simply come across and undergo, external obstacles to their successful adaptation. I have done this by showing that immigrants and their children do not just inherit race and ethnicity but consciously and deliberately shape what *Mexican*, *Filipino*, and/or *American* mean and therefore how these identities are experienced. I have also elucidated how "gender enters the picture" and affects second-generation outcomes by demonstrating how ethnic womanhood is constructed and used to exercise influence on daughters and to try to shield them from "the threats posed by discrimination, narrowing labor market options and street culture" (Portes and Rumbaut 2001b: 62). At the same time, my research shows how such immigrant strategies of resistance are prone to producing essentialist forms of race and gender that can restrict the autonomy of members of the second generation, especially if and when they do not conform to rigid internal definitions of what it means to be good Filipino or Mexican women and men.

Exploring the production and outcomes of Filipino American debuts and Mexican American quinceañeras also adds something entirely new to sociological understandings of how immigrant families confront and overcome barriers to their success: the concept of emotional operating capital. I conceive of emotional operating capital as the affective resources required to motivate and facilitate the acquisition, maintenance, and effective use of one's human, social, and cultural capital. In Chapter 6, I explain how potent and positive experiences such as debuts and quinces help create and grow emotional operating capital. Without such a concept, sociologists cannot fully understand why and how immigrants and their children find the inner capacity to persist and transform obstacles to their successful assimilation.

The cultural transformations that take place within immigrant families and communities, and that manifest themselves and/or are produced at their female coming-of-age rituals, also have important implications for how we currently imagine how and where cultural reproduction and change happens. My findings on the debuts and quinceañeras of Filipinas and Mexicanas in the United States lend powerful support to theories implying that social ambiguity helps produce social change; for example, Ann Swidler (1986) contends that actors question culture more actively during "unsettled" times; Maria Lugones (1987) proposes that moving in between various subcultures, or "worlds," enables resistance to hegemonic cultures; and William Sewell, Jr. (1996), writes that transformative historical events are activated by a (series of) social crises.

My research suggests that people with multiple, liminal identities located in transitory life stages and social situations are well positioned to challenge, redefine, and rearticulate existing cultural understandings and how they structure people's lives. Multiliminal individuals and groups who are "betwixt and between" multiple worlds are better able to "disconnect" from established schemas and to discover new and innovative ways of responding to situations. At the same time, multiliminal people who are also within multiple worlds are more capable of reacting to their circumstances in novel ways because their multiliminality gives them access to numerous repertoires, or cultural "toolkits" (Swidler 1986) and "rules" (Lugones 1987) from which they can build a response. Recent cognitive science even lends support to this notion; researchers have found that people who speak more than one language "seem to be more adept than monolinguals at solving certain kinds of mental puzzles" (Bialystock and Martin 2004, quoted in Y. Bhattacharjee 2012).

My findings also indicate that rituals play a vital role in articulating and disseminating new or novel cultural ideas because they are formalized, public performances that charge new notions with more import and a broader audience. Because rituals can endow new ideas with a greater sense of authority and the perception that these have been collectively heard, they enable people to better visualize a new concept as having the potential to be deployed and regarded as an "appropriate" response to a situation. This is vital because as Marian Wright Edelman, founder of the Children's Defense Fund, has been attributed as saying, "You can't be what you can't see." Finally, because rituals generate emotional operating capital, they can inspire actual incorporation of new concepts into practice.

Using debutantes and quinceañeras to highlight the many ways immigrants and their children are creatively constructing cultural identities and maneuvering (and occasionally inventing new) obstacles to their success clarifies how immigrants and their families are not simply received into U.S. society, with invariable sets of resources that slate them for one outcome or another. It restores agency to Mexican and Filipino Americans by putting on view how such work is often strategic, creative, and both contradictory and effective. It underscores, again, how much of the labor involved in incorporating U.S. immigrant populations is kin work that relies on women's work and women's bodies. And it suggests who and what social circumstances are most likely to produce real cultural change. All of these theoretical implications raise possible future lines of inquiry that include deeper examinations of other immigrant rituals, of how gender is constructed for young men, of how traviesos complicate and enhance the process of assimilation for minority immigrant groups, and of how else emotional operating capital is generated and operates in people's lives.

A Feminist Ethnic Study: Methodological Implications

This project has been an ambitious attempt to comparatively study the two largest immigrant populations in the United States, using an interdisciplinary lens and approach, during a period when interdisciplinary programs such as ethnic studies, gender studies, and queer studies have come under the heaviest fire since their inceptions. When I was just starting to conceptualize this project, I was one of hundreds of University of California, Berkeley, students supporting a hunger strike to protest massive cuts in the university's ethnic studies program and to demand increased funding, the hiring of more faculty who represented and could teach about our state and institution's diverse populations, and the creation of an ethnic studies research center (Lee 1999). Critics back then derided the strike as emblematic of the fact that "ethnic studies was not a scholarly field but a platform for angry kids with an ax to grind" (Saunders 1999). As I was finishing this book, the state of Arizona, reflecting widespread xenophobia triggered by a national recession, signed into law Arizona House Bill 2281, which outlawed ethnic studies, arguing that "public school pupils should be taught to treat and value each other as individuals and not be taught to resent other races or classes of people" and that ethnic studies classes "promote the overthrow of the U.S. government; promote resentment toward a race or class of people; are designed primarily for pupils of a particular ethnic group; [and] advocate ethnic solidarity instead of the treatment of pupils as individuals" (Senate Engrossed House Bill 2281 2010).

Months later, in response to the firing of Ethnic Studies Department staff as a result of "a comprehensive audit of university operations," UC Berkeley students again went on strike to try to call attention to how ethnic studies was under threat (Most 2011). Shortly after that protest, the conservative Manhattan Institute accused the "useless diversity infrastructure" of the University of California of "suck[ing] money away from the university's real function" and reduced "the cultivation of 'a student's understanding of her or his identity' . . . through the 'framework' of 'race, ethnicity, gender, religion, sexuality, language, ability/disability, class or age'" to an exercise in "narcissism" that diverted students from learning "about the world outside their own limited selves" (H. MacDonald 2011). This, in spite of the fact that even Republican governor Arnold Schwarzenegger noted and condemned several "intolerable acts of racism and incivility" at University of California campuses the year before, including the discovery of a noose hanging in a UC San Diego library and a swastika carved into a Jewish student's dorm room door at UC Irvine ("UCSD Suspends Student" 2010).

In view of all this, I offer this book as an unabashed public, feminist ethnic studies project to demonstrate the continued value of and need for such work. Although my training and background is in one field, I have borrowed ethnographic methods from anthropology, cultural studies, feminist studies, postcolonial studies, and even psychoanalysis to gather, analyze, and write research that is thick, anti-essentialist, and closely attentive to my subjects' standpoints, feelings, and experiences. I have deliberately and rigorously compared two populations of color to highlight how the experiences of the significant and growing "racial middle" in the United States have been shaped by their relationships with not only white America but also each other—in good and bad ways. And I have aimed to better distinguish the real workings of patriarchy, racism, ageism, and other systems of oppression, as much as I have tried to refine theoretical sociological understandings of contemporary U.S. immigrant experiences.

I have done all this not because I have "an ax to grind" but because I believe—as other interdisciplinary scholars do—that inviting and listening to the voices of those traditionally marginalized or excluded from the mainstream promote dialogue and respect between (rather than "resentment toward") individuals and groups as well as disciplines. Furthermore, it helps articulate more complete, honest understandings of our institutions, culture, and people. Philosopher of science Thomas Kuhn affirmed that the latter was one of the primary tasks of any scholarly enterprise when he wrote, "Attempts to increase the accuracy and scope with which facts . . . are known occupy a significant fraction . . . of experimental and observational science" (1996: 25). I also have done this because contrary to characterizations as "useless," I am confident that such knowledge has become increasingly important to understanding ourselves *and our world* as we rapidly move toward a "majority-minority" future when people of non-European ancestry will compose more than 50 percent of the American population.[1] Finally, like the most brazen traviesos, including our ethnic and women's studies pioneers, I still believe that such "rule breaking" and "border crossings" are one of the most effectual ways academe can contribute to inspiring and promoting visions of a better world.

Practical Suggestions

By situating this project as a public intellectual one, I assume the responsibility of making sure that my findings "are publicly available or useful to some group or institution outside the scholarly world" and that "it seeks to engage the public in dialogue" (Bellah 1985: 38). I also view this as a personal obligation because this book could not have been written—and my career could not have been established—without my subjects (literally) freely sharing their experiences and expertise.[2] Therefore, as I bring to this book to a close, I attempt what Burawoy calls "traditional public sociology" (2005); that is, I attempt to enumerate the main conclusions that should be taken from this study *while* making at least a modest slice of this book directly relevant to the people whom it is about—immigrant families who are organizing debuts or quinceañeras—by addressing the question "How can Filipino American debutantes and Mexican American quinceañeras help promote best outcomes for the immigrant families who organize them?"

Before I attempt a response, I should clarify what sociologists might describe as a best outcome and what I believe family and community members probably would say is a best outcome. If pressed, sociologists would probably describe the ideal assimilation experience as one that starts with immigrants entering the United States legally with a valued set of skills, knowledge, and experiences into a community that is not prejudiced and that is composed of a reasonable number of stable people from the same ethnic background. In addition, both parents would be present and able to maintain authority, with little conflict, over their children, and parents and children would be comfortable with and within the mainstream, English-speaking community and their own bilingual ethnic community. If all of these conditions were present, then children would have sufficient family and community resources to meet and overcome racism, the challenges of the labor market, and the allure of precarious subcultures. And they would ultimately be able to do well academically and professionally and to socially advance themselves (and their families) without losing too much of their culture. In short, sociologists would say that the best outcome for immigrant families would include stable parents who have the ability to influence their children, bilingual households, multicultural friendships and connections, and a secure sense of cultural identity. On the basis of what I observed and was told while I was performing my fieldwork, I conclude that most community members would probably agree that this would be ideal, *and* they might add to the list open and honest relationships between parents and children, high self-esteem, and the feeling that they truly belong to and can fully participate in both American culture and Mexican or Filipino culture.

Given such aspirations—secure parents, respectful relations between generations, dependable and diverse social networks, a bicultural sense of identity, and a strong sense of self-worth—I offer the following tips (in no particular order) for families organizing debuts, quinces, or similar events:

1. Understand that although they are framed as "for the girl," quinceañeras and debuts are *family* endeavors. Recognize that different family members may have different goals and desires and that if they are reasonable, these can improve the experience and outcomes of such events for everybody. So be willing to talk openly and negotiate a common vision for your event early during your planning.

2. Allow preparation to be a time for entering into meaningful exchanges and dialogues about your experiences as a parent or child in the United States. As I discuss in the book and as other migration and settlement scholars have noted, respectful, trusting relationships between generations is one key to healthy immigrant families. So is developing a bicultural sense of identity. Both these goals can be met if and when parents and children take advantage

of opportunities such as working together on a quince or debut, to ascertain more about each others' challenges, desires, and lives.

One benefit of learning how the world looks from another generation's point of view may also be the development of greater empathy. This would be timely, since a recent study reports that American college students are 40 percent less empathetic than the generation before them (Konrath, O'Brien, and Hsing 2011), and low empathy has been associated with loneliness, depression, violence, and other antisocial behaviors. On the other hand, empathy is the basis for meaningful bonds with others—"the best antidote to the downs of life and the single most reliable up" (Seligman, cited in Hooper 2011: 99). And empathy contributes to group and social well-being because it is what allows members and citizens to identify the risk and suffering of others, and it is what motivates people to promote social justice and the common good (Trout 2009: 4–12).

3. Parents: Allow girls to take some financial and/or organizing responsibilities—and let them (respectfully) disagree with you. As the experiences of some of the daughters in my study have shown, such experiences allow girls to develop leadership, personal money management know-how, communication skills, conflict-management, and *gratitude*—important aptitudes for their adult lives.

4. Daughters: Respect your parents—even when you disagree with them. This should not get in the way of your ability to honestly share your own goals and desires if they diverge from those of your parents. But it is important to recognize that most immigrant parents "want the best for their children, have high aspirations for their future, and invest extraordinary resources in them" (Portes and Rumbaut 2001b: 62). Therefore, they usually make choices and decisions that might affect you with your best interests at heart. Remember that second-generation children under sufficient parental supervision have been shown time and time again to achieve better professional, educational, and professional outcomes.

5. Consider your guest list and participants carefully. Debuts and quinceañeras are exceptional opportunities for building, managing, and restricting the strain of your social networks. Do you want to use this event to publicly, meaningfully thank and strengthen relationships you already have? Then be sure to designate the most important people in your lives with special roles, and do not leave

any best friends off your list. Or do you want to use your quince or debut to make new connections? Then, if you're not already part of a group cotillion, be strategic about the "outsiders" you invite by identifying what kinds of new relationships might most enrich your social network (e.g., someone who attends a college you would like to apply to, someone in a profession you are interested in pursuing, or someone who holds a great deal of homeland knowledge). And if there are certain relationships in your life that you know you need to end or distance yourself from, remember that *not* inviting people to events like quinces and debuts sends a clear message. Just be aware of possible fallout.

6. Remember that everyone is beautiful at fifteen and at eighteen. Quinces and debuts call for a lot of attention to preparing and presenting young women who appear physically "beautiful" and "perfect." And it can be fun for females to get ready and be admired. But the American Psychological Association has reported that an overemphasis on beauty "increases girls' vulnerability to the pitfalls that most concern parents: depression, eating disorders, distorted body image, risky sexual behavior" (cited in Orenstein 2011: 6).

7. Ritualize it. Quinceañeras and debuts set apart what is said and done at these events as special and even sacred. So if there is someone or something you want to formally recognize and/or make publicly known, this is the time and the place. This is why designating someone as a padrino or madrina is an effective way of establishing a relationship with kinship obligations, why girls who announce their personal and career goals at their debuts or quinces feel far more accountable to pursue them, and why the Scene Stealers I describe in Chapter 5 felt that reappropriated versions of debutantes and quinces were good vehicles for proudly proclaiming their nonconformist Mexican or Filipino identities.

8. Have fun! Immigrants and their children do not often avail themselves of (or have) many opportunities for "renewal." Worse yet, they sometimes find themselves in positions that make them feel degraded, powerless, and/or invisible. A quinceañera or debut offers a space and an occasion to be creative, and to freely experience and enjoy the various benefits of "play"—without which we deplete our abilities to efficiently problem-solve, communicate, and be productive (National Institute for Play 2003). These are also the perfect occasions for generating and building up your

reserves of emotional operating capital—the stuff that will give you the resiliency and motivation to get you through to the next opportunity for recreation and replenishment.

9. *But not too much fun.* You (or your parents) earn your money, so you (or your parents) can spend it. But it probably is not wise to spend to the point where you diminish your capacity for meeting your family's needs (e.g., everyday food, shelter, and clothing and such needs as transportation and college tuition). And organizing an event that emphasizes the material trappings of success, rather than the journey to success (i.e., a young woman's accomplishments and promise), risks passing on a "rah-rah mentality" to young people that separates and emphasizes "rewards," rather than genuine achievement (Cleaver 2007). Psychologists caution that when self-esteem is not understood as an outcome based on real accomplishments, individuals can develop a "skewed sense of self and overconfidence [that] affects their ability to make decisions" and to complete tasks—including graduating from college (Cleaver 2007).

10. Remember that there is no script. There is no "right" or "wrong" way to celebrate a debut or quinceañera—just as there is no "right" or "wrong" way to be Filipino or Mexican American. Writing about another popular form of cultural expression, college Pilipino Culture Nights, Theodore S. Gonzalves points out the danger of such performances in presenting "essentialist," or rigid and unchanging, forms of culture. As we seek advancement for our entire communities and for all people, as well as ourselves, we need to concede and allow for "a view of culture that is open to the possibilities of change and editing" (Gonzalves 1997: 178) and that in due time can be enlarged to comfortably accommodate all expressions of Filipino and Mexican American culture.

Finally, I would be errant as a sociologist if I did not make clear that individuals and families alone cannot be expected to help produce better social worlds for immigrants and their children. My research on quinces, debuts, and social networks suggests that ethnic community association cotillions were most effective at enhancing family social networks (especially to a diverse group of people with the same ethnic background), meaningfully connecting ethnic communities with mainstream institutions, and teaching debutantes-to-be about both their parents' homeland cultures and how to successfully navigate American society. On this basis, I highly encourage

Mexican and Filipino families considering quinces and debuts, as well as organizations (including places of worship) working with immigrant communities, to help revitalize ethnic community associations and to "bring back" group coming-of-age celebrations. Older members of the second generation have left the organization of such groups to their aging parents but should consider "taking up the torch." This would not only allow such valuable cultural organizations to carry on; it would also provide a rare and much-needed space for continued intergenerational and intercultural contact and exchanges to help ensure that as U.S. immigrants, their children, and their children's children come of age, they can all effectually contribute to what it means to be Mexican, Filipino, and American in the United States.

Appendix
Nandiyan Lang/Just over (T)Here:
Ethnographic Reflections on Researching
American Immigrant Families

Although I write that debutantes and quinceañeras are *ventanas* into the lives and identities of the individuals, families, and communities who celebrate them, peering into these windows would never have been enough to help me earnestly investigate and attempt to understand the events and people that are the subject of this book. In fact, engaging in this study forced me to abandon the idea that I should or could play the role of a detached, value-neutral observer, since doing so often raised the suspicions of early potential subjects and thus prohibited me from finding people outside my circle who would allow me to interview and/or observe them. As a result, I eventually adapted a more engaged approach that follows and has been informed by forty years of "decolonial social science," a method most commonly employed by women and scholars of color (see, e.g., Davalos 1998; Keohane, Rosaldo, and Gelpi 1982; Leong 1995; Rosaldo 1989; Russel y Rodríguez 2001; L. Smith 1999).

I considered a "decolonized methodology" (L. Smith 1999) to be most useful for this project because most of the immigrant families I studied were unfamiliar with sociology, research interviews, and doctoral students. Before they agreed to participate in the study, many of them could not imagine that their lives might be of interest to anyone other than members of their own families and communities and, perhaps, state officials and agents. So when I first used my institution-approved spiel to find outside research participants—by distributing church and community announcements and approaching strangers in dress and accessory shops and at community events—my advances were either brushed off or ignored entirely.

One day, after weeks of rejection in the field and a long afternoon of getting lost in a medium-sized shopping district popular among Las Querubes quinceañeras and their families, I entered a store and approached the Latina salesperson behind the counter. Throwing my spiel and my Spanish-speaking inhibitions out the window, I introduced myself—in Spanish—and asked her if she would mind talking to me about her work to help me in my research for a "book about Mexican quinceañeras and

Filipino debutantes." It was a breakthrough: for the first time since I'd started trying to locate subjects in Las Querubes, someone was willing to talk to me! The woman spoke excitedly about her observations of quinceañera customers, referred me to several other possible sources (including her manager), and asked where I grew up, how I came to speak Spanish, and whether I was Catholic. As I wrote up my field notes, I realized that her openness may well have been, in good part, a response to my transition from a cold, systematic approach to a less formal style that included a willingness to share some of my own personal information. It even dawned on me that before that encounter, my demeanor may have caused some to mistake me for an Immigration and Naturalization Service (INS) agent posing as an interviewer to sweep out undocumented community members.

From that time on, I was convinced that a far less impassive demeanor, a little self-disclosure, and some thoughtful reflection about the effect of my identity and behavior on my research were necessary if I wanted to (1) find new subjects and (2) pursue the study of debutantes, quinceañeras, and those who participate in the celebration of both. My preparation before entering the field (literature reviews, pilot interviews, and multiple visits to Las Querubes) had helped me identify key sites where I might find local "authorities" on debuts and quinceañeras—such as churches, shopping districts, and community associations. I spent months cold-calling vendors, parish offices, and ethnic community organizations to request their help in the research for my book. After several successful interviews, I gained more than expert insights on debutantes and quinceañeras. I also earned my interviewees' trust, their referrals, and their valuable endorsements, which greatly facilitated my ability to locate, and even be warmly received by, additional research participants.

The result was a snowball effect: referrals from previous subjects led me to new subjects, who led me to still other subjects. Given the obstacles to obtaining a random sampling from the undefined universe of immigrant families who organize debutante and quinceañera celebrations, this proved an ideal way for me to generate my sample of immigrant and second-generation subjects. The approval of mutual, respected social connections made potential subjects far more willing to consider participation in my study and actual subjects far more willing to honestly share with me the details of their lives.

I arranged all my subsequent interviews and family observation via telephone. Typically, I continued to introduce myself as a UC (University of California) Berkeley student writing a book on Filipino debuts and Mexican quinceañeras, mentioned that I had been referred to them by a specific participant, and asked whether I might interview them (at a location of their choice) for about an hour to an hour and a half. I also assured participants that I would not use their real names in my book or in any reports or presentations. Remarkably, of the subjects I contacted in this manner, the only ones who did not participate were those whose schedules did not coordinate with my own.

With the exception of a few vendors who requested that we meet in their workplaces or over coffee, I interviewed all of my subjects in their homes. I found this to be the ideal setting, since it put my subjects at ease and allowed me to view their neighborhoods (to understand who and what made up their local milieu), to observe the interior landscapes of their homes and family lives (to understand the priorities reflected in their communal spaces), to view items that subjects mentioned casually in their interviews (e.g., photos, letters, and videos), and to meet family and friends (all potential subjects) who formed the cast of characters in the stories they shared with me.

Because the immigrant families I studied were almost as reluctant to share personal details with members of their community as they were with outsiders (for fear that the information might become community *chisme* or *tsismis* [gossip]), I attempted to convey enough familiarity with their cultures and neighborhoods to be trustworthy but not enough to signal the risk of a slip that might reveal any of their personal information. I presented myself as a young adult who was out of the age range of both the parents and the teenagers I interviewed but who (through my race, language, and family background) had experienced what it was like to be the teenage child of immigrants and to have immigrant parents who work hard for their family's advancement.

For the most part, this role—which was, in fact, my identity—came quite easily. At the time that I was collecting data, I was in my mid-twenties—almost a decade removed from high school and highly cognizant of the exceptional sacrifices my immigrant parents had made to help me become one of the few first-generation minority graduate students at UC Berkeley. As the product of a working-class Southern California suburb that was primarily Mexican, white, and Filipino, I was well acquainted with the etiquette involved in gaining the trust and respect of Filipino and Mexican elders and young people alike. During my interviews and observations, I usually wore my everyday clothes—jeans, comfortable shoes, and a casual (but not revealing) top. I addressed the Filipino immigrants in my study as "Auntie" or "Uncle" (as I, and others in the community, would normally address those belonging to my parents' generation), and I spoke with them in English (the same language I would normally use with older Filipinos) but responded to them in Tagalog on the occasions when they chose to use Tagalog with me. I also addressed the Mexican immigrants in my study as I normally would, calling them "Señora" or "Señor," and I usually interacted with them entirely in Spanish. Although I sometimes had to ask my Mexican interviewees to speak more slowly and I always explained that Spanish was a relatively newly acquired second language for me, I believe that they greatly appreciated my use of their native language and that it encouraged them to honestly and generously share with me their experiences as immigrant parents in America. With my younger participants, I almost always spoke in English (although I followed the lead of my subjects in the use of Spanish or Tagalog terms to describe people or items, especially for elements of their own debuts and quinceañeras), and we called each other by our first names.

At my first meeting with each research subject, I reiterated that I was a Berkeley student writing a book on Filipino debuts and Mexican quinceañeras. I also shared that I was the eldest daughter of Filipino immigrants and that my interest in my research topic stemmed largely from my upbringing in a city with comparably sizable Mexican American and Filipino American communities. If my subjects asked me questions about my own life, I tried to answer them honestly but with enough generality to prevent them from forming preconceived notions that might influence their responses. After assuring them that I would keep their identities confidential (in my personal, as well as professional, work and interactions), I asked them to sign a voluntary consent form, to provide a pseudonym (if they so desired), and to keep in mind that I was not searching for "right" or "wrong" answers—just honest accounts that would help me better understand debuts and quinces. In an effort to build further rapport and trust, I started each interview by simply asking my subjects to tell me about themselves.

I believe that all of these factors—my appearance, my limited self-disclosure, and my ability to speak in the native languages of the participants—helped convey that I was someone who was *nandiyan lang*, a Tagalog phrase that is used to describe the location of someone or something in a nonspecific way. Because Tagalog is a language of not only words but also many subtle mannerisms, not-so-subtle gestures, singsong tones, and animated velocity, Filipinos have countless (and confusing) ways of describing location. *Doon* is often used to indicate a place or point that is far away, and *diyan* is often said to indicate a place or point that is not "here" but is relatively nearby. When *nandiyan* is pronounced in a drawn-out manner ("*nandiyaaaan*"), with one's eyes wide open and one's gaze aimed in a particular direction, it can mean "there, somewhat close by" or "right there, obviously."

In relation to my research subjects, my "position" as *nandiyan lang* indicated that I was both close *and* at a safe distance. This notion has been heavily influenced by the *ni de aquí, ni de allá* researcher approach employed by a long history of critical Chicano/a scholars (see, e.g., Anzaldúa 1999; Cantú and Nájera-Ramírez 2002; Hondagneu-Sotelo 1994; Moraga and Anzaldúa 1981; Romero 1992). However, whereas *ni de aquí, ni de allá* emphasizes a liminal location that is "neither here nor there," *nandiyan lang* conveys an indistinct omnipresence. Being *nandiyan lang* meant that I was "inside" enough for my research participants to feel at ease and "outside" enough not to pose the threat of divulging information that might become grist for the local gossip mill. My clothes placed me at a safe, but not too remote, distance from both the trendy Las Querubes youth and their more buttoned-up parents. My ability to speak some Tagalog—unlike most young Filipinos in Las Querubes—distinguished me as somewhat more culturally mature than the teenaged participants, but having been born and raised in the United States likened my background to that of the Filipino teens. Although my Latino subjects and I never lost sight of the fact that my background is not Mexican, my ability to speak Spanish fluently combined with my familiarity with Mexican culture (from having been raised in a border city and having resided in central Mexico for a period) gave validity to my sincere understanding of, respect for, and support for Mexican culture and people. Finally, my identity as a UC Berkeley researcher gave me both shared status as a student with my younger subjects and shared status as a responsible adult with my older subjects.

Clearly, however, my status as in-between and a bit of both generations, communities, and cultures does not eliminate the cultural differences that existed between my subjects and me or the effect of these differences on my presentation of the participants' experiences. For example, my identity as a woman influenced both what my subjects chose to share with me and how I chose to interpret and present my findings. James Clifford argues that such partiality is unavoidable in ethnographic research because "culture is not an object to be described, [and] neither is it a unified corpus of symbols and meanings that can be definitely interpreted" (Clifford and Marcus 1986: 19). He writes that it is therefore impossible for researchers to find and report "complete truths"; at best we produce "partial truths" (Clifford and Marcus 1986: 7) that examine how they have been informed by our subjectivities.

Nevertheless, I believe that my *nandiyan lang* identities and research approach enabled me to obtain a great deal of rich information about the people and events presented here and that they helped me understand my data from multiple perspectives. As a partial insider to the communities I was examining, I was more attuned to the intricate layers of my subjects' accounts, and I was able to probe and interpret them in effective and culturally sensitive ways. At the same time, as someone who was also partially outside the communities I studied, I had more leeway in seeking clarification of terms and customs that participants might otherwise have presumed were understood.

This is not to say that being an insider-outsider did not have its occasional drawbacks. My role as a researcher was occasionally challenged when my subjects allowed my partial insider status to cause them to slip into treating me as a full-fledged community member. For example, I became an unwitting center of "drama" when—much to his girlfriend's consternation—a male teenage entourage member told his friends he thought I was "cute." And I was asked by more than one "auntie" to advise her daughter to postpone dating until after college—which was at odds with my ideas on female autonomy and had not been my own experience. Then there was the question of how to present my scholarship. I have had to wrestle with creating accurate, but critical, portraits of the people I have studied—portraits that some of them might find unflattering or, at worst, as betrayals. I have also had to struggle with finding a writer's voice that is neither so intellectual that it renders my research inaccessible (not to mention boring) to people like those I studied and lived with in Las Querubes nor so colloquial that it is not taken seriously by my colleagues in academia. Finally, I have had to learn to trust that the snapshot I have created of the communities in my study will be understood as representative of only their particular communities, *at one moment in time*—and not as defining and everlasting representations of *all* Filipino Americans or Mexican Americans.

Despite these challenges, I feel privileged to have had the opportunity to collect the fascinating stories that my subjects shared with me and to be able to present them to a wider audience. I hope that readers will learn from the whole and partial truths that I have gathered and use them to achieve improved understandings of debuts, quinceañeras, and the lives of the immigrant families who celebrate them.

Notes

CHAPTER 1

1. To honor and reflect the language of those in my study, throughout this book I use the term *quinceañera* to describe both the event and the celebrant. I also follow the study participants by referring to the event as a "quince," a "fifteen," and a *"quince años."*

2. Again, as is customary, and out of respect for my subjects' language, throughout this book I use the term *debutante* to describe both the event and the celebrant.

3. In 2008, *USA Today* reporter Eric Gorski reported that "a $400 million-a-year industry has sprouted up catering to Hispanic immigrants seeking to maintain cultural traditions while showing they've made it in their new countries, offering everything for Quinceañera planners and cruises to professional ballroom dancers to teach the ceremonial waltz."

4. Much of the historical narrative in this section was first published in *"Primerang Bituin*: Philippines-Mexico Relations at the Dawn of the Pacific Rim Century," an article I published in *Asia Pacific: Perspectives* 6, no. 1 (May 2006): 4–12. *"Magkasama,"* the title of this section is a synonym for "interconnected." It is Tagalog/ Filipino for "together" or "in the company of."

5. *Mexica* is the Nahuatl term for what we refer to today as Aztec.

6. Spain was quite successful at doing so in the Philippines; the only reason the destruction was less extensive in Mexico is that during the demolition of precolonial Mexica cities and temples, the Spaniards left various places and objects only "superficially" ruined so that they could find, steal, and hoard indigenous "treasures." Mexican anthropologist Guillermo Bonfil Batalla writes, "The colonial enterprise engaged in destroying Mesoamerican civilization and stopped only where self-interest intervened" (1975: 29).

7. The uniqueness is a result of the persistence of indigenous folk beliefs and practices.

8. In exchange, the United States paid Mexico $15 million to compensate for war-related damage to Mexican land.

9. The Treaty of Paris was signed on December 10, 1898, and went into effect on April 11, 1899. Under its provisions, Spain surrendered the Philippines, Puerto Rico, and Guam to the United States and gave up all rights to Cuba.

10. This is because, although the Treaty of Guadalupe-Hidalgo specified that legitimate Mexican land titles would be recognized by the United States, the 1851 Land Act declared that Spanish-speaking citizens of the Southwest had to prove their property rights in court, which was difficult, because "Mexican[s] usually had not kept adequate records for their grants" (Quinn 1994: 104). As a result, "many of them lost their land. They could not prove they owned it—even though they had lived on the land for years" (Starr 1980: 83).

11. In addition to the country's war for independence and the Mexican War, the Mexican Revolution, a ten-year civil war, wreaked chaos on Mexico's people and economy and fostered the "second wave" of Mexican American migration between 1910 and 1920.

12. A *pensionado* is a Philippine scholar whose expenses are paid by the government while he or she studies aboard.

13. *Ilustrado* is the Spanish word for "learned," the term used for members of the Filipino educated class during the Spanish colonial period.

14. Mexicans and Filipinos working *lado a lado* as farmhands on the West Coast formed the UFW/AFL-CIO (United Farm Workers/American Federation of Labor–Congress of Industrial Organizations) to help American farmworkers protest inadequate wages and working conditions and to "achieve an ideal: mutual understanding, sincere cooperation and true brotherhood" (Scharlin and Villanueva 2000: 112). The UFW/AFL-CIO was essentially the union of the primarily Chicano National Farmworkers Association (NFWA) and the Filipino-formed Agricultural Workers Organizing Committee (AWOC).

15. The Tydings-McDuffie Act guaranteed the Philippines independence after a ten-year "transitional period" and reclassified Filipinos as aliens so that an annual quota of fifty immigrants from the Philippines to the United States could be instituted.

16. Before World War I, Filipino enlistees served "in a range of occupational ratings," but after the war, "the Navy issued a new ruling restricting Filipinos . . . to the ratings of officers' stewards and mess attendants" (Espiritu 1995: 29).

17. About sixty-five thousand Filipino "war veterans, war brides, and male *and* female students, workers, and their dependents" (Bonus 2000: 42) were allowed to enter the United States during the second wave, after the Filipino Naturalization Act enabled Filipino Americans to petition family members to immigrate.

18. Between the 1920s and 1930s, about six thousand Filipinos enlisted in the U.S. Navy; by World War II, about 30 percent of Filipinos in the United States were in the U.S. armed forces.

19. About three hundred thousand Mexican Americans also directly contributed to the war effort by serving in the U.S. armed forces.

20. Under the 1790 Naturalization Act, only people considered "white" could become naturalized citizens.

21. However, the families of some Mexican American World War II veterans were able to join the middle class by using their G.I. benefits for college and to purchase homes.

22. In 2010, the median individual income for all Americans was $25,185, 15.3 percent of all Americans were living below the federal poverty line, and only 17.7 percent of Americans held bachelor's degrees (see Figure 1.1).

23. I do not include these observations and interviews in the book's analysis, although they provided invaluable comparisons. My observation that the same events in the Philippines and Mexico did not carry the same work, obligations, and meanings for parents and daughters (e.g., coming-of-age celebrations in the Philippines and Mexico resembled ordinary parties more than extraordinary rituals in that they did not place nearly as much emphasis on presenting daughters as dutiful and chaste and they usually included only guests within a family's existing social networks) helped corroborate that the responses I observed in California debuts and quinces were indeed unique to immigrant life in the United States.

24. Also not officially counted, but crucial to my analysis, were informal observations and interviews made at quinceañeras and debuts in Latin America and the Philippines and separate, formal interviews that I conducted with one man who shared that he seriously wanted to have a "coming-out" party and with his mother, one man who had a coming-of-age celebration when he turned thirty, and one woman who had a coming-of-age celebration when she turned fifty.

25. Readers will note that I use the term *dalaga* for one Filipina as well as for more than one Filipina. In Tagalog, placing *mga* before a word indicates the plural. To avoid such awkward expressions as "señoritas and mga dalaga," however, I drop the Tagalog plural marker.

CHAPTER 2

1. All translations are mine.

2. *Freaking* is defined by the *Urban Dictionary* as a style of dancing that "involves two or more people making extremely close physical contact, and facial expressions and physical movements that are sexually provocative and/or that imitate sexual intercourse" (http://www.urbandictionary.com). This term was used by both Mexican and Filipino youth to describe the kind of provocative dancing they often used with contemporary popular music.

3. The feminine form is *madrina* (godmother).

4. None of the quinceañeras I interviewed or observed directly reported that they changed shoes or received a doll during their party, although I did note that a few dress shops in Las Querubes sold *muñecas* that could be outfitted with miniature replicas of girls' quinceañera dresses.

5. *Piña* is fabric that is sheer, lightweight, and hand-loomed from pineapple leaf fibers. Dresses made from this material are often worn by Filipina women for formal occasions.

6. This line is in the original script but not in the movie.

7. The feminine form is *tita*, Tagalog/Filipino for "aunt."

8. This is the national dress of the Philippines, traditionally made out of expensive materials and consisting of an ample floor-length skirt, a wide-sleeved (or *kimona*) blouse, and a *pañuelo* (or shawl) starched to stay raised behind a woman's neck.

9. The Barong Tagalog is a delicately embroidered long-sleeved shirt traditionally made out of *piña* that is worn untucked over a T-shirt.

10. This is the traditional garment of the southern people of the Philippines, a tubular piece of multicolored cotton fabric decorated with finely woven geometric patterns.

11. This is an instrument made up of "sets of graduated gongs laid in a row," usually across a wooden frame, which is used in the traditional music of the southern Philippines (Canave-Dioquino 2006).

12. This is a Filipino dance that originated in Mindanao, the southernmost region of the Philippines. Originally, chiefs' daughters performed this dance at public celebrations to demonstrate their grace to would-be suitors.

13. *Scratching* refers to shifting a record back and forth in small, quick motions on a turntable to produce distinctive sounds. It is often done while manipulating the crossfader on an audio mixing console (a *mixer*) to enhance hip-hop music and exhibit a deejay's turntable skills.

14. I did not come across any Mexican group cotillions during my research, although I did hear of at least one parish that offered group quinceañera masses in Texas.

15. This gown is a variation of the baro't saya, named after a fictional female character who is considered to epitomize Filipina womanhood.

CHAPTER 3

1. Belinda was the only Latino parent I interviewed who was not of Mexican descent. She was born and raised in El Salvador but married a Mexican man in the United States. Though they did not deny their Salvadoran heritage at the time of their interviews, her children, who lived in a predominantly Mexican and Mexican American community, strongly identified as Mexican.

2. Mark Granovetter writes, "The strength of a tie is a . . . combination of the amount of time, the emotional intensity, the intimacy (mutual confiding), and the reciprocal services which characterize the tie" (Granovetter 1973: 1361). Hence, "strong ties" describes interpersonal relationships that can be characterized by not only relatively long durations but also greater emotional intensity, "mutual confiding" or intimacy, and "reciprocal services." And "weak ties" describes more passing relationships, which do not involve significant investments of time, social commitment, and trust.

3. *Compadrazgo* is a Latin American form of fictive kinship, with roots in medieval European Catholicism, which institutionalizes parents' close friends or relations as co-parents, or "godparents," to their children, especially through the godparents' sponsorship of the child during an important religious ritual, such as baptism or first communion. See Dill 1994; Kana'iaupuni et al. 2005.

4. These articles are sometimes used during the quinceañera's religious ceremony at church. They are often blessed by the priest during the mass and formally presented to the quinceañera during the mass and/or the reception. Michele Salcedo writes that the medallion "proclaims her [the quinceañera's] Christianity," the ring "represents the unending circle of God's love," the rosary and Bible "keep the word of God in her life," and each flower in the offering to the altar of the Virgin Mary "represents a year of the girl's life and stands for her blossoming into a young woman" (1997: 38–39).

5. Other common court variations included either fourteen damas, fourteen chambelánes, and one chambelán de honor or seven chambelánes and one chambelán de honor.

6. After agreeing to become a padrino, female sponsors were subsequently addressed as "madrina" by the quinceañera celebrant and as "*comadre*" (literally, "co-mother") by the celebrant's parents. Male sponsors were subsequently addressed as "padrino" by the quinceañera celebrant and as "*compadre*" (literally, "co-father") by the parents.

7. The largest debutante court I observed had thirty-seven members: eighteen ladies, eighteen escorts, and the debutante's escort.

8. Occasionally, the debutante and her family provided these as gifts.

9. Here I quote text from an exposition I did not attend, in an effort to conceal the location of my study.

10. To reflect the socioeconomic self-identifications of the subjects in my study, I use terms that roughly correspond to the class categories used by the *New York Times* in its 2005 series *Class Matters*. In the series, "class" was reported to be a social status that reflected one's occupation, education, income, and wealth, and U.S. society was divided into five categories: the top fifth, the upper middle, the middle, the lower middle, and the bottom fifth. Those in the top fifth were in the most high-status occupations and had the highest levels of education, income, and wealth, while those in the bottom fifth were in the lowest-prestige occupations (e.g., providing transportation, preparing food, and/or doing maintenance work), had not completed high school, earned less than $20,000 per year, and had a household net worth of less than $5,000. To describe socioeconomic status, I use the term *lower working class* to refer to what the *New York Times* index would categorize as the top of its bottom-fifth category, the term *working class* to refer to the index's lower-middle category, the term *middle class* to refer to the index's middle-class category, and the term *upper class* to refer to the index's upper-middle and top-fifth categories.

11. Although I did not observe one during my research, upper-class Latinos certainly hold large quinces that may not be organized and/or used in the same ways. For instance, after my fieldwork, it was reported that the daughter of a Mexican celebrity celebrated her "sweet fifteen" at a cost of "over $100,000," with a guest list of "over 700 people" and free performances by her father's famous "connections" ("Francia Raisa's Sweet 15" 2011). Although the quinceañera was clearly used to display and fortify some social networks, it is likely that the quinceañera's family did not need "strong ties" for the same reasons that a working-class family might.

12. The Ladies' Association admitted girls up to twenty-one years old.

13. The inflation rate from 1988 to 2011 was approximately 90 percent.

14. For more history and background on the church controversy over quinceañera masses, see "Explaining the Quinceañera" in Davalos 1996.

15. Although criteria for my sample of primary interviews included having at least one immigrant parent, through these and my secondary interviews I heard numerous stories of non-immigrant Mexican American and Filipino American families deliberately rejecting involvement in debuts and quinces from lack of interest and the perception that they were "old-fashioned." Furthermore, when asked if they thought they could see themselves coordinating a debutante or quinceañera for their own daughters

in the future, all of the second-generation women in my sample expressed uncertainty and agreed that they would not "force" one on their daughters.

CHAPTER 4

1. A *tilma* is a cactus-fiber cloak used by Mexican *indios*.

2. This should not suggest that debutantes and quinceañeras unequivocally submit to their parents' demands during and after their coming-of-age celebrations. I discuss instances in which daughters question and/or dispute their parents' choices in Chapter 5.

3. LRPS girls were required to wear a *balintawak*, a rural Philippine costume popular in the early part of the twentieth century. Like the baro't saya (described in Chapter 2), a *balintawak* features bell-shaped sleeves and is worn with a *pañuelo*. However, a *balintawak* has a shorter, simpler skirt; is made with brightly colored, woven cloth; and is worn with the *pañuelo* draped over one shoulder.

4. Whether or not *don* is truly a Spanish word, Mrs. Favino used it, and translated it as such when a student asked her its meaning.

5. MAC (Makeup Art Cosmetics) is a high-end cosmetics company, founded in 1984, that was highly popular and esteemed among the young people in my study.

6. Here I do not consider rentals for the church and reception venue as purchases.

7. The Maria Clara ensemble technically includes a fourth piece that the debutantes did not wear, a knee-length *tapis*, or overskirt, worn over the floor-length skirt.

8. During Catholic Prayers of the Faithful, a reader proposes several intentions for the congregation's prayers; after each one, they collectively respond, "Lord, hear our prayer."

9. These lessons were further reinforced during later parts of the program, which often included a formal thank-you speech by the honoree and/or a special performance dedicated to the debutante's or quinceañera's parents (e.g., SCUFA debutantes performed "You Are the Wind Beneath My Wings").

10. *Tinikling* is a pre-Spanish Filipino dance in which bamboo poles are alternately beaten against the ground and raised and clapped together over and between dancers. The *tinikling* is the national dance of the Philippines.

11. None of the debutantes or quinceañeras that took place more than five years before my study included modern dances; neither did any of the group cotillions.

12. Referring to a *telenovela*, a televised Spanish soap opera.

13. Further illustrating the mini-drama aspect of quinceañeras, the Spanish network Televisa produced the soap opera series *Quinceañera* in 1987. In the show, lower-class Maricruz (Adela Noriega) and wealthy Beatriz (Thalía) are classmates and best friends who are eager for their quinceañeras and the transition to womanhood. Notably, *Quinceañera* is the only "classic" Mexican *telenovela* that has been dubbed in three Philippine languages and aired on multiple Philippine television stations. In April 2012, a new series "inspired" by the 1980s *Quinceañera* series, *Miss XV*, was launched on Nickelodeon Latin America and Canal 5. ("Todo Listo" 2012).

14. This section's title, "*Espejo, Salamin*," includes the words for *mirror* in Spanish and Tagalog, respectively.

15. Downward assimilation is the act of becoming incorporated into U.S. society at a lower socioeconomic level than that of the immigrant generation.

16. The Mexican Migration Project database (http://opr.princeton.edu/archive/mmp) reports that since the *bracero* program's termination, males constitute between 72.2 percent and 78.7 percent of undocumented migration from Mexico and between 40.9 percent and 52.2 percent of documented migration.

CHAPTER 5

1. To review how I have classified families socioeconomically, see Chapter 3.

2. However, the fact that quinceañeras and debutantes are used to claim U.S. cultural belonging should not imply that debutante and quinceañera organizers wish to renounce ties to Mexico or the Philippines. As previously noted, for most Filipino Americans and Mexican Americans, debuts and quinceañeras are ways of signifying and reaffirming ongoing, meaningful connections to the Philippines or Mexico.

3. They have been at least moderately successful, if the appearance of several quinceañeras on the widely watched MTV program *My Sweet Sixteen* is any indicator of increasing public consciousness around Latinos organizing such occasions.

4. *Cumbia* is a percussive, fast-paced Latin music genre.

5. *Coconut* is a derogatory Filipino American term for someone who is "brown on the outside, white on the inside" and who does not perform or embrace his or her Filipino cultural identity.

6. This is an inadequate translation of *bastos ka*, since the Pilipino word *bastos* cannot be literally translated into English and its meaning varies with its context. Usually, it refers to a person or behavior that is offensive, rude, and vulgar. Here it is used almost as an expletive toward Augusto.

7. In the film, Magdalena's pregnancy is explained by an online message board response to a user named "Pregnant Virgin": "Sperm are very determined beings whose sole reason to exist is to get inside the fallopian tubes. Whenever sperm is sprayed near the vaginal opening, there is a chance they can swim inside."

8. The fact that most Filipino and Mexican parents seem to sanction their daughters rather than outright ostracize them—*unless they become pregnant*—further supports this viewpoint.

9. At the time of this writing, I could not verify this statistic.

10. The brand is worth mentioning, since it is a relatively young line that claims to be committed to innovation, "to push[ing] the boundaries, evolving our core DNA and challenging our designers to investigate new materials, styles, and cuts" (G-Star Raw 2011).

11. Junior Reserve Officers' Training Corps (JROTC) is a federal program in U.S. high schools sponsored by the U.S. armed forces.

12. LGBT stands for "lesbian, gay, bisexual, and transgender."

13. The celebration of *cincuentañeras* by Latina women has been documented, however (see Cantú 2002). Ariel made this discovery after her own celebration as well.

14. Gonzalves writes about young Filipino Americans who are literal "scene stealers"—college activists who attempt to reformat traditional Pilipino Cultural Night shows (annual hours-long theatrical presentations, which students organize to exhibit Pilipino culture through skits and indigenous, colonial, and "modern" Philippine and Filipino American dance).

CHAPTER 6

1. The constitution of immigrants as noble and well bred via the construction of debuts and quinces as traditions is discussed at greater length in Chapter 4.

2. The church did give those involved in quinceañeras some background information about quinces as Mexican traditions. However, the church's historical (versus religious) information was usually viewed as redundant by and for the quinceañera, her court, and her padrinos.

3. I discuss in Chapter 3 how debuts and quinces impressed on their celebrants the extent and dependability of their social networks.

4. To be clear, the upward mobility experiences by nearly all my subjects indicate no definitive correlation between ethnicity or class and environments that require more emotional ballasting.

CHAPTER 7

1. As of 2011, this was already the case in three states: Nevada, Texas, and California, where this study was completed.

2. Russell Leong (1995) describes *not* fulfilling such obligations as "academic pimping." He writes, "Academic pimping (for those outside academia) involves the following: utilizing the communities' 'bodies' as informants, studying, collecting, and using community culture as material for research, publishing essays, articles and books based on the above—without giving anything back."

References

"About Us: *Quinceañeras Magazine*." 2010. *Quinceañeras Magazine*. Available at http://www.quinceanerasmagazine.com/about.php.

AMC. 2012. "*The Debut* (2001)." *Movie Guide*. Available at http://movies.amctv.com/movie/2001/The+Debut.

Ana. 2010. "The Intimate Details: What to Wear under Your Quince Dress." *Uniquely Quince*, May 18.

Anzaldúa, Gloria. 1999. *Borderlands/La Frontera*. San Francisco: Aunt Lute Foundation Books.

Baehr, Peter, and Randall Collins. 2005. "Review Forum: The Sociology of Almost Everything—Four Questions to Randall Collins about Interaction Ritual Chains." *Canadian Journal of Sociology Online*, January–February. Available at http://www.cjsonline.ca/reviews/interactionritual.html.

Batalla, Guillermo Bonfil. 1975. "The Problem of National Culture." In *The Mexico Reader: History, Culture, Politics*, edited by G. M. Joseph and T. J. Henderson, 28–32. Durham, NC: Duke University Press.

Bell, Catherine M. 1992. *Ritual Theory, Ritual Practice*. New York: Oxford University Press.

Bellah, Robert N. 1985. "Creating a New Framework for New Realities: Social Science as Public Philosophy." *Change* 17:35–39.

Best, Amy L. 2000. *Prom Night: Youth, Schools, and Popular Culture*. New York: Routledge.

Bettie, Julie. 2003. *Women without Class: Girls, Race, and Identity*. Berkeley: University of California Press.

Bhattacharjee, Anannya. 1992. "The Habit of Ex-nomination: Nation, Woman, and the Indian Immigrant Bourgeoisie." *Public Culture* 5:19–44.

Bhattacharjee, Yudhijit. 2012. "Why Bilinguals Are Smarter." *New York Times*, March 17. Available at http://www.nytimes.com/2012/03/18/opinion/sunday/the-benefits-of-bilingualism.html.

Bialystock, Ellen, and Michelle M. Martin. 2004. "Attention and Inhibition in Bilingual Children: Evidence from the Dimensional Change Card Sort Task." *Developmental Science* 7:325–339.

"The Big Day: Beauty Countdown." 1998. *Debutante and Bride Philippines*, July, p. 17.

Bonus, Rick. 2000. *Locating Filipino Americans: Ethnicity and the Cultural Politics of Space*. Philadelphia: Temple University Press.

Bourdieu, Pierre. 1984. *Distinction: A Social Critique of the Judgment of Taste*. London: Routledge and Kegan Paul.

"Bridal Industry Statistics." 2005. *The Knot*.

Burawoy, Michael. 2005. "2004 Presidential Address: For Public Sociology." *American Sociological Review* 70:4–28.

Burge, David. 2011. "Mexico Fuels El Paso Economy, Expert Says." *El Paso Times*, June 2. Available at http://www.elpasotimes.com/news/ci_18186908.

Cajayon, Gene, dir. 2001. *The Debut*. Los Angeles: 5 Card Productions.

Cajayon, Gene, John Manal Castro, and Dawn Bohulano Mabalon. 2001. The Debut: *The Making of a Filipino American Film*. Chicago: Tulitos Press.

California Department of Finance. 2005. "Governor's Budget 2005–06." Available at http://www.dof.ca.gov/html/Budget_05-06/Budget05-06pdfMenu.html.

Cameron, Julia. 2002. *The Artist's Way: A Spiritual Path to Higher Creativity*. New York: J. P. Tarcher/Putnam.

Campomanes, Oscar V. 2005. "Filipinos in the United States and Their Literature of Exile." In *A Companion to Asian American Studies*, edited by K. A. Ono, 296–318. Malden, MA: Blackwell.

Canave-Dioquino, Corazon. 2006. "Philippine Music Instruments." National Commission for Culture and the Arts, Philippines. Available at http://www.ncca.gov.ph/about-culture-and-arts/articles-on-c-n-a/article.php?i=155&igm=1.

Cantú, Norma Elia. 1995. "La Quinceañera." *Louisiana's Living Traditions*. Available at http://www.louisianafolklife.org/LT/Articles_Essays/la_quinceanara.html.

———. 2002. "Chicana Life-Rituals." In *Chicana Traditions: Continuity and Change*, edited by Norma Elia Cantú and Olga Nájera-Ramírez, 15–34. Urbana: University of Illinois Press.

Cantú, Norma Elia, and Olga Nájera-Ramírez. 2002. *Chicana Traditions: Continuity and Change*. Urbana: University of Illinois Press.

"Car Prices Top $30,000 on Average." 2004. *CNN Money*, January 22. Available at http://money.cnn.com/2004/01/21/pf/autos/prices/.

Carter, Bill, and Jacques Steinberg. 2006. "Anchor-Advocate on Immigration Wins Viewers." *New York Times*, March 29. Available at http://www.nytimes.com/2006/03/29/politics/29dobbs.html?_r=0.

Chavez, Leo R. 2001. *Covering Immigration: Popular Images and the Politics of the Nation*. Berkeley: University of California Press.

———. 2008. *The Latino Threat: Constructing Immigrants, Citizens, and the Nation*. Stanford, CA: Stanford University Press.

Clarke, John, Stuart Hall, Tony Jefferson, and Brian Roberts. 1976. "Subcultures, Cultures, and Class." In *Resistance through Rituals: Youth Subcultures in Post-war Britain*, edited by S. Hall and T. Jefferson, 9–74. London: Hutchinson.

Cleaver, Samantha. 2007. "Too Much of a Good Thing?" *Scholastic Instructor*, October. Available at http://www.scholastic.com/teachers/article/too-much-good-thing.

Clifford, James, and George E. Marcus. 1986. *Writing Culture: The Poetics and Politics of Ethnography: A School of American Research Advanced Seminar.* Berkeley: University of California Press.

Collins, Patricia Hill. 1990. *Black Feminist Thought: Knowledge, Consciousness, and the Politics of Empowerment.* Boston: Unwin Hyman.

Collins, Randall. 2004. *Interaction Ritual Chains.* Princeton, NJ: Princeton University Press.

Connell, R. W. 1987. *Gender and Power: Society, the Person, and Sexual Politics.* Stanford, CA: Stanford University Press.

Connerton, Paul. 1989. *How Societies Remember.* Cambridge: Cambridge University Press.

Davalos, Karen Mary. 1996. "La Quinceañera: Making Gender and Ethnic Identities." *Frontiers* 16:101–127.

———. 1998. "Chicana/o Studies and Anthropology: The Dialogue That Never Was." *Aztlán: A Journal of Chicano Studies* 23:11–45.

de la Garza, Mercedes. 2003. "El matrimonio, ámbito vital de la mujer maya." *Arqueología Mexicana*, March–April, pp. 30–37.

Dill, Bonnie Thornton. 1994. "Fictive Kin, Paper Sons, and *Compadrazgo*: Women and the Struggle for Family Survival." In *Women of Color in U.S. Society*, edited by M. B. Zinn and B. T. Dill, 149–170. Philadelphia: Temple University Press.

"Do the Waltz: Perfect Rhythm." 1998. *Debutante and Bride Philippines*, July, p. 36.

Downes, Celia. 2005. "Filipinas Come of Age." *Honolulu Advertiser*, August 28. Available at http://the.honoluluadvertiser.com/article/2005/Aug/28/il/FP508280319.html.

Durand, Jorge, Douglas S. Massey, and Emilio A. Parrado. 1999. "The New Era of Mexican Migration to the United States." *Journal of American History* 86:518–536.

Durkheim, Émile. (1912) 1965. *The Elementary Forms of the Religious Life.* New York: Free Press.

———. 1995. *The Elementary Forms of the Religious Life.* Translated by K. E. Fields. New York: Free Press.

Ebert, Roger. 2002. "*The Debut.*" RogerEbert.com, March 22. Available at http://rogerebert.suntimes.com/apps/pbcs.dll/article?AID=/20020322/REVIEWS/203220303/1023.

Erevia, Angela. 1980. *Quinceañera.* San Antonio, TX: Mexican American Cultural Center.

Erickson, Bonnie. 2003. "Social Networks: The Value of Variety." *Contexts* 2:25–31.

Espiritu, Yen Le. 1995. *Filipino American Lives.* Philadelphia: Temple University Press.

———. 2001. "'We Don't Sleep Around like White Girls Do': Family, Culture, and Gender in Filipina American Lives." *Signs* 26:415–440.

———. 2003. *Home Bound: Filipino American Lives across Cultures, Communities, and Countries.* Berkeley: University of California Press.

———. 2010. "Migration and Cultures." In *Handbook of Cultural Sociology*, edited by J. R. Hall, L. Grindstaff, and M. C. Lo, 659–667. London: Routledge.

Espiritu, Yen Le, and Diane L. Wolf. 2001. "The Paradox of Assimilation: Children of Filipino Immigrants in San Diego." In *Ethnicities: Children of Immigrants in America*, edited by A. Portes and R. G. Rumbaut, 157–186. Berkeley: University of California Press.

Fernandez, Joyce L. 1998. "Letter from the Editor." *Debutante and Bride Philippines*, July, p. 15.

"Francia Raisa's Sweet 15." 2011. *Latina*, May, p. 98.

Gabaccia, Donna. 1994. *From the Other Side: Women, Gender, and Immigrant Life in the U.S., 1820–1990.* Bloomington: Indiana University Press.

Gamson, Joshua, and Laura Grindstaff. 2010. "Gender Performance: Cheerleaders, Drag Kings, and the Rest of Us." In *Handbook of Cultural Sociology*, edited by J. R. Hall, L. Grindstaff, and M. C. Lo, 252–262. London: Routledge.

Gandara, Patricia C. 1995. *Over the Ivy Walls: The Educational Mobility of Low-Income Chicanos.* Albany: State University of New York Press.

Garcia de Angela, Alicia. 2012. "Beauty Secrets from Top Model Ines Rivero." Quinceañera.com, December 18. Available at http://www.quinceanera.com/index.php/lang-en/fashion-a-beauty/beauty/beauty-tips.

Garey, Anita Ilta. 1995. "Constructing Motherhood on the Night Shift: 'Working Moms' as 'Stay-at-Home Moms.'" *Qualitative Sociology* 18:415–437.

Garza, Saul. 2011. "In Texas, Quinceañeras Remain a Recession-Proof Industry." *FOX News Latino*, March 22. Available at http://latino.foxnews.com/latino/community/2011/03/21/texas-quinceaneras-remain-recession-proof-industry/.

Geertz, Clifford. 1973. "Thick Description: Toward an Interpretive Theory of Culture." In *The Interpretation of Cultures: Selected Essays*, edited by C. Geertz, 3–30. New York: Basic Books.

Gennep, Arnold van. 1960. *The Rites of Passage.* Chicago: University of Chicago Press.

Gerson, Kathleen. 1993. *No Man's Land: Men's Changing Commitments to Family and Work.* New York: Basic Books.

Gillis, John R. 1997. *A World of Their Own Making: Myth, Ritual, and the Quest for Family Values.* Cambridge, MA: Harvard University Press.

Glatzer, Richard, and Wash Westmoreland. 2006. *Quinceañera.* Los Angeles: Sony Pictures Classics.

Gonzalves, Theodore S. 1997. "The Day the Dancers Stayed: On Pilipino Cultural Nights." In *Filipino Americans: Transformation and Identity*, edited by M.P.P. Root, 163–180. Thousand Oaks, CA: Sage.

Gorski, Eric. 2008. "Quinceañera Ritual Divides Catholics." *USA Today*, January 3. Available at http://usatoday30.usatoday.com/news/nation/2008-01-03-3270065355_x.htm?csp=34.

Granovetter, Mark S. 1973. "The Strength of Weak Ties." *American Journal of Sociology* 78:1360–1380.

———. 1983. "The Strength of Weak Ties: A Network Theory Revisited." *Sociological Theory* 1:201–233.

Greene, Gayle. 1991. "Feminist Fiction and the Uses of Memory." *Signs* 16:290–321.

G-Star Raw. 2011. "About G-Star RAW Denim." Available at http://www.g-star.com/en/about/#/en-us/about/.

Guerin-Gonzales, Camille. 1994. *Mexican Workers and American Dreams: Immigration, Repatriation, and California Farm Labor, 1900–1939.* New Brunswick, NJ: Rutgers University Press.

Hagan, Jacqueline Maria. 1998. "Social Networks, Gender, and Immigrant Incorporation: Resources and Constraints." *American Sociological Review* 63:55–67.

Halbwachs, Maurice. 1992. *On Collective Memory.* Translated by Lewis A. Coser. Chicago: University of Chicago Press.

Hobsbawm, Eric. 1983. "Introduction: Inventing Tradition." In *The Invention of Tradition,* edited by E. Hobsbawn and T. Ranger, 1–14. Cambridge: Cambridge University Press.

Hochschild, Arlie Russell, and Anne Machung. 1989. *The Second Shift: Working Parents and the Revolution at Home.* New York: Viking Press.

Hondagneu-Sotelo, Pierrette. 1994. *Gendered Transitions: Mexican Experiences of Immigration.* Berkeley: University of California Press.

Hooper, Joseph 2011. "It's Time to Flourish." *Whole Living,* May, pp. 98–103.

Hune, Shirley. 2000. "Doing Gender with a Feminist Gaze." In *Contemporary Asian America: A Multidisciplinary Reader,* edited by M. Zhou and J. V. Gatewood, 413–430. New York: New York University Press.

Huntington, Samuel P. 2004a. "The Hispanic Challenge." *Foreign Policy,* March–April, pp. 30–45.

———. 2004b. *Who Are We? The Challenges to America's National Identity.* New York: Simon and Schuster.

Iglesias, Julio. 1981. "De Niña a Mujer." Miami, FL: Sony U.S. Latin.

Ignacio, Abraham Flores. 2004. *The Forbidden Book: The Philippine-American War in Political Cartoons.* San Francisco: TBoli.

"I Want You to Say 'Happy Birthday,' to Me!" 2007. *Super-Sized Chicana Blog.* Available at http://supersizedlatina.wordpress.com/14/.

Juarez, Ana Maria, and Stella Beatriz Kerl. 2003. "What Is the Right (White) Way to Be Sexual? Reconceptualizing Latina Sexuality." *Aztlán: A Journal of Chicano Studies* 28: 5–37.

Kana'iaupuni, Shawn Malia, Katherine M. Donato, Theresa Thompson-Colon, and Melissa Stainback. 2005. "Counting on Kin: Social Networks, Social Support, and Child Health Status." *Social Forces* 83 (March): 1137–1164.

Katzew, Ilona, and Susan Deans-Smith. 2009. *Race and Classification: The Case of Mexican America.* Stanford, CA: Stanford University Press.

Keohane, Nannerl O., Michelle Zimbalist Rosaldo, and Barbara Charlesworth Gelpi. 1982. *Feminist Theory: A Critique of Ideology.* Chicago: University of Chicago Press.

Kiang, Lisa, Andrew J. Supple, Gabriela L. Stein, and Laura M. Gonzalez. 2011. "Gendered Academic Adjustment among Asian American Adolescents in an Emerging Immigrant Community." *Journal of Youth and Adolescence* 41 (3): 283–294.

Kim, Elaine H. 2000. "Foreword." In *Philip Vera Cruz: A Personal History of Filipino Immigrants and the Farmworkers Movement,* edited by C. Scharlin and L. V. Villanueva, ix–xv. Seattle: University of Washington Press.

Kim, Ryan. 2001. "Princess for a Night/Filipina Rite of Passage Growing Popular in Bay Area." *San Francisco Chronicle,* February 25, p. A1.

King-O'Riain, Rebecca Chiyoko. 2006. *Pure Beauty: Judging Race in Japanese American Beauty Pageants.* Minneapolis: University of Minnesota Press.

Kondo, Dorinne K. 1997. *About Face: Performing "Race" in Fashion and Theater.* New York: Routledge.

Konrath, Sara H., Edward H. O'Brien, and Courtney Hsing. 2011. "Changes in Dispositional Empathy in American College Students over Time: A Meta-Analysis." *Personality and Social Psychology Review* 15 (2): 180–198.

Kuhn, Thomas S. 1996. *The Structure of Scientific Revolutions.* Chicago: University of Chicago Press.

Kurashige, Lon. 2002. *Japanese American Celebration and Conflict: A History of Ethnic Identity and Festival, 1934–1990.* Berkeley: University of California Press.

Lamont, Michèle. 2000. *The Dignity of Working Men: Morality and the Boundaries of Race, Class, and Immigration.* Cambridge, MA: Harvard University Press.

Lee, Henry K. 1999. "UC Berkeley Hunger Strike Enters 5th Day/School's Offer to Ethnic Studies Dept. Rejected." *San Francisco Chronicle,* May 4. Available at http://www.sfgate.com/education/article/UC-Berkeley-Hunger-Strike-Enters-5th-Day-2932855.php.

Leonardo, Micaela di. 1987. "The Female World of Cards and Holidays: Women, Families, and the Work of Kinship." *Signs* 12:440–453.

Leong, Russell. 1995. "Lived Theory (Notes on the Run)." *Amerasia Journal* 21:ix–x.

Lim, Shirley Jennifer. 2005. *A Feeling of Belonging: Asian American Women's Public Culture, 1930–1960.* New York: New York University Press.

López, David E., and Ricardo D. Stanton-Salazar. 2001. "Mexican Americans: A Second-Generation at Risk." In *Ethnicities: Children of Immigrants in America,* edited by A. Portes and R. G. Rumbaut, 57–90. Berkeley: University of California Press.

Lowe, Lisa. 1996. *Immigrant Acts: On Asian American Cultural Politics.* Durham, NC: Duke University Press.

Lugones, Maria. 1987. "Playfulness, 'World'-Traveling, and Loving Perception." *Hypatia 2 (2)*: 3–19.

Lukacs, John. 1986. *Immigration and Migration: A Historical Perspective.* Monterey, VA: American Immigration Control Foundation.

Mabalon, Dawn. 2001. "The Making of 'The Debut.'" In The Debut: *The Making of a Filipino American Film,* by G. Cajayon, J. M. Castro, and D. B. Mabalon, 1–23. Chicago: Tulitos Press.

MacDonald, Heather. 2011. "Less Academics, More Narcissism." *City Journal California,* July 14. Available at http://www.city-journal.org/2011/cjc0714hm.html.

MacDonald, Jeffrey L. 1997. *Transnational Aspects of Iu-Mien Refugee Identity.* New York: Garland.

Maira, Sunaina. 2002. *Desis in the House: Indian American Youth Culture in New York City.* Philadelphia: Temple University Press.

Mann, Susan Archer, and Douglas J. Huffman. 2005. "The Decentering of Second Wave Feminism and the Rise of the Third Wave." *Science and Society* 69:56–91.

Martin, Karin A. 1998. "Becoming a Gendered Body: Practices of Preschools." *American Sociological Review* 63:494–511.

Martino, Al. 1967. "Daddy's Little Girl." Los Angeles: Capitol.

Massey, Douglas S. 1987. *Return to Aztlan: The Social Process of International Migration from Western Mexico.* Berkeley: University of California Press.

Menjívar, Cecilia. 2000. *Fragmented Ties: Salvadoran Immigrant Networks in America.* Berkeley: University of California Press.

Migration Policy Institute. 2009. "US Historical Immigration Trends." Available at http://www.migrationinformation.org/datahub/historicaltrends.cfm#source.

Mills, C. Wright. 1959. *The Sociological Imagination.* New York: Oxford University Press.

Moraga, Cherríe, and Gloria Anzaldúa. 1981. *This Bridge Called My Back: Writings by Radical Women of Color.* Watertown, MA: Persephone Press.

Moreno, Jose. 2001. "Costume at the Fin de Siecle: Maria Clara." *Filipino Heritage.* Available at http://filipinoheritage.zxq.net/costumes/findesiecle/maria_clara.htm.

Most, Jonah. 2011. "Going Hungry in Berkeley for Ethnic Studies." *Berkeley Daily Planet,* May 4. Available at http://www.berkeleydailyplanet.com/issue/2011-05-04/article/37791?headline=Going-Hungry-in-Berkeley-for-Ethnic-Studies--By-Jonah-Most-NAM-.

Nakano-Glenn, Evelyn. 1983. "Split Household, Small Producer and Dual Wage Earner: An Analysis of Chinese-American Family Strategies." *Journal of Marriage and Family* 45:35–46.

———. 2009. *Shades of Color: Why Skin Color Matters.* Stanford, CA: Stanford University Press.

National Campaign to Prevent Teen and Unplanned Pregnancy. 2008a. "Fast Facts: The Consequences of Unplanned Pregnancy." Available at http://www.thenational campaign.org/resources/pdf/fast-facts-consequences-of-unplanned-pregnancy .pdf.

National Immigration Law Center. 2006. "Paying Their Way and Then Some: Facts about the Contributions of Immigrants to Economic Growth and Public Investment." Available at http://v2011.nilc.org/immspbs/research/research003.htm.

National Institute for Play. 2003. "Play Science: The Patterns of Play." Available at http://nifplay.org/states_play.html.

New York Times. 2005. *Class Matters.* New York: Times Books.

O'Brien, Eileen. 2008. *The Racial Middle: Latinos and Asian Americans Living beyond the Racial Divide.* New York: New York University Press.

Oishi, Nana. 2002. "Gender and Migration: An Integrative Report." Working Paper. San Diego, CA: Center for Comparative Immigration Studies, University of California.

Omi, Michael, and Howard Winant. 1994. *Racial Formation in the United States: From the 1960s to the 1990s.* New York: Routledge.

Orenstein, Peggy. 2011. *Cinderella Ate My Daughter: Dispatches from the Front Lines of the New Girlie-Girl Culture.* New York: HarperCollins.

Otnes, Cele, and Elizabeth Hafkin Pleck. 2003. *Cinderella Dreams: The Allure of the Lavish Wedding.* Berkeley: University of California Press.

Our Sunday Visitor's Catholic Almanac. 1998. Huntington, IN: Our Sunday Visitor.

Pascoe, C. J. 2007. *Dude, You're a Fag: Masculinity and Sexuality in High School.* Berkeley: University of California Press.

Pastor, Cristina D. C. 2004. "Debutante's Ball: The Economics of Turning 18." *Philippine News,* February 11.

Pavlakovich-Kochi, Vera, and Alberta H. Charney. 2008. "Mexican Visitors to Arizona: Visitor Characteristics and Economic Impacts, 2007–08." Tucson: University of Arizona, Eller College of Management.

Paz, Octavio. 1950. "The Sons of la Malinche." In *The Mexico Reader: History, Culture, Politics,* edited by G. M. Joseph and T. J. Henderson, 20–27. Durham, NC: Duke University Press.

Pew Hispanic Center. 2004. "Latino Teens Staying in High School: A Challenge for All Generations." Available at http://www.pewtrusts.org/uploadedFiles/www

pewtrustsorg/Fact_Sheets/Hispanics_in_America/pew_hispanic_education_ fact_sheet_persistence.pdf.

Poinsett, Joel. 2002. "The Mexican Character." In *The Mexico Reader: History, Culture, Politics*, edited by G. M. Joseph and T. J. Henderson, 11–14. Durham, NC: Duke University Press.

Portes, Alejandro. 1998. "Social Capital: Its Origins and Applications in Modern Sociology." *Annual Review of Sociology* 24:1–24.

Portes, Alejandro, and Leif Jensen. 1989. "The Enclave and the Entrants: Patterns of Ethnic Enterprise in Miami before and after Mariel." *American Sociological Review* 54:929–949.

Portes, Alejandro, and Rubén G. Rumbaut. 2001a. *Legacies: The Story of the Immigrant Second Generation*. Berkeley: University of California Press.

———. 2001b. "Not Everyone Is Chosen: Segmented Assimilation and Its Determinants." In *Legacies: The Story of the Immigrant Second Generation*, edited by A. Portes and R. G. Rumbaut, 44–69. Berkeley: University of California Press.

Prida, Dolores. 2007. "15 Gone Wild: Supersized Quinceañeras Have Hijacked a Latino Tradition." *New York Daily News*, August 8, p. 19.

Qin-Hilliard, Desirée Baolian. 2003. "Gendered Expectations and Gendered Experiences: Immigrant Students' Adaptation in Schools." *New Directions for Youth Development* 2003:91–109.

"Quinceañera: Is This Right [*sic*] of Passage Sending the Wrong Message?" 2004. *Latina*.

Quinn, Arthur. 1994. *The Rivals: William Gwin, David Broderick, and the Birth of California*. New York: Crown.

Reed, Philip, and John DiPietro. 2001. "How to Get a Used Car Bargain." Edmunds .com, March 8. Available at http://www.edmunds.com/car-buying/how-to-get-a-used-car-bargain-part-one.html.

Rivard, Robert. 2010. "Mexican Nationals Enrich City's Culture, Economy." *San Antonio Express-News*, November 27. Available at http://www.mysanantonio .com/news/local_news/article/Mexican-nationals-enrich-city-s-culture-economy -836404.php.

Rizal, José. (1887) 2004. *Noli Me Tangere* [The Lost Eden]. Makati City, Philippines: Bookmark.

Rodriguez, Clara E. 1997. *Latin Looks: Images of Latinas and Latinos in the U.S. Media*. Boulder, CO: Westview Press.

Rodriguez, Evelyn I. 2006. "*Primerang Bituin*: Philippines-Mexico Relations at the Dawn of the Pacific Rim Century." *Asia Pacific: Perspectives* 6:4–12.

Rodriguez-Scott, Esmeralda. 2002. "Patterns of Mexican Migration to the United States." Paper presented at the 82nd Annual Meeting of the Southwestern Social Science Association, New Orleans.

Romero, Mary. 1992. *Maid in the U.S.A.* New York: Routledge.

Rondilla, Joanne L., and Paul Spickard. 2007. *Is Lighter Better? Skin-Tone Discrimination among Asian Americans*. Lanham, MD: Rowman and Littlefield.

Rosaldo, Renato. 1989. *Culture and Truth: The Remaking of Social Analysis*. Boston: Beacon Press.

Russel y Rodríguez, Mónica. 2001. "Confronting the Silencing Praxis in Anthropology: Speaking of/from a Chicana Consciousness." In *The Qualitative Inquiry Reader*, edited by N. K. Denzin and Y. S. Lincoln, 347–376. Thousand Oaks, CA: Sage.

Saito, Hiro. 2010. "From Collective Memory to Commemoration." In *Handbook of Cultural Sociology*, edited by J. R. Hall, L. Grindstaff, and M. C. Lo, 629–638. London: Routledge.

Salcedo, Michele. 1997. *Quinceañera! The Essential Guide to Planning the Perfect Sweet Fifteen Celebration.* New York: Henry Holt.

Sandoval, Chela. 1982. "The Struggle Within: Women Respond to Racism." New York: Center for Third World Organizing.

San Juan, E. 1998. *From Exile to Diaspora: Versions of the Filipino Experience in the United States.* Boulder, CO: Westview Press.

Saunders, Debra J. 1999. "Activism Drowns Out Academia." *San Francisco Chronicle,* May 7. Available at http://www.sfgate.com/opinion/saunders/article/Activism -Drowns-Out-Academia-3317769.php.

Scharlin, Craig, and Lilia V. Villanueva. 2000. *Philip Vera Cruz: A Personal History of Filipino Immigrants and the Farmworkers Movement.* Seattle: University of Washington Press.

Schippers, Mimi. 2007. "Recovering the Feminine Other: Masculinity, Femininity, and Gender Hegemony." *Theory and Society* 36:85–102.

Schulte, Bret. 2008. "Mexican Immigrants Prove Slow to Fit In." *U.S. News and World Report.* Available at http://www.usnews.com/articles/news/national/2008/05/15/ mexican-immigrants-prove-slow-to-fit-in.html.

Seligman, Martin E. P. 2011. *Flourish: A Visionary New Understanding of Happiness and Well-being.* New York: Free Press.

Senate Engrossed House Bill 2281. 2010. Arizona State Legislature, House of Representatives. 49th Leg., 2nd Reg. Sess.

Sewell, William H., Jr. 1996. "Historical Events as Transformations of Structures: Inventing Revolution at the Bastille." *Theory and Society* 25:841–881.

Shah, Bindi. 2007. "Being Young, Female and Laotian: Ethnicity as Social Capital at the Intersection of Gender, Generation, 'Race' and Age." *Ethnic and Racial Studies* 30:28–50.

Smith, Linda Tuhiwai. 1999. *Decolonizing Methodologies: Research and Indigenous Peoples.* New York: St. Martin's Press.

Smith, Robert C. 2002. "Gender, Ethnicity, and Race in School and Work Outcomes of Second-Generation Mexican Americans." In *Latinos: Remaking America*, edited by M. M. Suárez-Orozco, M. Páez, and David Rockefeller Center for Latin American Studies, 110–125. Berkeley: University of California Press.

Stack, Carol B. 1974. *All Our Kin: Strategies for Survival in a Black Community.* New York: Harper and Row.

Starr, Kevin. 1980. *California!* Santa Barbara, CA: Peregrine Smith.

Steinberg, David Joel. 1982. *The Philippines, a Singular and a Plural Place.* Boulder, CO: Westview Press.

Strategic Events. 2011. "Latino Bridal and Quince Girl Expo." Available at http:// www.quincegirlexpos.com/losangeles.html.

Swidler, Ann. 1986. "Culture in Action: Symbols and Strategies." *American Sociological Review* 51:273–286.

Takagi, Dana Y. 2000. "Maiden Voyage: Excursion into Sexuality and Identity Politics in Asian America." In *Contemporary Asian America: A Multidisciplinary Reader*, edited by M. Zhou and J. V. Gatewood, 547–560. New York: New York University Press.

Takaki, Ronald T. 1993. *A Different Mirror: A History of Multicultural America*. Boston: Little, Brown.

Thalia. 2011. "Thalia's Quinceañera Beauty Tips." Available at http://www.mis quincemag.com/quinceanera-beauty/makeup/thalia-quinceanera-beauty.

Thorne, Barrie. 1993. *Gender Play: Girls and Boys in School*. New Brunswick, NJ: Rutgers University Press.

Tierney, Jim. 2006. "Quinceañera Elegante Launches Web, Print Catalogs." *Multichannel Merchant*, October 10. Available at http://multichannelmerchant.com/crosschannel/Quince_Girl_catalog_10102006/.

"Todo Listo para el Estreno de 'Miss XV.'" 2012. *Televisa*, March 29. Available at http://www.televisa.com/noticias-espectaculos/423765/todo-listo-estreno-miss-xv/?country_code=US.

Trout, J. D. 2009. *The Empathy Gap: Building Bridges to the Good Life and the Good Society*. New York: Viking Press.

Turner, Victor. 1977. "Symbols in African Ritual." In *Symbolic Anthropology: A Reader in the Study of Symbols and Meanings*, edited by J. L. Dolgin, D. S. Kemnitzer, and D. M. Schneider, 183–194. New York: Columbia University Press.

———. 1987. "Betwixt and Between: The Liminal Period in Rites of Passage." In *Betwixt and Between: Patterns of Masculine and Feminine Initiation*, edited by L. C. Mahdi, S. Foster, and M. Little, 3–22. La Salle, IL: Open Court.

"UCSD Suspends Student Linked to Noose Found on Campus." 2010. 10News, February 27. Available at http://www.10news.com/news/ucsd-suspends-student-linked-to-noose-found-on-campus.

Ueda, Reed. 1994. *Postwar Immigrant America: A Social History*. Boston: Bedford Books of St. Martin's Press.

"The Ultimate Planning Timeline." 2011. *Latina*, May, p. 96.

U.S. Census Bureau. 2007a. "The American Community—Asians: 2004." Washington, DC: U.S. Census Bureau. Available at https://www.census.gov/prod/2007pubs/acs-05.pdf.

———. 2007b. "The American Community—Hispanics: 2004." Washington, DC: U.S. Census Bureau. Available at https://www.census.gov/prod/2007pubs/acs-03.pdf.

———. 2010a. "Place of Birth for the Foreign-Born Population in the United States." Available at http://factfinder2.census.gov/faces/tableservices/jsf/pages/product view.xhtml?pid=ACS_10_3YR_B05006&prodType=table.

———. 2010b. "Selected Characteristics of the Total and Native Populations in the United States." Available at http://factfinder2.census.gov/faces/tableservices/jsf/pages/productview.xhtml?pid=ACS_10_1YR_S0601&prodType=table.

———. 2010c. "Selected Population Profile in the United States: Filipino Alone or in Any Combination." Washington, DC: U.S. Census Bureau.

————. 2010d. "Selected Population Profile in the United States: Mexican." Washington, DC: U.S. Census Bureau.

Vida, Vendela. 1999. *Girls on the Verge: Debutante Dips, Gang Drive-bys, and Other Initiations.* New York: St. Martin's Press.

Vinson, John. 1992. *Immigration Out of Control: The Interests against America.* Monterey, VA: American Immigration Control Foundation.

Vives, Olga. 2001. "Latina Girls' High School Drop-out Rate Highest in U.S." *National NOW Times*, Fall. Available at http://now.org/nnt/fall-2001/latinas.html.

Voynar, Kim. 2006. "Sundance Review: *Quinceañera.*" *Moviefone*, January 24. Available at http://blog.moviefone.com/2006/01/24/sundance-review-quincearnera/.

Waldinger, Roger. 1997. "Social Capital or Social Closure? Immigrant Networks in the Labor Market." Los Angeles: Lewis Center for Regional Policy Studies, School of Public Policy and Social Research, University of California.

Weinberg, Sydney S. 1992. "The Treatment of Women in Immigration History: A Call for Change." *Journal of American Ethnic History*, Summer, pp. 24–46.

Yahoo! Answers. 2009. "I Don't Want a Quinceanera What Should I Do?" Available at http://answers.yahoo.com/question/index?qid=20090621141303AA3zRjU.

Yancey, George A. 2003. *Who Is White? Latinos, Asians, and the New Black/Nonblack Divide.* Boulder, CO: Rienner.

Zhou, Min, and John Logan. 1989. "Returns on Human Captial in Ethnic Enclaves: New York City's Chinatown." *American Sociological Review* 54:809–820.

Index

Evelyn Ibatan Rodriguez is an Associate Professor of Sociology at the University of San Francisco.